THE MEANING OF PSYCHOLOGY

THE MEANING OF PSYCHOLOGY

by

C. K. OGDEN
Magdalene College, Cambridge

GYAN

Published by

GYAN

Gyan Publishing House
5, Ansari Road
Daryaganj, New Delhi-110002
Phone: 011-47034999, 9811692060
E-mail: books@gyanbooks.com

Distribution Network
gyanbooks.com
India, USA, Canada, UK, Australia, France

ISBN : 978-81-212-6033-6 (PB)
First Published, 1926

2nd Impression 2021

Printed at: Gyan Press, Delhi.

The Meaning of Psychology
Author: C. K. Ogden

THE MEANING OF
PSYCHOLOGY

BY

C. K. OGDEN
Magdalene College, Cambridge

Director of "THE INTERNATIONAL LIBRARY OF PSYCHOLOGY, PHILOSOPHY AND SCIENTIFIC METHOD," *and Editor of* "PSYCHE"

ILLUSTRATED

CONTENTS

CHAPTER I: PRELIMINARY

CHAPTER II: THE MIND AND THE BODY

CHAPTER III: IMPULSE AND INHIBITION

CHAPTER IV: HOW THE BRAIN WORKS

CHAPTER V: PURPOSE AND INTEREST

CHAPTER VI: THE GROWTH OF THE MIND IN ANIMALS

CHAPTER VII: THE MENTALITY OF APES

CHAPTER X: BEHAVIOR

CHAPTER XI: LOOKING INWARDS

CHAPTER XII: LOOKING OUTWARDS

CHAPTER XIII: HOW WE THINK

CHAPTER XIV: EMOTION AND CHARACTER

CHAPTER XV: HOW THE MIND GOES WRONG

CHAPTER XVI: THE ABNORMAL

ILLUSTRATIONS

PLATES

PREFACE

A FEW years ago the word Psychology was a technicality covering a field of inquiry in which none but specialists and perhaps a few enterprising teachers were expected to take an interest. But at the present time it would be hard to find a general reader of current literature who has not at any rate browsed through one or more of the books on psychological topics which appear every other day.

There are, however, among these readers many who feel a difficulty in comparing and combining together the views, opinions, and information thus casually obtained. Although interested, they have no leisure for the study of voluminous works on first principles. They would like to read Shand's *Foundations of Character*, Marshall's *Consciousness*, Mitchell's *Structure and Growth of the Mind*, Wundt, Lipps, and Stumpf, Hobhouse's *Mind in Evolution*, Dumas' *Traité*, the *Analytic Psychology* of Professor Stout (having dipped perhaps into a volume with almost the same title by Dr. Jung), Urban's exhaustive treatise on *Valuation*, Baldwin's *Thought and Things*, or Professor Ward's *Psychological Principles;* but they have no ready means of discovering which is about what.

It seems probable, therefore, that many who are seriously approaching Psychology for the first time, and who are vaguely aware that many hundreds of important volumes have appeared since the last of these works was written, will welcome a brief account of the nucleus of accredited opinion from which the growing science is tending to develop. In what follows will be found an endeavor to deal in the simplest possible language with the subject in the light of the most recent advances; and to deal with it more concisely than has been done by any comprehensive introduction hitherto.

My object, however, has not merely been to cover the field on accepted lines. No conscientious teacher could to-day put his own Outline forward without taking account of the existence of admirable summaries such as those of Woodworth, Warren, McDougall, Stout, Angell, Hunter, Pillsbury, Yerkes, and Titchener. Each of these has its own advantages, and it would be no service to the public to attempt to combine their distinctive merits, or to forget that the two volumes of William James' *Principles* are generally accessible for reference with their abundance of unsurpassable descriptions. Nor can the physiological side of sense-perception, or the statistical handling of intelligence tests, for example, be usefully described in brief compass. For these the reader will be better advised to go direct to the original authorities, and I have therefore appended a short Bibliography of works available in the English language for his guidance in fuller reading.

It would be gratuitous to pretend that psychologists as a body are agreed on many fundamental issues. On this point the first fifty volumes of the

"International Library of Psychology, Philosophy, and Scientific Method" or the pages of *The Psychological Review*, on which much of the present work is necessarily based, are alone conclusive. The reader who compares this Outline with right- and left-wing works such as Fox's *Educational Psychology* (1926) on the one hand, and Watson's *Behaviorism* (1925) on the other, will also be able to judge to what degree departure from tradition or undue conservatism is in evidence in the following pages.

There remains always the probability that some apparent differences of opinion are actually but differences in formulation; this aspect of the problem, however, has already been discussed in *The Meaning of Meaning* (1923), to which the present work might serve as a stepping-stone for the linguistically inquisitive. On this occasion I have had the advantage of discussing numerous points with my former collaborator, Mr. I. A. Richards of Magdalene College, Cambridge, to whose *Principles of Literary Criticism* I also owe much.

C. K. OGDEN.

ROYAL SOCIETIES CLUB,
ST. JAMES'S STREET,
January, 1926

THE MEANING OF PSYCHOLOGY

THE MEANING OF PSYCHOLOGY

CHAPTER I: PRELIMINARY

Reasons for the Study of Psychology. There are four and a half good reasons for studying Psychology seriously.

There are many more reasons for studying it in other ways. It may help us to pose more readily as profound thinkers, to write more telling advertisements—or resist being taken in by them—to detect failings in our friends, and to discover new Wonders in our Offspring. But none of these things will carry the student through two hundred and fifty pages. Fortunately there are stronger motives.

1. WHAT ARE WE? Psychology is the only means by which this momentous question can ever be fully answered. Conchology cannot do it, nor yet Ontology: nor can Physics. Physiology can only help us in part. Only by a study of that portion of us which we call the mind can we ever learn what the mind is. This may seem a simple saying, but its significance has only lately been generally accepted. Psychology is the youngest of the sciences, and the most attractive:

> "O latest born and loveliest vision far
> Of all Olympus' faded hierarchy"

says Keats in his "Ode to Psyche." The study of the psyche, of mental processes, besides its universal appeal, has this further advantage that we each carry perpetually about with us all the subject matter which it requires.

2. WE GO WRONG. Even if we do not, we are always in a position to say with Richard Baxter: "there, but for the Grace of God, goes Richard." And psychology is beginning to point out both how we may avoid disaster and how regain the right track. The labors of Gall, Esquirol, Carpenter, Maudsley, Charcot, Ribot, Hughlings Jackson, Stanley Hall, Goltz, Creighton, Ferrier, Havelock Ellis, Janet, Freud, Adler, Rivers, and a thousand others have already made modern psycho-therapy a powerful resource against the worst afflictions to which man is liable.

3. WE CAN BE IMPROVED. If the reader was ever a child he will fully realize how much room for improvement not only we, but our outworn educational methods, allow. "It is quite true," wrote Professor James Harvey Robinson in 1921, "that what we need is education, but something so different from what now passes as such that it needs a new name." And in the last five years the Walls of the World, the bounds of human imagination and knowledge, have again been swept back by the further triumphs of Einstein, Eddington, Jeans, Rutherford and Bohr; while at the very heart of our being new and intricate mechanisms and possibilities are being revealed by fresh applications of such researches as those of Pavlov, Bose, Lapicque, Westermarck, Malinowski,

and the newer psycho-analysts. At the same time international, economic, and social affairs, and the contacts between minds, between types, races, and classes, which they entail, grow ever more bewildering. When confronted by these problems, or by our ignorance with regard to them, we must confess our inadequacy. We must learn how to learn—and our name is Legion. Democracy must face its problems. New millions of participants in the control of general affairs must now attempt to form personal opinions upon matters which were once left to a few. At the same time the complexity of these matters has immensely increased. The old view that the only access to a subject is through prolonged study of it, if true, has consequences for the immediate future which have not yet been faced. The alternative is to raise the level of communication through a direct study of its conditions, its dangers, and its difficulties. The practical side of this undertaking is, if communication be taken in its wide sense, education.[1]

4. THE MIND IS A STARTING-POINT. Psychology ultimately provides a basis for all other studies—Ethics, Economics, Æsthetics, Ethnology, Grammar, Politics, and Mathematics. Even Physics is ultimately driven back on hypotheses which are essentially matters of psychological criticism and construction. All our research is the exercise of our thinking powers, and in the long run the test for thinking lies with those whose business it is to study the processes of

[1] *The Meaning of Meaning* (1923), by the Author and I. A. Richards, p. xxx.

thought. This has, of course, always been realized by those physicists whom the world acclaims as at once the most prudent and the most daring; and in Chapter XII quotations will be found which illustrate their views.

To turn to the science which seems the most removed from Physics—namely Ethics. As fashions have changed in psychology men's theories of the good have followed them. This is inevitable, for ever since the days of Aristotle it has been agreed that only *experiences*[1] can be 'good' or 'bad,' and in describing the differences between good and bad experiences it is desirable to know how experiences may differ. The most commonplace view—"The greatest *happiness* of the greatest number"—no less than the most transcendental, "*Self*-realization", depends upon discussions which figure largely in every psychological treatise. Indeed, such a work as Westermarck's *Origin and Development of Moral Ideas* has led many to an Ethical Relativity in which the whole problem of morality reduces to a study of human types and desires in their social setting.

Nor is the science of the Beautiful (Æsthetics) capable of being divorced from Psychology. What we are really talking about when we criticize a poem, a picture, or even a statue are essentially the states

[1] The reader who is approaching psychology for the first time must not be disturbed by the special associations which certain simple terms such as *experience* (= 'a terrible experience'), *sensation* (cf. 'sensational'), and even *perception* and *adaptation* have acquired in daily life and in the press. He will soon get accustomed to their more general uses.

of mind (including pleasure, emotion, ecstasy, synæsthesis, and so forth) which they cause in us, so that the central problem of Æsthetics is to decide which of the states of mind that arise as our response to a given work of art are relevant.

Finally, as Mr. Belloc wrote:

> "The Path of Life, men said, is hard and rough
> Only because we do not know enough.
> When Science has discovered something more
> We shall be happier than we were before."

If this be really true, Psychology, in virtue of its unique position among the sciences, would gain another half point.

The Subject-Matter of Psychology. Clearly, however, Psychologizing is not one of the 'instincts.' It cannot be embarked on *ab ovo*, or from the cradle. Introspection (Lat. *introspicio* = look inward) is its main instrument, and a certain amount of training is necessary in introspection as in most other pursuits. Before commencing a detailed study we may make a brief preliminary survey of the field. The subject matter of Psychology is perhaps best indicated by an example.

As the reader reads these words he will probably agree that many things happen "in his mind."

He *attends* to the marks on the paper, he *thinks* and *understands*, he takes up an *attitude*, he *remembers*, he is *interested* or *bored* as a consequence, his *instinct* of curiosity is perhaps aroused, or possibly he is *irritated* by the obscurity of the style. He *endeavors* to persevere, until eventually he feels *tired*, and to avoid pain he falls *asleep*. But even then he may *dream*, and on awakening may *forget* his dream—though if hypnotized he may rescue it from the *unconscious*.

All these are psychological events described in current psychological language, and in psychology we are either engaged in classifying such events and elaborating our descriptions of what takes place, or in seeking for their causes, *i.e.*, explaining why just that particular process took place at just that time in just that way.

The Genetic Approach. The first of these, classification, is academic psychology—useful when wanted, but receding in favor of genetic (Gk. *genesis*=origin) and causal treatment. By genetic treatment is meant the treatment which seeks for light upon the things with which it deals through the study of their origin, their history and development. When we thus approach the mind we find that the importance of past history is far greater than it is with physical processes. A teacup, for instance, is little affected in its behavior by what has happened to it in the past, though the researches of Sir Jagadis Bose on responses in metals and plants show that the phenomena of biological memory may be more far-reaching than has hitherto been supposed; certainly nothing that a mind does, or that can be done by a mind, is unaffected by its previous experience.

It is, in fact, the first principle of psychology to recognize the peculiar way in which experience leaves effects behind it. Whenever we think of anything as being this or that, there are, as Professor Stout puts it, "processes of interpreting, identifying, classifying, recognizing, etc., by which the object is brought into relation with the results of previous experience as retained and organized in performed dispositions." Just what these dispositions are we shall have to consider later in this work. Similarly, anything we do by habit we do only thanks to our past experience. Thus we never think or feel or act quite freshly and spontaneously, for the character of our thinking, our feeling, and our acting is always due, in part at least, to the ways in which we have thought and felt and acted in the past. What exactly this dependence in any particular case may be is the main question which psychology attempts to answer, and it is chiefly in order to trace these connections more easily that it adopts a special vocabulary.

Technical Distinctions. Popular language in all matters that are connected with the mind is apt to be vague and misleading. Psychologists have, therefore, felt obliged to introduce terms freer from irrelevant associations than those in ordinary use, and these often make the subject seem dry and abstract to the beginner. But if it is realized that they are only names for what must from the nature of the case be processes familiar to everyone as part of ordinary experience, a little patience is all that is necessary for the mastery of current opinions.

Thus we find *Psychosis* ('state of mind', and sometimes 'abnormal state of mind': much as *phenome-*

non='appearance' and sometimes 'abnormal appearance'), *Conation* (striving), *Volition* (will), *Affect* (feeling), *Cognition* (knowing), *Engram* (impression), *Presentation* (sensation), *Ideation* (thinking), *Hedonic tone* (pleasure-pain), *Endo-somatic* (inside the skin), *Coenæsthesia* (sensibility of the whole body); and so on. Some of these terms will of course be found in the present work; others are not of much use.

Adaptation. From the most general standpoint, the business of the mind is to adapt the organism to its environment. The process of continual change from adaptation to adaptation is what is known as *Conation* (Lat. *conor*=try). In cases where there is conscious effort this process is popularly known as 'willing.' It is, however, now widely held that there is no essential difference, beyond a difference in complexity, between automatic responses to the environment and those responses which, owing to a conflict of tendencies, seem to involve the efforts of something which may be called the 'Will.' There are difficulties in admitting such an agent as the Will into psychology as a science, but on the view that all mental change is conative, we must of course admit that we are 'willing' even when we are asleep, and much of the work of modern psychologists, such as Freud, is devoted to showing that we constantly have volitional (Lat. *volo* = wish) processes of which we are unconscious. The 'libido' which now appears so prominently in psycho-analytical writings, is a name for this general striving activity, which throughout life is never suspended.

How this stream of striving proceeds in any individual depends partly on sensations impressed by the external world, but also partly on internal factors. Certain of the latter are of particular importance, because their character determines the direction of the stream. It is to these factors the terms *Instinct*, *Impulse*, *Interest*, *Need*, refer. Pleasantness and painfulness clearly play a great part in controlling our behavior, and this pleasure-pain aspect of experience is what is generally spoken of as feeling-tone.

Consciousness. Where in such an account does consciousness (Lat. *conscio* = know) appear? It cannot be too clearly realized that much of what is quite properly to be called mental activity is not conscious. Only some of the elements involved have the peculiar character which we name consciousness. But we should be careful when we use the term 'element.' A mental state is not built up of items as a wall is of bricks. This is an error which has long haunted psychology, and is known as associationism or atomism. What were supposed to be the bricks were mental occurrences of two kinds, sensations and images. They have received a disproportionate amount of study because they are the mental events which are most easily introspected. Sensations are [1]

[1] In this form the statement is highly controversial. We raise the point here because it is important that the student should realize as soon as possible that the basic assumptions of psychology are still matters of dispute. The alternative views are discussed in Chapter II.

happenings in the nervous system, due to stimuli from outside the body, *e.g.*, in vision, or to the stimulation of one part of the body by another. A toothache, or a colic, is the same in its mode of origin as the sensation obtained, *e.g.*, by clenching the fist. The importance of these sensations, due to the action of one part of the body on another, will be clear when we come to discuss *emotions* and they have much bearing upon the growth of self-consciousness and of our knowledge of other minds.

It is obvious that not all effects of stimuli are, or give rise to, conscious perceptions. What may be the difference between effects which give rise to consciousness and those which do not is a matter upon which no light has yet been thrown. It illustrates the relative unimportance of the idea of consciousness in psychology that this problem is rarely discussed. Consciousness is supposed to be associated with the higher parts of the nervous system, the bringing in of these higher systems accompanying the act of *attending*. It is plain that attention may make conscious what has hitherto been present but unperceived. If we keep our eyes motionless, we can discover, by merely attending to the edges of the field of view, that we are all the time seeing far more than we are ordinarily conscious of seeing. Similarly with all our senses. Without changing anything in our stimulation we can bring into explicit awareness much that lies ordinarily outside it—*e.g.*, the feel of our clothing on the skin and the rhythmic tension and relaxation of our breathing. Thus at all times there is a large field of inattention (stimulation not attended to) which is affecting us without causing consciousness.

Images. The other kind of 'element' which invites introspection is the *image*, the representative of perception which occurs without the stimulus required for the perception. A great deal of work has been done on images since Galton's *Inquiry into Human Faculty* drew attention to the vast range of difference between individuals both as to the images they habitually employ, and as to their powers of forming imagery of any kind. To-day, however, psychologists of all schools lay less stress upon images as an essential feature of mental life; and there are some, such as Professor Watson, in his *Behaviorism* (1925), who deny that any kind of imagery is necessary, or indeed occurs at all. There is also an interesting controversy as to how far thought can be conducted without it. But in most people all kinds of imagery undoubtedly occur—visual, auditory, tactual, olfactory, gustatory, motor, kinæsthetic, thermal, and organic. In fact, it is possible to form images corresponding to every kind of sensation.

The reader should discuss imagery with his friends, getting them to describe what they see when they imagine—*e.g.*, a monkey riding a bicycle, and asking them to give the monkey a top hat with a red rosette, etc. He will find that they differ greatly both in the vividness of their imagery and in their power of controlling it. It seems likely that special powers of imagery in one direction or another are due in large part to early trends of interest; and if, as seems probable, various abilities depend largely on these trends and the imagery to which they give rise, it should eventually be possible to avoid much disappointment and waste of time due to the later selection of unsuitable occupations.

These great differences between the types of imagery which are employed by different people raise a special problem, as to how far people with different imagery can be said to have the same thoughts. If my consciousness is filled, say, with mental pictures (visual images) and your consciousness is filled with the mental echoes of the sounds of words, how can we be said to have the same thoughts? And yet there is plainly a sense in which people who use quite different images can be said truly to be in agreement, to be thinking similarly.

Ideas. This problem, which is very important both historically and theoretically, is the same as the old question, "What is an Idea?" when this question is asked in Psychology. The full answer is very complicated, but an outline may be given which shows how the difficulty we have raised, which would result from an attempt to identify ideas with images, may be avoided.

For this purpose we require the biological notion of adaptation with which we began. All thinking, all mental activity, occurs in the course of adaptation. When we have an image, the actual occurrence (which appears to us as an image) is a step in an actual or possible adaptation. It is a repetition of a step in a previous adaptation, namely, that which we made when we had the original sensation of which the image is sometimes said to be a copy.

An adaptation involves something to which we are adapting. If, for instance, I am thinking of St. Peter's by means of an image of its dome, and you are thinking of it by means of the words 'St. Peter's,' we shall each be adapted to something. If this is the same, then we can be said to be thinking of the same thing, and so to be having the same thoughts —*i.e.*, adaptations—the same ideas, in spite of the difference in our imagery. Thus an *idea* (an ambiguous word which is synonymous with a 'representation,' a 'conception,' a 'concept,' a 'notion,' or a 'universal') is a way of thinking applicable to something, and as is implied by the term 'adaptation,' all 'thought' is determined by the necessity of reacting to situations and determines action of some kind or other.

Emotions. We may now, bearing in mind this idea of adaptation, turn to the active side of mental processes, to striving, and consider instincts and the emotions. The distinctive feature of emotional as opposed to other experience is the presence of certain organic sensations, due to physiological changes in the internal organs of the body, such as a quickened pulse and arrested breathing. These, or images of them, give their peculiar flavor to experiences such as anger, fear, love, or wonder.

Instincts. But it must not be supposed that these sensations are all that constitutes such an emotion as anger. We have to examine the causes to which the sensations themselves are due. We then find that there are apparently a small number of primitive drives or inborn arrangements of the organism, which lead it to respond to special situations in a special manner. These are, or may give rise to, the so-called *instincts.* Thus if a jaguar rushes suddenly upon us, our instinctive adaptation takes the form of *flight.* But to facilitate flight the internal conditions of the body (the heart-beat, the breathing, the glandular activities, etc.) are modified; and these modifications give rise to the sensational part of the emotions above indicated. In other words, we are sorry, as James put it, because we cry, rather than *vice versa.* But a fly in the eye will make that organ water, yet we do not necessarily experience grief. That is to say, it is only bodily sensations, instinctively originated, which constitute emotions, or 'affects,' as they are often called by modern writers; and there is much more in an emotion than a mere organic disturbance. In some such way as this the chief objection to William James's view, namely Stout's contention that a stomach-ache is not an emotion, is avoided. Yet it is fairly clear that instinctive activity may be unaccompanied by emotion in the sense in which we have used the term. Some, however, would maintain that emotions do accompany such instincts even when not consciously experienced, but are "in the unconscious" to which we may now turn.

The Unconscious. The recognition, chiefly since the opening of the present century, that most of our mental life has not the character of consciousness, is responsible for much of the present popular interest in the subject. The laws of the interconnections of conscious 'elements' had been elaborately studied a hundred years ago by writers like Hartley, and already by the time of John Stuart Mill it seemed unlikely that much more could be added. Authorities like Bain were producing definitive treatises on the intellect and the emotions, and, though there were sporadic attempts to found a science of animal psychology, and laboratory methods were being developed, it hardly appeared possible to do more than put the finishing touches on so monumental a structure.

At this point morbid psychology, through the work of medical men and alienists, specialists in the treatment of those who are beside themselves (Lat. *alius* = other), began to force upon the attention of the official representatives of the science the necessity for fresh hypotheses.

As so often, advance was due to the fresh stimulus provided by strange occurrences for which accepted theories could suggest no explanation. Hypnotism, alternating personalities, automatic writing and psychical research, hysteria, phobias and neuroses in general, particularly those relating to sex, became the central points of interest. Resemblances between the phenomena of dreams and those of mental diseases led to a completely new account of what happens in the mind when conscious control is relaxed.

The facts thus brought to light show that only a small part of our mental life is under conscious control, *i.e.*, controlled by processes which are themselves conscious. This has emphasized the fact that consciousness is the exception rather than the rule in the processes studied by psychology. In dealing, however, with 'The Unconscious' which is becoming too ready a resource in psychological difficulties, the first necessity is to decide precisely how we are going to use our language. Most discussions of the unconscious proceed as though there were two distinct realms, the conscious and the unconscious; as when it is said that what was in the unconscious can be brought into consciousness or what is conscious may be repressed into the unconscious. The mind is thus regarded as composed of separate strata, and in addition to the Unconscious we hear of the Sub-conscious, the Fore-conscious, and so forth. This metaphorical language is convenient for some purposes, but no clear understanding of the problems can be reached unless we are prepared to go behind such verbal devices.

Metaphors and Facts. The result of rash speculations on the contents of the Unconscious has been a revival of almost mediæval views of 'possession'—whereby from time to time the personality is invaded and occupied by what amounts to a separate spirit. Or, as Bertrand Russell in his *Analysis of Mind* well puts it, "the unconscious becomes a sort of underground prisoner, living in a dungeon, breaking in at long intervals upon our daylight respectability with dark groans and maledictions and strange atavistic lusts"; his own view being that an unconscious desire is merely a law of our behavior, namely, "that we remain restlessly active until a certain state of affairs is realized, when we achieve temporary equilibrium. If we know beforehand what this state of affairs is, our desire is conscious; if not, unconscious. The unconscious desire is not something actually existing, but merely a tendency to a certain behavior; it has exactly the status of a force in physics."

Arising out of the metaphor of 'force' in physics we have an extensive metaphorical vocabulary of impulsions, resistances, impacts, pulls and pushes, which at a certain level of analysis have their usefulness, but are carefully excluded by the physicist from any exact statement. Similarly, we may use the metaphors of 'unconscious desires,' 'the censor,' 'repressed complexes,' and we then get the following representative psycho-analytic description of a dream: "The barriers of the Freudian unconscious are less tightly closed during sleep, and elements from behind these barriers, as well as ordinary elements from the foreconscious, from the marginal zone, and from the primary unconscious may all play their part." It is hardly necessary to point out that all this metaphorical language will vanish as the science advances. But just as the scaffolding erected by builders is often more interesting to the public than their final architectural achievements, so the psychology of desire and memory in its early stages has lent itself to a picturesque treatment which, now that its work has been done, can profitably be discarded.

With these general considerations before us we may come to grips with our subject by introducing the momentous problem of Mind and Body.

CHAPTER II: THE MIND AND THE BODY

Mind, Soul, and Spirit. Upon the most interesting of all questions, "What is the mind?" psychologists are as yet by no means agreed. And it is unlikely that any amount of mere discussion and argumentation will lead to agreement. More facts are needed, and time for a realization of the bearing of these facts upon the general problem. The question has not yet become, as it must if it is to be solved, a purely scientific matter. Men's prejudices, preferences, and desires still intervene to make cool judgment difficult.

It is usual in psychology to include under the term 'mind' what in ordinary speech would be regarded as special attributes relating not to thought alone, but to the 'emotions,' the 'passions,' the 'affections,' the 'heart,' to 'intuition,' to the 'soul,' and to the 'spirit.' Popular opinion often assumes that these things are distinct from mind, which is regarded as chiefly concerned with the intellect, and it is sometimes convenient to distinguish emotion and will as 'spiritual,' and thought or intellect as 'mental.' But all these, as we shall see in Chapter XI, are, of course, inseparable aspects of the same stream of activity.

Even psychologists, however, have felt that the too exclusive preoccupation of academic thinkers (such as Mill, Mach, Meinong, Moore, Marty, and

Maier—to confine ourselves to one letter of the alphabet only) with intellectual analysis has unduly warped the subject, and that some term more comprehensive than 'mind' might be desirable. The term 'psychical,' as applied to 'psychical development,' 'psychical qualities,' etc., has long been familiar, though the advance of Psychical Research, the study of supernormal mental phenomena, has tended to give it and particularly the word 'psychic' a supernatural tinge.

But if we oppose the brain to the 'mind' in its narrower sense, some more general term, the 'psyche,' would be opposed to the body, the 'soma,' as a whole; it need hardly be pointed out that an experience is not connected solely with the brain, for the stomach, and the solar and sympathetic ganglia (Chapter XIV), may be playing their part. The indiscriminate use of technicalities is to be deprecated, and the bandying about of such terms as 'endo-somatic' where 'bodily' would do just as well is one of the vices of latter-day experimentalists. In this work the term 'mind' will often be used, for convenience, in a comprehensive sense.

The Seven Theories. To approach psychology through the Body-Mind controversy is one of the best ways of going quickly to the heart of the matter. Many conflicting views are still held by thinkers whose opinions are worthy of respect and consideration. The number of theories theoretically possible as to the relations of mind and matter is, it may surprise the reader to learn, only seventeen, and the parent of many of them[1] slays six of his offspring in a single paragraph; but of those which concern the psychologist only seven are of importance.

(1) MATERIALISM AND BEHAVIORISM. There is the view of the Behaviorists and the Materialists that what appears to be mental is in reality physiological processes. Thinking, for example, according to Professor Watson, is *sub-vocal talking*; that is to say, silent internal discourse—very slight muscular movements in the organs of speech or elsewhere in the body. Mental events, on this view, simply do not exist. What has always been regarded as experience, as the working of the mind, is an illusion, like the malevolence attributed by the savage to a pistol. All that we do is to respond by activities of our muscles and glands to the situations which we encounter. The main motive of this school is a passionate desire to avoid all mention in psychology of items which are in the least degree obscure or inaccessible to standard methods of observation. This is a laudable desire, especially in view of the extent to which unverifiable speculations have occupied psychologists in the past, but it has led to a bias as extraordinary as that which it was designed to avoid.

Moreover, there can be no doubt, and Professor Watson and his fellow Behaviorists should be the last to deny it, that the happenings in our brains and more generally in our nervous systems are at least as important in 'thinking' as any movements which we

[1] C. D. Broad, *Mind and its Place in Nature* (1925), pp. 611-612.

make. It is true that it is still more difficult to discover what exactly these happenings are than to observe muscular movements. Yet Watson's 'sub-vocal movements' are themselves at present not accessible to observation. Their sponsor has lately extended the doctrine. The sub-vocal movements which are 'thought' itself need not, he now holds, occur in the throat. Movements in any other part of the body may, by 'conditioning' (see Chapter IV), take their place. We cannot be certain that an individual is not engaged in thought unless we are certain that no such movements are taking place in him.

The inaccessibility of happenings in the nerves, with which we shall be much occupied in the following chapter, is not a good reason for denying that they are the essential things in thinking. Thus the majority of neurologists (Gk. *neuron*=nerve) give the movements so much stressed by Behaviorists a subordinate place and regard mental events as being actually processes in certain parts of the brain. To quote a popular account of this doctrine: "As soon as 'mental states' are resolved into reflexes among some of the 10,000,000,000 cortical neurons, it becomes obvious that the word 'mind' is no more than shorthand for neuronal action and interaction when influenced from the outside or by internal stimuli."[1] When Materialism is inverted we get the various forms of Spiritualism (philosophically termed Ideal-

[1] Morley Roberts, *Warfare in the Human Body* (1924), p. 229.

ism) according to which matter is an illusion and the only 'reality' is mental.

(2) ANIMISM AND INTERACTIONISM. In vigorous opposition to the materialists are the Animists (Lat. *anima*=soul), of whom Professor McDougall is the most uncompromising. They maintain that whatever may be the status of these material phenomena, however far neurology may go in explaining the processes which occur in the body, none the less, there is a mind or soul also: a spiritual thing utterly different in nature from the body, which *interacts* with the body, being affected by it and likewise affecting it. The old view that the Conservation of Energy made this interaction impossible is now abandoned; but the nature of the interaction which occurs remains so obscure, owing to an ignorance both of mind and of body, that the doctrine is at present almost without significance. On the other hand, there are many phenomena—from a dose of chloroform to a cure at Delphi—which, if we are not too particular about knowing exactly what we are saying, may seem clear proofs that mind and body act after one another. None the less, both the psychologist and neurologist are reluctant to accept this view because it would involve for each the intervention in his science of factors which in no way belong to it; and the more closely either psychology or neurology is studied the less place there is in either for extraneous explanations.

Various hypotheses have been devised to avoid either of these opposed positions, to escape both

Materialism and Animism. The most widely adopted is Parallelism.

(3) Psycho-neural Parallelism. According to parallelists there is a mind quite distinct from the body, but mind and body do not influence each other in any degree or at any point. Instead, it is supposed that every event in the higher parts of the nervous system is accompanied by a mental event, and *vice versa*. The two streams, neural and mental, run parallel to each other, but in complete independence: like two clocks, back to back, keeping time. This is perhaps the safest view in psychology; on the other hand it does not fully satisfy many of its adherents.

(4) Epiphenomenalism. On this view mind would be a by-product, an epiphenomenon, of neural processes, not reducible to such processes, but still quite unable to influence them. It would be like a phosphorescent glow due to the neural processes which would go on regardless of it; or, to adopt a perhaps more appropriate metaphor it would be like the light emitted by an arc-lamp as the current passes across the gap between the carbons. This view, associated with the name of T. H. Huxley, has lately receded somewhat in favor of

(5) The Double Aspect Hypothesis. Both mind and brain might be equally real, neither reducible to the other but each of them 'aspects' of something else. Both what we experience—*i.e.*, our mental processes—and what others, if they could look into our heads, would observe, are on this view

equally signs of more fundamental happenings. The very same event which *appears to me* as my thought would *appear to you*, if you could see it, as my nervous system in agitation. The evident disadvantage of such a double aspect theory is that the fundamental happenings are left in such obscurity. They would seem to be things we could know nothing about.

(6) NEUTRAL MONISM. To avoid such unknowables, a new suggestion has recently been put forward by Bertrand Russell. Mind he reduces to sensations and images, and these are regarded as probably reducible to physiological events; at the same time his treatment of matter, including the body, turns the universe into sensations and sensibilia—*i.e.*, possible sensations. Thus the two meet in *one* (Gk. *monos*=one) kind of neutral stuff, those changes in this stuff which follow psychological laws being mental, those which follow physical laws being physical. Much interest is certain to center round this view, which is, however, far from representing a stable position.

It is fortunately not necessary for psychology to decide at the outset between these rival hypotheses. Almost all its results can be stated in terms of any of them with more or less trouble in different cases: and perhaps the most interesting point in the controversy is the extreme difficulty of finding any facts which might decide between them when apparent differences due to the prejudices which they invite have been eliminated. This circumstance has suggested a seventh view which is much akin to the Double Aspect theory and is gaining ground.

(7) THE DOUBLE LANGUAGE HYPOTHESIS regards neurology and psychology as being concerned with the very same facts, but concerned to describe them in two different languages.

A child thinks that an orange looks yellow and has a size when there is no one there to see it. But, as Professor Mitchell well puts it, the orange "is a real thing which we only know in this physical or sensory way. Our own mind and its experiences we may know in this way as the brain and its processes, and in this way other people can know us equally well, or better than we know ourselves. But we also know our mind and its experience directly, and this no one can do but ourselves, who are our mind and have its experience."[1] Every remark in the one science can theoretically be translated into terms of the other. The two accounts deal not with different aspects of some further unknowable event, but with the very same event, which is known in two ways: directly, in introspection, when we are or enjoy an experience; indirectly, in neurology, when through the interpretation of signs we infer an event in the brain. As Professor Piéron in introducing his masterly survey of modern research, *Thought and the Brain*, admirably remarks:

"Whatever certain theorists may assert to the contrary, neurophysiology does undoubtedly often

[1] *Structure and Growth of the Mind* (1907), p. 22.

provide an adequate representation of the laws established by psychology; the study of the functions of the brain frequently supplies satisfying explanations of psychological phenomena. In fact, we often pass from one form of representation—or rather, from one form of expression or language—to the other.

"To these and similar advances made by science beliefs will always adapt themselves. If it is a materialistic doctrine that seeks support from the new data, the adaptation presents no difficulty. But even a spiritualistic creed, if free to remold certain articles of faith, could well accept the facts now established. There will always be a sufficient residue of the unknown for scientific facts to be accommodated to the various systems of beliefs; and in any case the mind can always take refuge in a transcendental idealism."

The New Orientation. Neurophysiology, on which so much of our understanding of psychological processes is based, is no longer studied only by scientists who mistrust the contribution of the student of mind. Medical men with a wide and intimate experience of human behavior both in health and disease are daily throwing light on problems of thought and emotion. The neurologist who has to grapple with the intricacies and implications of aphasia (loss of speech) or of epilepsy is to-day competent to meet psychologists on their own ground. And on the mind-body problem the modern neurologist is for the most part in agreement with Professor Piéron:

"The tendency either to take an extremely psychological or an extremely material view of certain forms of sickness is partly due to the old conception of *causation* in the etiology of disease. . . . The integration of the nervous system, the integration of the endocrine system, and the integration of the conscious and unconscious realms of the human psyche, are not independent phenomena. Man is the supreme integration of every system, nervous, vascular, glandular, or psychological."[1] And, adds Dr. Kinnier Wilson, editor of the *Journal of Neurology*, "to interpret psychological phenomena in terms of bodily movement is a truly objective method. . . . The psyche must be interpreted and understood in terms of action and behavior. . . . And by action is meant not only voluntary movements and speech, but also implicit action such as bodily postures, attitudes, gestures, tensions, and autonomic disturbances" (*Ibid*, p. 344).

Many adherents of the Double Aspect formulation would probably subscribe to the Double Language view if they considered the alternative more closely. Thus Professor Warren assumes "that conscious and neural phenomena constitute one single series of events, and that their different appearance is merely due to different ways of observing them"; but he does not posit a further something of which both are aspects. "Consciousness," he continues, "'belongs to' the activity of neurons as truly as the

[1] *The Journal of Neurology and Psycho-pathology* (editorial), vol. i, 1920-21, p. 165.

intensity or form of neural impulses belongs to this same activity. . . . They form part of the 'total description' of nerve activity."[1] And it is significant that the *Gestalt* psychologists "consider mind, or rather mental processes," in the words of Professor Koffka,[2] "not as something outside of nature, but as just such natural events as any other. They are links in the chains of reactions produced by an organism in an environment, and cannot legitimately be isolated from this context. . . . The total reaction of the organism of which mental processes are parts is surely a physiological event."

A peculiar effort of the imagination is required before this view becomes plausible. An experience and an agitation in the body seem so unlike one another that the suggestion that they are one and the same, and that the difference is merely in our mode of access to them, is often treated as outrageous. Yet it is the very uniqueness of experience which suggests this view; and those who dismiss its advocates as unable to appreciate the obvious fact that experience is unique are frequently unaware of the weight of considered opinion in favor of the linguistic solution. We approach all other happenings from without; but our experience is a happening in ourselves. Thus it should naturally seem to us totally distinct from the happenings which we observe through signs; and if, as this view holds, an *experience* be observed from without, it must be un-

---

[1] *Human Psychology* (1919), by Howard C. Warren, p. 415.
[2] *Psyche*, vol. v, 1924-25, pp. 80-81.

recognizable as an experience. The unlikeness, therefore, would only be an argument against treating the experience and the nervous disturbance as identical if the psychologist introspecting and the neurologist making his conjectures were using the same kind of observation. Language itself (always awkward when things which have been traditionally regarded as different have to be identified) and the absence of parallel instances, which could be used as analogies, are further difficulties. Thus it is often objected that we can ask questions about the brain—its shape, for example—which we cannot ask about the mind. It is true that such questions at present sound awkward; but, to take a rough parallel, we do not, if we are wise, conclude that because the remark, "Parliament is hungry," sounds awkward, Parliament must therefore consist of something other than the human beings who forthwith proceed to lunch.

As Professor Dewey well puts it, "our language is so permeated with consequences of theories which have divided the body and mind from each other, making separate existential realms out of them, that we lack words to designate the actual existential fact. . . . Body-mind simply designates what actually takes place when a living body is implicated in situations of discourse, communication, and participation."[1] It is from a position similar to this that many adherents of the theory of 'emergent evolution' proceed. At various points in the evolutionary

[1] Dewey, *Experience and Nature* (1925), pp. 284-285.

process there have arisen, according to this view, which is associated with the name of Lloyd Morgan and is a development from the earlier vitalistic formulation of Bergson, new or emergent 'factors.' Thus purely physical processes, as they increase in complexity, give rise to chemical emergents, and similarly the organic emerges from the inorganic. In the same way, it is suggested, 'mind' (conation) emerges out of life, and consciousness out of mind—first, most probably, in the form of pain. This is in many respects a convenient way of describing evolution, if we remember that the new or emergent factor need be nothing other than a new arrangement or integration of what was already in being; in which case 'mind' is not to be contrasted with body in the Mind-body controversy, but is a shorthand term for a certain mode of working of some bodies. Advocates of the vocabulary of 'emergence,' therefore, need not dissent from the Double Language explanation, since they are not concerned to deny that psychology and some parts of neurology are ultimately describing the same processes.

Advantages of the Linguistic Solution. The Double Language view retains the advantages of the physical approach while avoiding its incompleteness; for on this view psychology is no more reduced to neurology than neurology is reduced to psychology.[1]

---

[1] As Professor Eddington puts it in his contribution to *Science, Religion, and Reality* (1925): "There is nothing to prevent the assemblage of atoms forming the brain from being a thinking-machine. . . . Because we see that our precise knowledge of certain aspects of the behavior of atoms leaves their intrinsic nature just

Both remain indispensable parts of a complete account. Introspection, metaphorically speaking, studies life from within, neurology from without. Each account supplements the other. Thus the natural prejudices on both sides have less play, and are less offended by this theory than by any of the rival views. Those who resent a solution which would reduce all mental life to a mere play of brain processes, governed by laws into which such things as hopes, desires, purposes, and aspirations do not enter, can find on careful consideration no ground for objection; for neural laws would be a translation of just these kinds of things into terms of neural action. At the same time those who feel a despair of a science whose methods and results do not admit of control and corroboration by the methods and results of the other sciences will find their demand met.

The Interchange of Methods. Whichever of the above views the reader elects to adopt provisionally, he will undoubtedly find his interest in psychology heightened and sustained by a habit of constantly regarding the facts with which he becomes acquainted in the light of the bearing they may have upon this all-important question. He will find, too, that the actual process of psychological investigation involves a constant interchange between the two methods, study of the body and the nervous system by obser-

---

as transcendental and inscrutable as the nature of the mind, so the difficulty of the interaction of matter and mind is lessened."—Or rather, the difficulties raised by the term 'interaction' vanish!

vation and the technique of the neurologist, and study of the mind by what is known as introspection. And in actual fact he will constantly be attempting to translate the results of the one into the terms of the other. If, for example, he has a headache he will consider whether lack of exercise, too much food, too little sleep, bad air, or some such physiological cause is likely to have so affected the brain as to cause the headache. That something is wrong he knows from within on purely psychological grounds. He then tries to arrive by physiological considerations at a probable explanation of this very state of affairs. Or again he may look up from his book some evening and be surprised to notice that it is long past his ordinary bedtime. This unusual behavior he will explain by saying: "I must have been unusually interested"—a psychological explanation for the prolonged continuance of the movements and adaptations of reading.

Now whether we regard these as instances of interaction between body and mind or as evidence for a double aspect or a double language view is at present unimportant. What *is* important is to notice how intimately observation of bodily behavior, together with inferences as to the working of the nervous system, are mingled in all our descriptions of the events in our lives with observations of our feelings, our thoughts, our interests, and the rest of our experiences. Our movements, etc., are public facts, our experiences are private. A complete account of a minute of any person's life would have to mention both public and private facts. Neither alone would be adequate. It is those who are most expert in inferring the one kind of fact from the other who succeed in the world. There is nothing so important as to be able to pass without mistake from observation of the behavior of other people to conclusions about their thoughts, feelings, and intentions; and conversely to pass without mistake from our own private experiences to conclusions about the external events which are influencing us and about the state of our bodies.

Program. This division between observations from within and from without, therefore, will guide us in the division of our subject-matter. And since the stock of common knowledge is far greater as regards internal observations than external, we will begin by describing in outline the part which is less familiar, namely the working of the nervous system so far as this concerns psychology: the more familiar part may then be considered in a new light. Keeping to the standpoint of external observation, we shall sketch the growth of the mind from its earliest forms to its present development in man. We shall, of course, unavoidably be using throughout a great deal of information which we only possess thanks to internal observation of experiences. This serves as a clue to external observation. We know before we begin to consider psychology at all a very great deal about the experiences which in ourselves correspond to certain forms of behavior. We cannot help interpreting certain noises made by a baby as meaning discomfort and certain others as meaning satisfaction. It would be folly to attempt to dispense altogether with this knowledge. Without such knowledge as a clue it is certain that neither neurology nor physiology would have got far on the road. We must be careful, needless to say, to avoid misinterpretations, as, for example, in dealing with animals unlike man.

We shall use this clue; and when we have carried our neurological account as far as possible, we shall turn to the psychological account and describe the mind as it appears *from within*. Knowledge gained by either method will be found invaluable in the development of the other.

CHAPTER III: IMPULSE AND INHIBITION

The Action of Neurones. The body is a vast society of living cells, many hundreds of thousands of millions in number; each of these cells has its special task, its contribution towards the activity of the whole society. Each, of whatever kind it may be, in skin or bone or muscle or gland, depends for its life upon the co-operation in numberless ways of other kinds of cells. But this co-operation does not come about of itself. Special arrangements are needed to adjust the different activities of separate groups of cells to one another; and, what is equally important, to put the organism as a whole into adjustment with what is happening outside it. From minute to minute the situation in which we find ourselves changes; we need to make suitable corresponding changes ourselves. Conversely, our own internal state changes and we need to make suitable changes in the situation. The principal agent whereby this is done is the nervous system.

The nervous system is itself made up of living cells which specialize as conductors, handing on disturbances which arise in one part of the body so that other parts of the body can deal with the situation. These cells (known as neurones) are of a fantastic variety of forms; some will be found illustrated in Fig. I. But since they are all essentially conductors, they have a common plan. Each consists

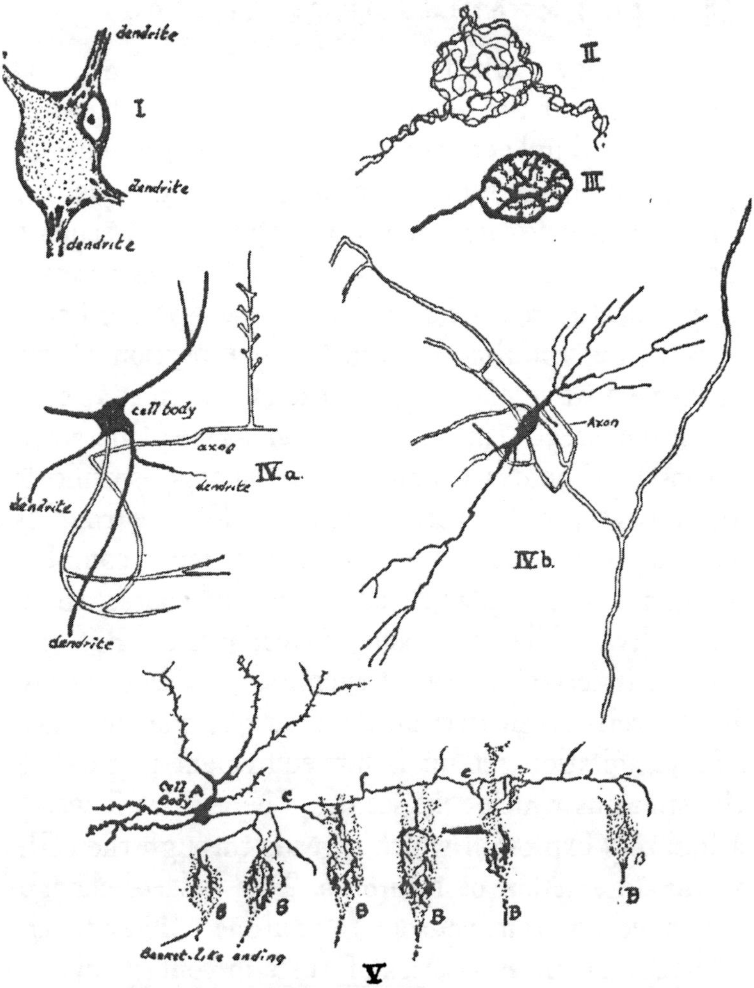

FIG. I.—VARIOUS TYPES OF NEURONES

(To illustrate the great variety of forms taken by the cells which make up the nervous system)

I. Nerve cell with beginning of its Axon and Dendrites.

II. Types of pericellular network around the cell-body of a neurone, illustrating ways in which one neurone forms synapses or connections with another.

III. Coarse variety of (II).

IV. *a.* Neurone of common type with short dendrites and single long axon (Golgi cell of first order).—Axon drawn in double line.

IV. *b.* Neurone of another type (Golgi cell of second order).

V. Synapses or junctions between a neurone (A) and a number of other neurones (B); branches of the axon (C) forming basket-like endings around their cell-bodies (Purkinje system).

of a *cell-body*, which is as it were the commissariat department of the whole cell looking after its nourishment and upkeep, and also of a varying number of prolongations in some cases of great length, as, for instance, when a neurone in the spinal cord sends a prolongation down to a muscle for the toe or receives one from the root of a hair in the back of the hand.

When a stimulus is applied to one portion of the neurone a wave of change spreads through it at considerable speed (in man as high as 125 meters a second). The exact nature of the change is difficult to discover, for several reasons. The neurone is microscopic; it is made up of the most complex substance on this planet; and it has, of course, to be kept alive while it is being investigated. But the change is certainly in part chemical. Latent energy in the cell is released on stimulation; the intensity of the agitation set up is not equivalent to that of the stimulus which releases it. There is, as it were, a leisurely explosion which spreads through the cell.

The Interaction of Neurones. This wave of change is handed on from neurone to neurone. They touch one another off as a series of fuses in contact might. The points of contact, known as synapses (Gk. *synapto* = join together),[1] seem to act as valves: they let

[1] Whether contact occurs, and whether there are not narrow thread-like structures which bridge the gap and so make the neurones continuous with one another, is disputed. In any case these meeting points are of peculiar importance. They are the points of greatest resistance in the path of the impulse, like hurdles in the track of a runner. For it is a curious fact that, though the impulse may, while passing through a synapse or series of synapses, be decreased in strength or extinguished, yet, if it passes the difficult piece of the

the impulse pass in one direction only; it is not allowed to return on its track. The neurone itself may have something to do with this. Among its prolongations (see Fig. I), however numerous, there is, as a general rule, one (known as the axon) which is different from the others (known as dendrites). It is finer and as a rule longer. And it is through the axon that the impulse passes on to the next neurone in the chain. The dendrites, or the cell-body, receive the impulse, either from a sense-organ or from the axon of another neurone; the axon conducts it elsewhere. It follows that if we stimulate the wrong end of a chain of neurones nothing happens at the other end.

The neurone is thus rather like a tree whose roots receive water and convey it to the stem and branches; for the axon commonly branches, and the impulse may pass out of it now through this branch, now through that, sometimes from one branch, sometimes from many. What happens in any particular case depends upon the state of the synapses, or upon the state of the neurones themselves. As to this, little has yet been definitely ascertained. The point to

---

track at all, it gets new life and goes on as before. An impulse is usually stopped at a synapse. And the synapse as a contact surface between cells is a point at which the most varied and the most important changes might be expected to take place. As Sir Charles Sherrington observes, "it might restrain diffusion, bank up osmotic pressure, restrict the movement of ions, accumulate electric charges, support a double electric layer, alter in shape and surface tension with changes in difference of potential, alter in difference of potential with changes in surface tension or shape, or intervene as a membrane between dilute solutions of electrolytes of different concentration or colloidal suspensions with different sign of charge."

notice is that there is always a bewildering variety of possible paths for the impulse, and which of them it takes is the all-important matter, since different paths lead to different responses and so to different behavior and different experiences. It may be added that however incomplete the physiologist's account of what happens at the synapse, the psychologist's own independent account of choice (for this is what is often psychologically in question) is just as scrappy and unfinished.

The Conflict of Impulses. The central problem, then, is this—How does it happen that an impulse takes one path on a given occasion and not another? To consider it we need a clear idea of the system as a whole (cf. Fig. II) and of the broad outlines of its working.

In the first place, it is an extraordinarily unified system; its various parts and their separate activities are interdependent in the highest degree. This must obviously be the case in an organ whose job is to *integrate* the body, to unite its activities into orderly co-operative behavior. But the rule that what is happening in any one part of the nervous system depends upon what is happening elsewhere holds good throughout, and we must strenuously resist the temptation to regard any particular impulse as an isolated happening.

If a wasp stings my finger I usually take the finger away from it, and it is tempting to analyze this impulse as though the rest of the goings-on in my nervous system were irrelevant. But if I were hang-

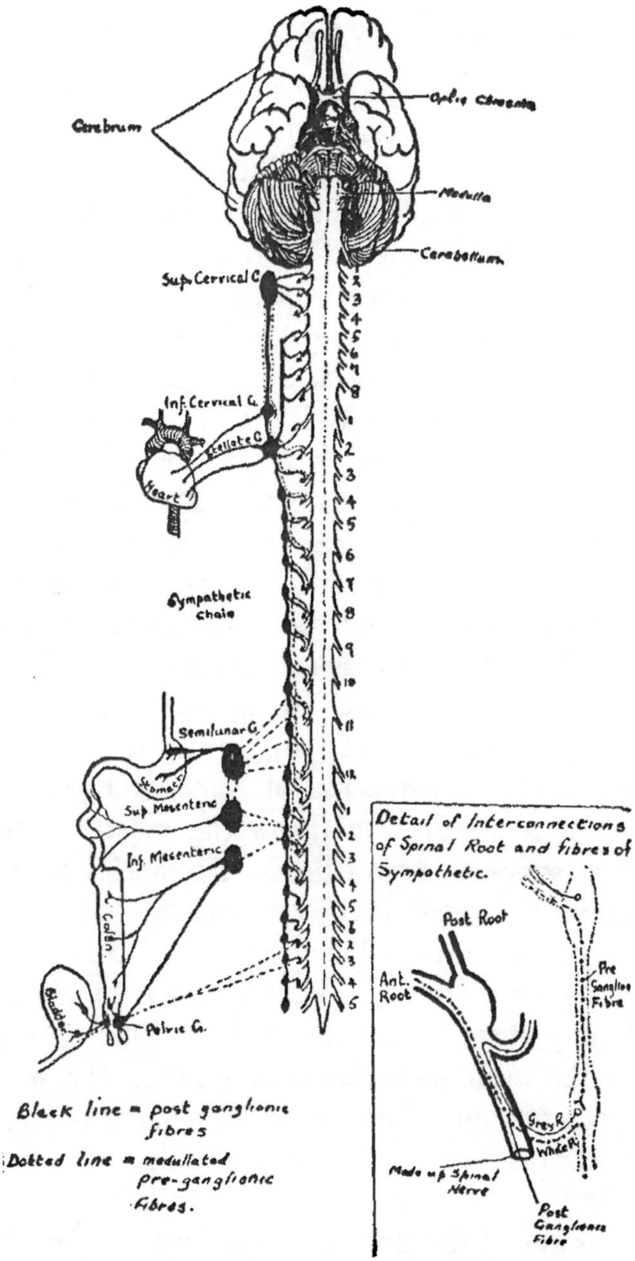

FIG. II.—GENERAL DIAGRAM OF THE NERVOUS SYSTEM
Showing the relationship of the central nervous system to the sympathetic.

ing over a precipice by that hand alone I should not wave it about, however busy the wasp might be. The fact is that even the impulses which seem most insistent and independent have merely a precedence *allowed* by the others. They take their course by consent and in the general interest, and may, if the situation is sufficiently exceptional, be overruled.

Adjustment through Clearing-houses. The instance suggests a point of view which is illuminating. The arm muscles of the wasp's victim are engaged for the moment in the task of holding on. A special set of neurones (motor neurones) running *down* to them from the spinal cord is keeping them in the right state of contraction. But the sting of the wasp sets up an agitation in another set of neurones (afferent or sensory neurones) which run *up* to the spinal cord, and this agitation would, if it did not find them already engaged, make use of some of those very same motor neurones to throw the muscles into a different series of contractions. At the entrance to these motor neurones two rival claimants for the use of them have arisen. Now the central part of the nervous system (the spinal cord, that is to say, and the brain) is an arrangement for adjusting precedences between such claims in view of the whole relevant situation. The motor neurone, or the similar apparatus in the case of a gland, is therefore sometimes called the "final common path." It is an apparatus at the disposal of an immense number of impulses from different sources, some of which can use it together while others obviously can only use it in turn. In between the sources of these impulses and the motor apparatus intervenes tier after tier of clearing-houses sorting out rival claims, combining some, holding up others. These are arranged in tiers because plainly the extent of the relevant situation varies from case to case; it may be comparatively narrow and simple, or it may embrace the whole nature of the universe as known to the individual. The situation relevant to the way we breathe, for example, is fairly simple. The main factors are the state of the atmosphere and of the blood and the position of the body. So the adjustment of the various claims can ordinarily be left to fairly lowly centers as a routine business. But for the singer and the Everest climber the matter is more complicated; higher-level clearing-houses have to take charge, and since these higher centers are less used to the business, a learning process is required.

The Importance of the Head. The highest centers are those which have to take note of the widest and most intricate situations and to order the largest and most varied sets of claims. For reasons which are clear enough in outline they lie in the head—in the 'cerebrum' and 'cerebellum.'[1] To quote the physiologist:

"The head is in many ways the individual's greater part. It is the more so the higher the individual stands in the animal scale. It has the mouth, it

[1] The cerebrum (see Fig. II) is the seat of the highest co-ordinations of sense and movement, whereas the cerebellum is concerned with the highest co-ordinations of the relations of the organism to space.

takes in the food, including water and air, it has the main receptive organs providing data for the rapid and accurate adjustment of the animal to time and space. To it the trunk, an elongated motor organ with a share of the digestive surface, and the skin, is appended as an apparatus of locomotion and nutrition. The latter must of necessity lie at the command of the greater receptor organs of the head."[1]

The nose for lower animals, such as the dog, the eyes and ears for man, are the sources of most of the claims which are going to be made upon the motor neurones that finally promote action. And the dominance of the brain, the organ for co-ordinating the impulses set going through these sense organs with the rest of the impulses ceaselessly flowing through the nervous system, is explained by this fact. What may be regarded as the conjunction of brain and spinal cord, the medulla, is itself the seat not only of very important nerve-centers, but also of the centers for breathing, vomiting, and of the vagus nerve, which is intimately related to the sympathetic nervous system dealt with in Chapter XIV.

The exact topographical site of the various orders of clearing-houses which occur in the brain (as to which a good deal is beginning to be known) is of no general importance for psychology. An idea of some of the areas which are known to be concerned with special functions can be gathered from Fig. III. It is the scheme of their relations to one another

[1] Sherrington, *The Integrative Action of the Nervous System* (1914), p. 350.

that matters. Each clearing-house is a fairly extensive region where innumerable cell-bodies with their dendrites and axons, interlacing and criss-crossing in every direction in a tangle of incredible com-

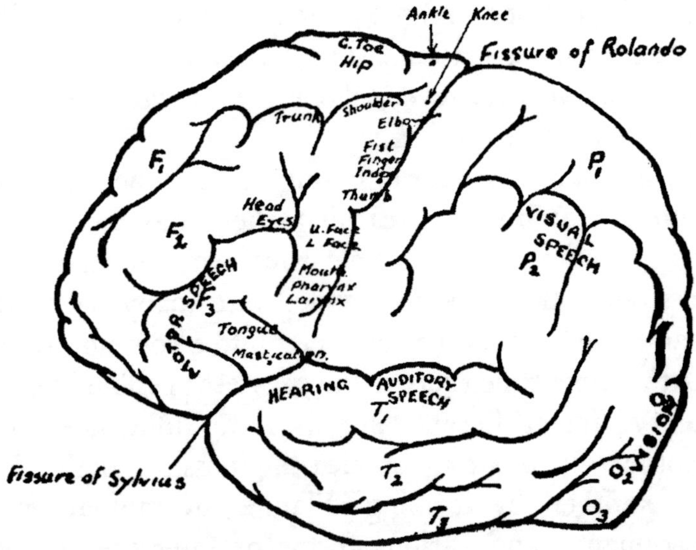

FIG. III.—THE LOCALIZATION OF FUNCTION IN BRAIN
(*Seen from the left side*)

The area thickly spotted with names just in front of the Rolandic fissure is the *motor* area, and if it is electrically stimulated voluntary movements of the parts indicated occur. The corresponding areas on the other side of the fissure are *reception* centers for touch sensations from the same parts. The visual reception area is at the extreme back of the brain. Between this and the tongue area lie, with innumerable others, the association centers for reading.

plexity, are massed together. Cell-bodies and dendrites are gray, axons are white in appearance; hence the name 'gray cells' or 'gray matter' for those parts of the brain in which the most complex transactions take place. The white matter consists of axons running, as a rule, lengthy courses and linking up more distant regions. Every part of the brain is so linked with every other part. It is rather fortunate that a very extensive region of gray matter (known as the cortex) stretches over the surface of the brain like the peel of an orange, just where it is most easily got at for investigation. There are other more deep-lying regions, however, about the precise functions of which much less is known.

Thanks to this intermingling of neurones in these centers any impulse reaching them has an almost infinite number of possible routes by which it can pass out. It can be subdivided into many paths, or many impulses can be combined into a common path. At the same time there is the greatest possible opportunity for different impulses to influence one another, by blocking or clearing possible paths for one another, by forming alliances, by mutual reinforcements, and various forms of interference and conflict.

The Spinal Cord. The exact way in which neurones interact is still largely a matter of speculation. What little we know of them comes chiefly from experiments upon what are known as 'spinal' reflexes. When the spinal cord is severed from the brain, its operations are no longer controlled by the higher clearing-houses, and a great simplification results; further, as there is clear evidence to show, consciousness, including pain, for the parts thus cut off, no longer occurs. It is then possible to elicit movements, say of the leg, by simple stimuli in a very uniform manner. By combining stimuli and noting the responses, something of the ways in which impulses combine or interfere with one another can be made out. For instance, as most children know, there is a scratch-reflex which can be elicited in a sleeping dog by gently pulling the hair or tickling the skin of his flank near the shoulder. Now there is a curious point which even experiments on the hearth-rug will bring out. The scratch has a rhythm of its own. It varies in vigor and in the amplitude of its sweep, but remains almost exactly the same in rate, however we space our ticklings; whether *we* scratch the dog slowly or rapidly, he scratches himself at a uniform rate. The responses are spaced out as compared with the stimuli by a central arrangement which completely transforms the rhythm of the impulses. The reason is evident; if it were not so, the leg might merely reach the point to be scratched and stay there. It must have time to return to the starting point.

Inhibition. But this return is really a complicated affair. The leg is moved by two sets of muscles opposite to each other. One set bends it, the other stretches it. When the leg is at rest both these sets are mildly active; each has a slight contraction which is known as the muscular tonus, and this is, in part at least, maintained through a series of impulses continually passing out through the motor neurones. When the leg is bent one set of muscles (the flexors) contracts more vigorously; the opposite set (the extensors) relaxes. So in every movement the motor neurones concerned have to see that one set of muscles contracts and the opposite set relaxes. In other words, introducing an important technical term for an idea which is fundamental in psychology, one set of muscles is excited and the other set is *inhibited* (Lat. *inhibeo*=check). Actually, the problem is less simple, for it has recently been claimed that voluntary muscles are innervated from the sympathetic nervous system (with which we deal in Chapter XIV) as well as by the cerebro-spinal.

It is tempting to suppose that there must be a special set of motor neurones or a special kind of impulse whose office is solely to inhibit. But the very same motor neurones are used sometimes to excite a muscle and sometimes to inhibit it. Inhibition is a shutting off of excitation from the motor neurones, not a special form of message which immobilizes the muscle. Excitation is a passing through, inhibition a cutting off, of impulses. As the dog scratches away, at every stroke spinal impulses are being turned *on* for the flexor muscles and *off* for the extensors and *vice versa* as the leg sweeps back. What, in terms of inter-neurone action in the spinal cord, is happening?

To study this two reflexes are taken which are antagonistic—that is to say, such that each tends to inhibit the other. For example, if we stimulate the sleeping dog's other hind foot while a hearty scratch is in progress, we shall probably wake him up, but under suitable conditions this stimulation simply puts an end to the scratch; the leg is thrust out instead.

This 'crossed extension-reflex' inhibits [1] the scratch-reflex, and does so, just as in the case of the unlucky tourist and the wasp, by making a rival demand for the use of the final common path, the motor neurones that excite the leg muscles.

A diagram will assist matters at this point. *M* and *M'* are motor neurones or sets of them going to the flexor and extensor muscles of the leg. *A* and *B* are neurones through which impulses come in from the two sense-organs stimulated. *A* by itself would excite *M* and inhibit *M'*, *B* by itself would excite *M'* and inhibit *M*. Remembering that 'inhibit' means

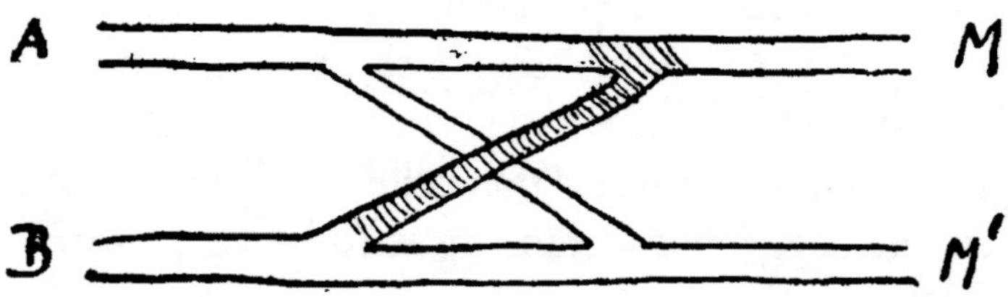

FIG. IV

merely 'leave quite unexcited,' what kind of an account can be suggested of how it is that whenever *M* is excited *M'* is inhibited, and *vice versa?*

Here we pass from the realm of fact to that of conjecture. But the part played by inhibition throughout the working of the nervous system is so extensive, and its importance for psychology is so

[1] This correspondence of excitation with inhibition for antagonistic muscles has been verified for inhibitions lasting no more than .004 of a second. The delicacy and refinement of the experimental work which has been done on this and allied problems is almost beyond belief. A good idea of some of the methods can be gathered from Sherrington's *The Integrative Action of the Nervous System* and from Keith Lucas' *The Conduction of the Nervous Impulse.*

great, that any approach towards an understanding of it is of value. What follows may, at first sight, appear alarming to the beginner; but is not really more difficult than a simple Cross-Word Puzzle. The reader may, however, with a good conscience, proceed rapidly to Chapter V, and return to this slightly more intricate section when its importance has become clear to him.

Four Theories of Inhibition. Four theories may be said to be in the running. One is that the impulse, or rather volley of impulses coming in through *A* liberates at some point on its path a substance which blocks all the other paths to the motor center, thus cutting out *M′* while going through itself to *M*. The substance would have to be very evanescent in its effect, but that is not impossible. The objection is that the suggestion is too vague to be very useful at present.

Another theory is that the impulse on its way to *M* drains away energy from the neurones leading to *M′* by lowering the resistance of synapses which lead out of *B* into *A*, thus cutting off *M′*. The assumption is that the passage of an impulse through a system of neurones lowers the resistance of the synapses leading into it. If we think of the neurones as connected pipes it is clear that lowering the pressure in *A*-*M* would cause water in *B*-*M′* to flow into it. This theory agrees with many facts which are otherwise hard to understand. Fatigue of the synapses would lead to the drainage-process being periodically reversed if the stimuli remain the same, thus giving a neat explanation of 'alternating' movements like the scratch-reflex. But some obvious difficulties arise. One of these concerns what is psychologically the most interesting consequence of the theory. Inhibition is represented as a kind of theft of energy. *A*, when it inhibits *M'*, which would otherwise be excited by *B*, steals some of *B's* energy. The more intense the excitation in *B*, provided it be not greater than that in *A*, the more energy *A* steals. But this result seems not to be experimentally verifiable. Another consequence would be that if, for example, I am writing, the louder a barrel organ plays beneath my window, provided that I do not attend to it, the better my work will go on. This again seems doubtful. But the most serious objection is that when an axon branches, there is no reason to suppose that conduction out of one branch affects what happens in the other branches. Thus the 'drainage' analogy seems hardly to work if examined closely. In view of the constant appeal by the theorists of psycho-analysis to overflow metaphors—as, *e.g.*, when the libido is said to be dammed up—this conclusion is of great importance.

A third, more recent, theory starts from the ascertained fact that the passage of an impulse leaves its track in a 'refractory state.' That is to say for a brief period no other impulse can follow. Now, it is supposed that the *B*— impulses (impulses from *B*) which inhibit *M* have to pass over part of the same track as *A*— impulses which would excite it, and that the going in the shaded parts is so bad that *B*—

impulses give up just before reaching *M*, and yet leave refractory states on *A's* path. Thus no *B*− impulses reach *M* to excite it and yet when *B*− impulses are not running *A*− impulses get through, since they are able to survive their shorter distance of bad going. Meanwhile whenever *B*− impulses block the path to *M*, *M'* gets excited, which was the principal fact to be explained. This beautifully ingenious theory (which is largely the work of Dr. E. D. Adrian) is likely to be developed further.

The fourth and most recent theory, due to Lapicque, is as speculative as the others, but it has the advantages that it is closer to the probable facts than the second, and is more helpful in imagining the subtler happenings in the nervous system than the third. It starts from comparing the times required to produce a response in different nerves and their muscles. The way in which it has been worked out is as follows:

Chronaxies. There is for each muscle and nerve a certain intensity of electrical stimulation which is the least that will excite a response, however long we give it. If this intensity is doubled and the times these doubled intensities take to excite the nerve or the muscle are measured, it is found that these times (known as 'chronaxies'—from *chronos*='time' and *axia*='value') have simple relations to one another. Every tissue has, as it were, its own private time-value.

For example, a muscle and its motor nerve have the same chronaxy; they are isochronous, but different muscles have different chronaxies. Neurones, too, have each their own chronaxy. When the chronaxies of neurones which work together are not the same, one is an integral number of times longer than the other—three times for instance. Now—and this is the interesting point—it is found that conduction only takes place when this normal relation between chronaxies holds. By poisoning a nerve, with strychnine or curare, for example, we can alter its chronaxy and then the excitation no longer passes to the muscle. It is the *difference* between their chronaxies which matters. If we lengthen or shorten both the chronaxies together, the conduction still goes on; it is only when we alter one without altering the other that it ceases. And similarly with the neurones. They get out of tune, as it were. The expression is not strictly correct since a change in chronaxy is very different from a change in a rate of vibration, but we shall use it for lack of a better and say two neurones are *in tune* when their chronaxies allow the impulse to pass, and out of tune when they don't.

Inhibition then might consist in a change of chronaxy throwing an afferent neurone and a motor neurone, for example, out of tune with each other. This would be a delightfully simple solution of the problem. And fortunately there seems good reason to accept it, for it has been shown that changes in chronaxy can be produced not only by poisons, by fatigue, and by hormones such as adrenalin (See Chapter XIV), but by neural influences themselves.

Cutting off the action of the brain commonly doubles the chronaxies in the spinal chord. Now this seems to imply that neurones, besides handing on impulses, have a further, quite distinct, way of influencing one another.

If this is confirmed it opens a completely new prospect of explaining thought in terms of the brain.

In much of what follows we shall assume the chronaxy theory or something like it to be true, and shall call the passage of trains of discharges 'impulses' and modifications of chronaxies 'influences.' A neurone can be discharged by other neurones and it can be influenced, tuned up or tuned down, by them. This last and especially the possibility of its being tuned back again to its former chronaxy is all important, as we shall see later. One further point should be noticed. A given difference from the normal tuning may stop a moderately strong impulse from passing, but a stronger will get by. Thus the normal channel for an impulse may be overflowed if the excitation is violent. This helps to explain why different intensities of stimulation may have such different effects; and, we may add, it is of great significance in connection with emotion.

Various other, even more intricate, theories of inhibition have also been put forward, and it is certain that whatever account is ultimately accepted will have to be very complicated indeed.

One other feature, which no theory yet satisfactorily explains, is probably of some considerable psychological importance. This is the 'rebound,' following inhibition, which is often experimentally discoverable. The inhibited activity starts again with renewed vigor when the inhibition is removed. Whether this is always the case it is at present impossible to know, but there are many obvious facts in everybody's experience which suggest that it may be very general; the increased vigor of a 'temptation,' for example, which is only momentarily quashed, and many of the phenomena unearthed by psycho-analysis.

CHAPTER IV: HOW THE BRAIN WORKS

The Relation of Higher and Lower Levels. We can turn back now to consider how the various higher- and lower-level clearing-houses in the nervous system are related. And we must be careful not to choose a point of view which presents the matter upside down, so to speak. Since the arrangements in the spinal cord are more easily investigated than the higher centers in the brain, it is easy to fall into the habit of thinking of them first and regarding the brain as something which they call into action only if they cannot get on without it. But if we want to understand a business it is better to begin by talking to the directors than by plaguing the office boy and the stenographers. We may otherwise tend to see the superior authorities merely as conveniences which the lower ranks call in only when they need them. But in fact it is the other way round.

Instead, then, of starting with one particular stimulus and asking how it comes to arouse a particular response, we must begin, as psychologists, with the total situation in which the body finds itself. Of the innumerable impulses which are coming in from the greater number of our sense organs all the while, only a small proportion ultimately reach the final common paths, the motor neurones which excite the muscles. But very many which themselves play no final part have yet, at one level or another, a say in what finally shall take place; typically by barring out other impulses which otherwise would get through. And only a small proportion of these finally give rise to consciousness in the form of mediating the individual's *awareness* of some part of the situation. A process of selection takes place quite early on in the afferent (incoming) course of the impulse. Further, a set of excitations which in themselves would each be unnoticed and have no central effects may, if they happen to come together in a certain pattern, get through and take effect at once; for example, a set of black and yellow streaks in the landscape when, and only when, coiled upon one another in the rattlesnake fashion, or a set of sounds in an otherwise unnoticed hubbub if they happen to be arranged in the pattern of our own name.

Receptive Centers. Thus the notion of *receptive centers* which act as a kind of selective sieve becomes necessary; and the actual location of some of these centers in the cerebral cortex has been discovered. Here a preliminary sorting out occurs. For example, other things being equal, a stimulus which is unlike its neighbors has a better chance of getting through, and certain kinds of impulses have almost invariable precedence. Again, impulses arising from stimuli harmful to the skin override all others. But hard upon this simpler kind of sorting out there follows a more complicated task—that of responding to certain patterns, as with the snake or the name, and not to others. The reception apparatus recognizes some patterns just as a lock 'recognizes' its key. It is not difficult to imagine this being done by a system of neurones which discharge other systems only when excited together or in a certain order. But the fact that we 'recognize' our names when spoken by very different voices raises a great difficulty which we shall note again in our chapter on Perception.

Co-ordination Centers. The receptive centers are in close connection then with *sensory co-ordination centers,* as these arrangements which pick out patterns among incoming impulses are called. Certain injuries, it is found, may incapacitate the co-ordination centers without disturbing the receptive centers. In such a case there might be nothing detectably wrong with the patient's vision, for example, in itself; he would not be blind, he would merely not recognize anything he saw.

But the different co-ordination centers are themselves in close touch with one another, as we see if we shut our eyes and attempt to recognize an unfamiliar object first by touch and handling alone, and then with our eyes open. The particular patterns which one center will pick out depend upon the patterns which other centers are picking out or have just picked out. How is this interdependence brought about?

Association Areas. There is here probably the same kind of rivalry for a common path (not in this case, of course, a *final* common path) that we encountered in the case of the motor neurones of the spinal cord. The various receptive areas in the brain are known to be linked together by tracts of nerve fibers in a very intimate manner; impulses leaving each are continually passing onwards a further stage towards their goal, the motor neurones. But they have a long way to go, many alliances to make and many competitors to deal with. Thus on the inner side of the sensory co-ordination centers there will be many further centers which carry out the same kind of transactions as the co-ordination centers; only this time with the products of the co-ordination centers and not with original impulses from the sense organs. We may call these higher clearing-houses the *association areas.*

Now imagine a co-ordination center which has received from the receptive centers let us say 7,003 impulses which together make up a certain pattern, and suppose that it hands on a much simplified pattern of 42 impulses as the result of the combined action of these 7,003. This 42 pattern is a candidate for passage through an association center. But at the entrance it has to pass through a set of neurones which are also being used by other patterns coming from other co-ordination centers. Suppose that it conflicts with them, that it cannot make an alliance and reinforce them, but is in some way incompatible. The situation will be similar to that which we have already considered in the case of the spinal reflexes. What will happen?

Evidently there is a bewildering number of possibilities. There may be other association centers into which it *can* discharge, so getting round the difficulty for the moment. But then the problem is shifted on to a yet higher association center in which the claims of the lower centers are adjusted. It may be that part of the pattern can get through and part not. It may be that it will as a whole supersede the other patterns and bar them out, or it may be barred out itself. In the last case the barring out may be permanent or temporary, and this will depend upon the degree of insistence of the pattern, a matter which we have yet to consider.

The most illuminating case, however, is that in which it is possible for the co-ordination center to pick out from its 7,003 impulses and send forward a different pattern which *can* combine with the others and get through the association center. Endless instances from perception suggest that this is what ordinarily happens. Whenever we first suppose ourselves to be perceiving one thing and then, since other sensory evidence makes this impossible, detect that we were mistaken, we have such a case. The interesting point is that then the thing, whatever it is, *commonly looks* quite different from what we supposed it to be. In such cases the co-ordination centers seem plainly to try again under a subsequent influence from the association centers. We need not suppose, however, that this subsequent influence actually goes through the same neurones which brought in the rejected pattern.

Expectation. So far we have been tracing the march of the armies of impulses inwards, but by the time the association centers are in play there must be corresponding movements outwards, from higher centers to lower, from association centers to sensory co-ordination centers. The influence of expectation on perception is clear evidence for this. If we are expecting a certain person to appear in the distance we are extremely likely to mistake other people for her. Now an expectation in such a case involves a special setting of a co-ordination center brought about by an association center, a certain preparedness to pick out one pattern rather than others. What we know from within as 'attention' is accompanied by a heightening of tone. An impulse or influence from above alters the lock—to use our former metaphor—so that the 7,003 impulses coming in from the receptive center may more easily turn it.

We must think, then, of these tides of impulses as having eddies, through which what has already reached the centers controls what is still coming in. There will be circuits of this kind not only from association centers to co-ordination centers but from higher to lower association centers. A typical case is the influence exercised by a general conception (which is the activity of an association center of relatively high level) upon the particular instances of experience which can be brought under it. When we know that a thunderstorm is an electrical phenomenon, it is no longer quite so easy to regard it as a judgment upon our actions. Even the most intricate intellectual play of ideas—the mastering of a psychological theory, for example—may be imagined as consisting of the same kind of transactions as those of the co-ordination centers and the reflex centers of the spinal cord, but carried out at higher levels and perhaps of even greater complexity.

The Influence of the Past. In one respect which has not yet been mentioned the complexity is certainly greater. The higher we go in the nervous system the more definite and the more subtle the influence of the past becomes. The spinal dog shows no signs of personal memory. Its reactions are fixed. It can be taught nothing. But in the intact dog, more in the ape, and still more in man, reactions are not fixed. What happened in even the remote past of the individual's history has its bearing upon what happens now.

What exactly memory may be in terms of the nervous system is a problem which is still a very long way from solution. It is better perhaps to speak of *retention* than memory, for memory may mean either recollection (I have a memory of Armistice Day) or that I now can do something (*e.g.*, swim) which I could not do if I had not done it before. The second is the sense in which retention is used. The first (recollection) is a special instance of the working of retention. Both offer many problems some of which we must now briefly consider.

Retention is already active at the level of the sensory co-ordination centers; it is essentially a matter of the repetition of certain co-ordinations even when the circumstances are no longer the same. It shows itself in two ways at every stage of co-ordination right up to the highest levels.

Retention and the Conditioned Reflex. The response on repetition may become quicker, smoother, more perfect of its kind, as we see happening in the formation of *habits*; or it may dispense with some part of the stimulation which was originally necessary, as we see most clearly in the formation of what are known as *conditioned* reflexes. Usually the two effects of retentiveness go together.

When two impulses have co-operated to produce a certain response it is found that after a sufficient number of repetitions one of them alone may bring it about, though formerly inadequate by itself. Such a response is said to be 'conditioned'; a new stimulus has been substituted for the old, and the response now occurs under new conditions. In man very few repetitions may be sufficient; but after infancy all his reactions are made to such complicated situations that it is far easier to study conditioned responses in animals. Even here, however, the most elaborate precautions are required to exclude disturbing factors.

The fundamental work on this subject has been done by Pavlov and his assistants at Leningrad, and the results already attained seem likely to be of the utmost assistance to psychology. They are the foundation of the theories of the Behaviorist School to which we devote a special chapter. Pavlov has found it best to work with one particular response. A dog secretes saliva when given food. It is his first step towards digesting it. Now all through the evolution of the dog (the same is true of man), he has been constantly on the lookout for signs of food. He is thus specially prepared for all kinds of different stimuli to become connected in his association centers with the presence of food. This gives the investigator his opportunity. Every time

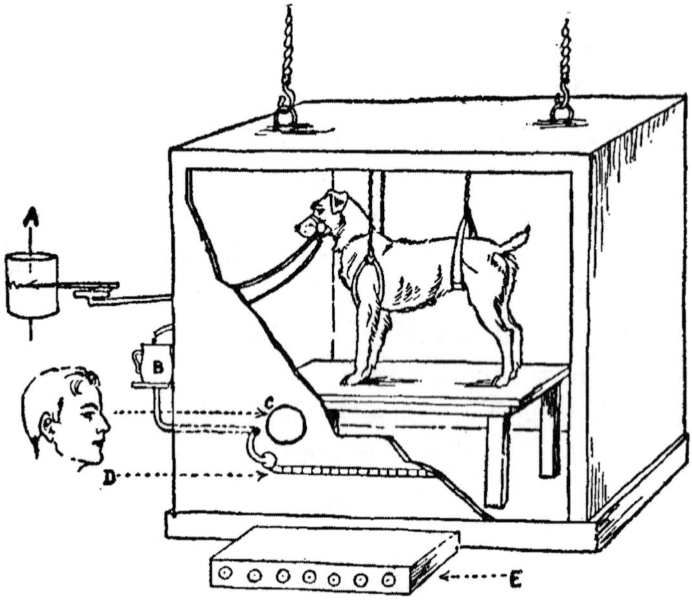

FIG. V.—PAVLOV'S DOG

A. Revolving drum for recording rate of secretion of saliva
B. Vessel for receiving salivary secretion
C. Observation window or periscope for observing the dog
D. Graduated scale for measuring quantity of salivary secretion
E. Electric contacts for setting into operation source of stimulus

food is put before the dog a particular note, for example, is sounded. After a certain number of repetitions of this combination the note is sounded alone. The dog's mouth waters. A conditioned reflex has been established. It may be added that the dog does not seem to be averse from this experiment, and jumps of his own accord on to the table where he appears in Fig. V.

By this method many very remarkable phenomena have been brought to light. For example, at first the conditioned stimulus (the note in the case we have taken) irradiates. By this it is meant that any similar stimulus produces some degree of salivation. But as the conditioned reflex becomes more and more established this irradiation is narrowed down until only notes very similar indeed to the conditioned note share its power of evoking the reflex. If such a note is now sounded repeatedly *without* the unconditioned stimulus (the food) it soon becomes 'inactive'; it loses this power. It has been shown that this loss is not a mere disuse, but an actual inhibition. The 'inactive' stimulus inhibits salivation. One fact which shows this clearly is very striking for further reasons. Suppose that just before or during the elicitation of a conditioned reflex we give the dog a strong extra stimulus which has not been conditioned in any way, the conditioned reflex is at once greatly reduced. This new external inhibiting activity superimposes itself on whatever process it encounters. If it meets with excitation it inhibits it; but, and here is the surprising fact, if it meets with inhibition it *inhibits this inhibition.* Thus an electric shock just before the sounding of a note which has been made 'inactive' causes this note to be no longer inhibitory and salivation reappears.

By progressively making notes nearer and nearer

to the conditioned note 'inactive' it is possible to investigate the dog's powers of *discrimination*. With pure tones it is found to be vastly superior to that of the best human musicians. A point of interest to educators arises with what is known as conditioned inhibition. In this case the conditioned stimulus is accompanied by some slight indifferent stimulus—not, as in the last case, by a strong stimulus which itself causes an unconditioned reflex. After a number of repetitions the extra stimulus causes inhibition, and this increases; in the former case the inhibition grows weaker. It is found that well-established discriminations are temporarily interfered with during the development of such conditioned inhibitions even when they concern quite different kinds of stimuli. But as soon as the new acquisition is firmly established, the interference ceases and the discrimination returns to its former state.[1] This phenomenon is met with constantly in education. As Anrep remarks, a child who, having mastered addition, is taught multiplication, will for a while make mistakes in addition. A dog which had failed to develop a discrimination did so almost at once after an easier conditioned inhibition had been acquired. The moral is perhaps that a child who fails at a problem will have a much better chance of solving it after a successful spell at an easier task.

Finally the extraordinary facts of experimental neurasthenia in dogs should be mentioned. If the dog is persistently given too difficult a task, for ex-

[1] G. V. Anrep, *Proc. Royal Soc.*, Series B, vol. iv, pp. 404 ff.

ample if he is forced to attempt a discrimination between shapes which are too similar for him, he little by little loses all his previously acquired conditioned reflexes. He even fails in the end to discriminate between what is edible and what is not. At the same time he becomes quarrelsome, dirty, and unmanageable, howls at the moon and finally ends up in a state of general incompetence. A prolonged rest cure at the farm is needed to restore him to his former good-tempered sanity. The general bearing of these results, when they are explained, upon human psychology is likely to be immense. But we must return to the problem presented by the simplest case of conditioning.

The point to note is that here we have a response, the watering of the dog's mouth, which would not have occurred if the conditioned stimulus (the note) and the unconditioned stimulus (the food) had not been combined in the comparatively remote past. The past conjunction has left some effect in the dog's nervous system through which the note alone produces the response which formerly required the presence of the food. How are we to conceive this effect?

The Image Theory. It is important *not* to think of it either as the storing in some neural archive of an image of food which bobs up to co-operate when the note is sounded, or as a mere track gouged out, or a channel in the neural pathways deepened or enlarged. Both theories have tempted many psychologists and both are unsatisfactory. The objections to the image theory are simple. There may be an image formed; but if so (and the point is very difficult to settle) it would be something itself needing explanation and could not be used *as* an explanation. And, further, images are *not* stored up; they are *not* persistent effects. They depend upon persistent effects, but the old theory that they themselves reside permanently in cells in the brain is long ago exploded. An image is a process, a transaction, just as much as a perception; it is a happening. And there is every reason to suppose that images differ only from the actual experiences by being aroused not through incoming impulses from the receptive centers but through impulses of central origin. We call them images because they correspond to perceptions, and they are due in some way to persistent effects[1] left behind by perceptions, but they are not, themselves, those effects. What lasts is not the image, but as Hering said, "the peculiar attunement (*Stimmung*) of the nervous substance in virtue of which it will give out to-day the same note that it gave out yesterday, if the strings be touched aright." The problem of the image is in part the same problem as that of the conditioned reflex itself. Namely, what is the nature of the residual effect?

[1] These have been called by Semon (*Mnemic Psychology,* Chapter VII) "engrams" and by Morton Prince (*The Unconscious,* p. 131) "neurograms," but the more usual term in psychology is 'disposition' or 'trace' (Stout, *Manual of Psychology,* p. 18 ff.). It is better to think of them not as imprints left behind by excitations, but as patterns or configurations to which the centers concerned return when the relevant conditions recur. The laying down of a trace is really a change in these relevant conditions.

But the conditioned reflex is more easy to investigate, and should be considered first.

The Theory of Lowered Resistance. The other explanation in terms of a deepening of nervous channels is much more on the right lines. But it is plainly not enough to suppose merely that the repeated passage of an impulse lowers the resistance of the synapses; and for the following reason. In come the two impulses, due to the note and to the food, close together. The note must be sounded before or contemporaneously with the giving of the food; otherwise the conditioned reflex is not established. No conditioning at all takes place, surprisingly enough, if the note be sounded after the food is given. After a number of these combined arrivals the note-impulse arrives alone and now goes through in the absence of its formerly indispensable colleague. It plainly will not do to say merely that the final common path (its entrance resistances having been lowered) has now got used to this particular intruder. If henceforth it always got through, that might be a possible account. But, in fact, if we go on sounding the note without the food, the salivation instead of becoming more and more copious, soon ceases altogether. The mere passage of the impulse does *not* of itself keep the resistance down; actual conjunction from time to time with the other impulse, from the food, is necessary.

But, it may be suggested, is it not sufficient to say that the two together lower the resistance to the one alone for a certain while? If I have no money and a friend goes with me occasionally to the opera and every time buys me a seat for the rest of the week, do we not have a situation somewhat like the conditioned reflex? If I begin by going alone my appeals have no effect on the box office; I do not get through. With my friend I do get through, and I get through afterwards for a limited while only, unless he comes again—when my privilege gets a new lease of life. The objection to this analogy as throwing any light upon the conditioned reflex is, however, that the proceedings in the box office are themselves also conditioned reflexes on a more elaborate scale, and just as much in need of explanation as the watering of the dog's mouth. It may be remarked that circular arguments and analogies of this kind are extremely hard to avoid in psychology. All the comparisons which are so popular between the nervous and the telephone systems are guilty of it in more or less serious degree.

McDougall's Drainage Theory. We are forced then to attempt more ingenious explanations. The most plausible extension of the 'lowered resistance' theory is McDougall's drainage hypothesis. We have already mentioned reasons for thinking that drainage theories will not work. None the less, in this case it is worth trying to work out such a theory because its failure helps us to see more exactly what it is that a better theory must do. For the conditioned reflex it might run roughly as follows:—The note when first heard by the dog causes a widely radiating impulse. It is followed immediately by the impulse set up by the food. We must suppose a number of side-channels connecting the path of the note-impulse with that of the food-impulse. Now the discharge of the food-impulse lowers the nervous potential in the path (through to the salivary glands) which it is taking. It creates a partial vacuum so to speak in this path. The note-impulses therefore rush in through the side-channels to fill up this vacuum, and this rush, whenever it happens, lowers the resistance in these channels. Now what has to be explained is how this rush still takes place, although no food-impulse is lowering the potential in the food-impulse path. We must obviously suppose that it is being lowered in some other way, by impulses from the viscera for example. The dog, in other words, is to some extent hungry. These impulses do not discharge into the final common path and make the dog's mouth water, but they may well be supposed to play a part in lowering the potential in that path, by draining it slightly themselves, for example. A diagram (Fig. VI) may help to make the matter clearer.

The discharge of the food-impulse down the middle is supposed to lower the pressure in the middle channel *F*, so draining its neighbors through *a* and a^1, inlet valves from *N* and *H*, synapses whose resistance becomes lowered with the passage of impulses. When no food-impulse is passing, impulses flowing down *H* from the visceral sense organs lower the pressure there and so drain *F* slightly through *b* (an inlet valve from *F*). Thus when pressure is raised in *N* through the note being sounded, the impulse flows into *F* and out to the salivation center *S*.

But we have still to grapple with the principal difficulty. Why does the flow from *N* to *F* cease to happen if the note is repeated too often and no food is given with it to the dog? What happens, then, to cut off the impulse from *N* to *F*? On this kind of theory it is clear either that the resistance at *a*

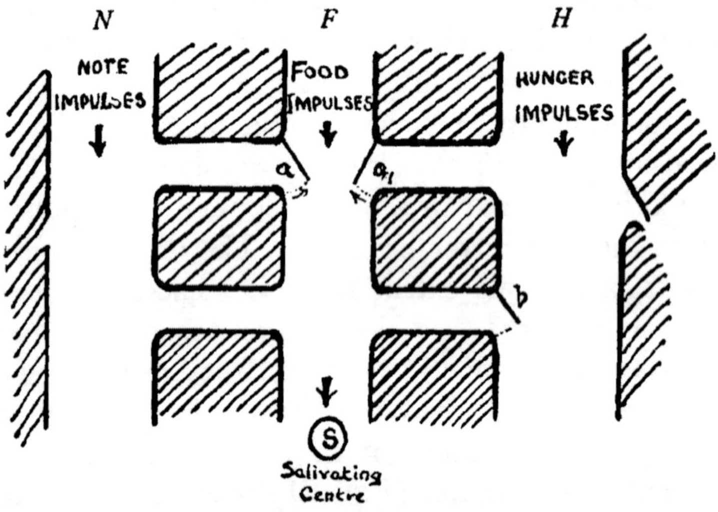

FIG. VI

must have gone up, or that too much of the energy in *F* has been drained elsewhere, through *H*, say, thus inhibiting *F*.

This second possibility seems to be the one worth considering. For no plausible account can be given as to why, if the mere passage of impulses from *N* to *F* lowers *a's* resistance, further passages should raise it again. Fatigue cannot be the cause, since the effect is the same no matter how the impulses are spaced out. But there does seem reason to think that the discharge of saliva *without food* may have as an indirect consequence the inhibition of the process which leads to this unsatisfactory state of affairs. For, as we have said, this watering of the mouth is a first step in the whole complex cycle of digestion. Further steps require the presence of something to be digested. Since this is lacking, these steps fail, and their failure may well have a back-wash effect by increasing drainage from *F* for example, of the kind required.

It will be plain that by this means we have only pushed the difficulty further on. We have still to work out a mechanism for this new transaction, and it seems as though this might go on indefinitely. For apart from the objection that it does not fit in with what is known about the conduction of the nervous impulse, the defect of the drainage hypothesis (though it represented a step in the right direction) is that it is too simple. There are other means (as we saw in discussing chronaxy) through which the paths taken by impulses are controlled besides the wearing down of resistances at synapses and the differences in potential (if such occur). We must take account of these other ways in order to reach a more satisfactory theory.

What has emerged from this consideration of the drainage view is that we must take account of the end-state of the whole process, the success or failure at the point which matters to the animal, if we are to explain the variations in the means by which this is brought about. In other words, all behavior is purposive, though it may often be so ill directed, incomplete, and confused that we cannot pick out the purpose. The mainspring of these conditioned reflexes is the dog's need for food. If we leave this out of consideration we shall naturally find the facts difficult to explain.

The drainage hypothesis was invented to meet a crucial problem. As McDougall very rightly said: "If no solution can be found physiological psychology is bankrupt."[1] But he was probably too hasty in assuming that if the drainage theory had to be abandoned the only alternative would be some kind of "psychical guidance of the neural impulse," in other words, "a directive power of psychical energy or 'mind' working in some way that we cannot at all conceive" (pp. 128, 134). Things working in ways which we cannot conceive should not be invoked by science, as McDougall in 1905 clearly realized. Possibly the growing doubtfulness of the drainage hypothesis in part explains a change of view on this fundamental point which has much perplexed many of his admirers.[2]

Success as Establishing Attunement. But to abandon the drainage theory is not in the least to give

---

[1] *Physiological Psychology* (1905), p. 126.

[2] It is interesting to note that in his latest work (*An Outline of Psychology*, 1923, pp. 179 and 280) McDougall still regards his hypothesis as "the only one that can interpret these facts of reciprocal inhibition in the higher brain levels," in spite of a difficulty of reconciling it with what is now known of the nature of the nervous impulse (cf. Bayliss, *Principles of General Physiology*, 1924, p. 424, for a discussion and references).

up hope of a physiological explanation. Let us see what can be done with the aid of the tuning or chronaxy theory. We must remember that the problem is not properly set if we merely ask how do the note-impulse and the food-impulse arrange affairs between them as regards the salivary discharge, and neglect the rest of the dog's impulses, notably those which would be modified if he had just gorged to repletion.

Neither the impulses from the note nor those from the food come into an indifferent brain. The latter find a center already tuned for them by the emptiness of the dog's viscera. The impulses from the note reach this center—and they must reach many other centers besides. The fact to be explained is that after a certain number of conjunctions in this center with the food-impulses, the center discharges on the arrival of the note-impulses alone. We must remember that practically any stimulus in place of a note can be conditioned in the same fashion. Even a painful stimulus can. All symptoms of fright or pain cease and a severe pinch or bruise merely causes abundant salivation. Nothing brings out the interdependence of the processes in the brain better than this astonishing fact. Whatever sensory stimulus—whether from a color, a noise, a touch, an electric shock, or what not—immediately precedes the giving of the food, the impulse it arouses comes to discharge the center in place of the food-impulse, given sufficient repetition.

The difficulty of understanding how this happens

is due to thinking of the center in two phases only—as it is when the note-impulse reaches it, and as it is when the food-impulse causes it to discharge. Instead, we must think of it in four phases—

(1) as it is when played upon by hunger-impulses before the note-impulse comes in,
(2) as it is when this impulse has altered it,
(3) as it is when the food-impulse discharges it,
(4) as it is when the consequences of the arrival of the food in the stomach are playing upon it.

This last seems to be the decisive phase in tuning the center to discharge henceforward on the mere arrival of the note-impulse. Evidently the food- and note-impulses together leave the neurones of the center in a peculiar state of tuning which lasts for a little while. The incoming of the impulses from the stomach fixes this state. Next time the note-impulse comes in it finds the center still tuned in the same way—tuned, that is, to be discharged either by the note or by the food, and the center discharges. As to how this particular tuning comes about, the simplest hypothesis is to suppose that the simultaneous or closely successive activity of two neurones in the center brings their chronaxies nearer together, so that next time, if this change is fixed, the one can now discharge the other. A number of steps may be needed for this approximation. Thus, in the dog, twenty or thirty may be required, and in the rat a much greater number. In man it can often be achieved at one stroke. Similarly, the time the fixation lasts varies greatly. In the dog, if we do not give him the note too often without the food, or otherwise bring in inhibitions, it lasts indefinitely, as it does in man. In the cockroach it seems to last at most half an hour. The memory of the cockroach is not very tenacious.

We can now see how it is that if we sound the note too often without food, we break down the conditioned reflex. The tides of impulses (phase 4) which come to the center after salivation, from an empty stomach or a full, are very different; the tuning there, instead of being fixed, is changed. The note henceforth, instead of exciting the final common path now inhibits it.

We have lingered somewhat over these intricacies, as we did over the theories of inhibition, so that the reader may take stock of the difficulties; and also that he may realize why the physiological explanation of the brain's activities does not stand or fall with the success or failure of any one particular theory. There is still much work to be done in the physiological laboratory whose results will undoubtedly have a direct bearing on these problems. The main attack has not yet been made. The work so far done amounts to 'getting the guns into position' for that attack. So that to assume special 'psychical' agents, or to maintain that the working of the mind is beyond the scope of any possible physiological explanation would be a rash procedure for a psychologist to-day.

CHAPTER V: PURPOSE AND INTEREST

Purpose and Foresight. There is another important reason for looking rather closely into the nervous mechanism of retention. Only so can we see its close connection with the *purposive* character of behavior. An activity is said to be purposive when the result which it is going to produce seems to influence its course; that is to say, when what is about to happen seems to be directing and controlling what is already happening. This kind of apparent causation by what does not yet exist, by the end or goal of an activity, is known in philosophical language as teleology and has always seemed a very mysterious affair. Many thinkers have regarded it as necessarily involving 'foresight,' meaning thereby something which no physical or physiological processes, however intricate, can explain. And unless we have an adequate conception of these intricacies, and especially of the ways in which retention complicates them, this view is very difficult to avoid. For this apparent foresight is entirely due to retention. It is due to the ways in which the effects of past activities control the present. When we seem to be influenced by what is about to happen, by the results to come from what we are doing, we are really being influenced by the lingering effects of what has happened on former occasions in similar situations. And we are constantly being so influenced; in fact, nothing that we do is immune from the influence of similar situations in our past or that of an ancestor. So it is perfectly correct to say that all our behavior has the peculiar character of purposiveness, a character not possessed by such physical processes as are involved when stones fall or clouds form or earthquakes rage. But we should realize that this purposiveness is a physiological characteristic, that it is due to retention in living tissues and preeminently in the living systems which form the higher nervous centers. Physiological processes are, in the opinion of the most circumspect authorities, merely extremely complicated physical processes. The more complex systems which make up living tissue naturally behave in more complicated ways than the simpler systems of physics.

Retention and Attunement. We take retention then as a fundamental fact in the working of the brain. We have seen that it does not necessarily involve any storing up of impressions or images, or any laying down or scouring out of new paths or channels. To say that the brain retains a response is to say that certain stimuli may find it in the state of attunement in which that response left it, and that therefore if the situation recurs it will respond in the same way. This, of course, does not bar out the possibility of persistent modifications.

Recognition. So far we have discussed retention only as it appears in the simplest form of conditioned reflex. We shall see how universal the influence of the past upon the present is if we reflect upon some of the less simple forms. Consider the sensory co-ordination centers which we discussed above, and the way in which they pick certain patterns out of the welter of incoming impulses. The center by which we recognize a series of sounds as being a certain tune is a good example. The first time this series of impulses comes into the center we do not, of course, recognize it. But, since we have presumably heard other tunes before, it does not find the center unprepared, and we have probably heard the same notes before. Each note has its own special effect upon the center and is handed on as a special set of impulses different from those due to any other note. Further, each note leaves the center ready to deal with some notes better than with others. As the tune proceeds a cycle of operations takes place in the center, easier for some people than for others (what is called "a good musical ear" is really a good center) and easier if the tune is of a familiar kind, and if the transactions required in passing from note to note are fairly simple. Quite early, on, after two or three notes perhaps, back into the center come the consequences of the passing through of these notes. Every impulse that the center hands on has a widespread reverberation all over the body and the effects of these reverberations come back to the center and take a share in handling the following notes. This is why the earlier notes seem to make so much difference to the later ones. The later notes have actually to be handled differently by the center because of the effects of the earlier.

Finally the tune is completed, the last of the reverberation effects comes in and the center is left more or less set for the handling of this tune in future, according as these reverberations are more or less satisfying to the whole organism. The process is quite parallel to that in Pavlov's dog. Of course what constitutes a satisfactory reverberation will differ enormously from man to man, varying from grade to grade of musical knowledge and taste, and from temperament to temperament, and an unsatisfactory tune may 'stick in the mind' for any one of a thousand extraneous reasons. A man may have heard it while burgling a till, for example. Or the tune, while in a crude sense unsatisfying, may be musically interesting in some way. Still in all these cases what determines whether the tune is retained or not is the character of the impulses playing upon the center from other sources, while the tune is going on or immediately after.

When the tune is heard again and recognized, it is not in the least necessary, as everyone knows, to recollect the occasion on which it was formerly heard. The burglar probably will, but most people commonly do not. All that is involved in mere recognition is that the center is, on the second occasion, after the first few notes, set ready for the rest of the transaction. It has been transformed into a lock, so to speak, for which that particular tune is the key. Clearly, one and the same center may be concerned in the handling of innumerable tunes.

This offers no difficulty if we realize its prodigious complexity.

On this second occasion not only are the later notes influenced by the earlier, but also the earlier by the later; to put it more accurately, they are influenced by the still enduring effects of the notes which followed on the former occasion. This explains why a tune, though recognized as the same, yet often sounds very different on repetition, and why it is so easy to hear some tunes too often.

We have taken this instance partly for its own interest, since an understanding of what is actually happening clears up much that is often considered mysterious, even miraculous, in music. But there was another reason. The recognition of a melody with the apparent knowledge of the future which it seems to entail is a favorite example with those psychologists who maintain that the mind must have powers beyond the capacity of the brain. We have seen that foresight (of a kind) does occur and also in what this foresight consists.

Interest and the Selection of Patterns. All recognition of other people, of our own name, of words, of places, of tables and chairs, of moods and emotions, of situations large or small, part or whole, is done in this fashion. The plan of the universe as we see it is the plan of the persistent accords in our nervous centers, the plan of the patterns by which we handle our stimulation. And as our instances have brought out, these patterns depend not only upon what is given in stimulation to our sense organs, but still more upon the relative satisfaction to us as integral individuals of picking out one pattern rather than another. The universe may be and probably is, shouting at us all the time the clearest and most unmistakable news. Perhaps news which in the long run might be of overwhelming importance to our welfare. But if the immediate consequence of picking out the pattern of these 'messages' is uncomfortable, or if it involves ceasing to pick out a pattern which suits us, we shall not hear them.[1] The world as we ordinarily regard it, the world of roads, gardens, motor cars, noises, colors, bodies, and even of brains, is the indirect reflexion of our interests, since it is these which ultimately pick out the groups of stimuli which we treat as single things.

Hence it is that the conceptions even of homely and familiar objects—the wood in the grate, the wine in the wood, the billiard table, or the household cat—entertained by people of different interests can vary so immensely. The accounts given of the wine by the chemist and the connoisseur are far removed. The ordinary man is satisfied with an idea of a cannon which the physicist (as a physicist, not as a billiard-player) rejects *in toto*. And how the physiologist regards the cat may be gathered to some extent from these pages. The problem of how we are to pick and choose among these points of view

---

[1] As Professor Thurstone puts it [*The Nature of Intelligence* (1924), p. 9], "while walking to your office . . . most of the signs, stores, vehicles, and people are indifferent stimuli which are not even perceived because you do not identify them with your purpose."

—which patterns to select—cannot be avoided by a psychologist. And he is, or should be, the man of all men who is best placed for considering it, since it is his job to study this choice between patterns and also the factors by which it is controlled.

In actual fact we pick out the pattern which best fits in with the dominant activity. Pavlov's dogs pick out the note and treat it as a signal for salivation because food-seeking is their dominant activity. The errand boy picks up the tune because whistling is his. The physicist at the billiard-table discards all thoughts of electrons because pocketing the white is his main aim for the moment. And the psychologist works out a conception of the nervous system because an intelligible account of behavior and experience is his concern. In all cases the pattern picked out depends upon the purpose (conscious or unconscious) or interest which it serves. This is not to reduce truth to convenience in any ordinary sense of the word 'convenience.'

But, to return, what are these dominant activities, these purposes, these interests, which pick and choose among possible patterns? Are they, too, conceivable in terms of the nervous system or have we here at last to abandon physiology and introduce something not of a physical order, in the form of psychic urges, instincts, wants, desires, strivings, an *élan vital* or a *libido?* Can these, too, be brought under our scheme of connected brain centers influencing one another and handing on impulses to one another, forwards and by backwash? And lastly how do these interests, besides selecting what shall come in, also decide what goes out, and how do they translate the inner swirl of impulses into overt action?

If we compare the body to a self-directing and self-regulating machine, however inappropriate from some points of view the comparison may be, we shall at least be reminded that, like an engine, it needs fuel. It uses up its supplies of energy and has to get more. Further, and here it differs from those simple physical systems we call engines, it dies unless it subdivides from time to time. In lowly animals the subdivision is simple; in man it is complex and involves endless to-do. Again, man is a social animal. He cannot get on by himself and has to live in a herd. This also involves a vast ramification of consequences among which speech, sanitation, war, and the great majority of mental diseases are examples. We might go on extending the list of man's needs. Food and sex are the original roots of a good many of them, but there are probably others, as we shall see in Chapter VII.

Man's Fundamental Needs. A Need is an internal disequilibrium. If it continues unappeased the efficiency of the organism often declines. The three needs we have mentioned, food, sex, and society, are apt to be fatal unless supplied. Reproduction as a way of escape from death strikes the ordinary man as unsatisfying—but from the point of view of the biologist a man may be said to live on in his offspring. Deprived of society, the infant only lives a few hours, the child a few days, and the adult is rapidly impaired in a number of ways.

On primitive needs derivative needs become grafted. For example, food-seeking, except for a very few fortunates, involves locomotion. Now unless the locomotor apparatus is employed a detrimental condition arises, so that even persons who are regularly fed by others find they have to take exercise. A derivative need arises. In general, though there are exceptions, the possession of a capacity involves a need to employ it. This is more obviously so when the capacity has developed special structures in the body—noteworthy biceps, for example: the sad state of the retired boxer or oarsman is frequently remarked. Where mental capacities are in question there is more doubt. The need of the mathematician to keep up his studies, or of the stamp-collector to go on collecting, is less certain. Even here it will perhaps be agreed that, other things being equal, if no other interests can be found, they will be well advised to continue.

Another way in which needs ramify involves the principle of the conditioned reflex again. If I continually drink tea while I am working I may find in time that I need tea in order to work. The centers involved have become tuned to work best in the tea-intoxication condition. Such drug addictions are a very clear example of acquired needs. My state, however, when deprived of tea is not of necessity detrimental to all my activities, but only detrimental to the work.

We all suffer from innumerable parasitic and conditioned needs of this kind. The lecturer who cannot get on unless he fidgets with the chalk, the dandy who cannot shine in conversation unless his attire is elegant, are obvious instances. The great Kant was not at his best unless his gaze was fixed upon a certain tower across the way; in the course of years a neighbor's tree grew up to intercept this vision; the owner had to cut it down before the Critical Philosophy could proceed.

Fixations. A very important group of these conditioned needs are what the psycho-analysts call fixations. A child whose tenderness and affection have for a long time been centered exclusively on its mother often finds it difficult to feel these emotions towards anyone who does not resemble the mother in certain respects. Many other instances from the pathology of the mind will arise for consideration later. We have said enough to make plain how universally operative conditioned needs are, and can pass to the problem of interests.

The Nature of Interest. An interest is an activity set going and maintained by a need. There is no mystery (as opposed to intricacy) about the way in which the need provokes the activity. The disequilibrium which is the need fires volleys of impulses into the centers, and their response to this bombardment is the activity. They respond when they can. But the rest of the situation has to be fitting. We often have intense needs about which nothing can be done. The interest then is latent except in so far as internal processes go on in the nervous system with a view[1] to finding some aspect of the situation or making some change in it which will allow something to be done. Sometimes we can only wait for a change. Then when the change comes, the activity starts in what seems an entirely spontaneous fashion. Our interest leaps to life, as we say. The change may seem to be utterly inadequate to account for it. We must not forget that the need is the other and the controlling factor. A man's needs are not necessarily the measure of his interest. For more than a mere need is required before an interest develops. There must also be the nervous organization necessary in order to translate the need into activity. A man in a coma is in a desperate state of need, but he shows the minimum of interest.

We should be on our guard constantly as to how we use quantitative terms in speaking of interest. The danger is that we easily get into a way of thinking of it as a fixed quantity of energy. But there is no physiological ground for such a view and the psychological evidence which suggests it can be better interpreted otherwise. For example, it is true that one interest can oust another, but this is not the same thing at all as a central fount of energy being turned into a new channel. It is a much more complex transaction involving a rearrangement of prec-

[1] Having now an account of purposive activity in terms of repetitions of previous sequences of experience, we need no longer hesitate to use such language. Note that these operations need not be *conscious.*

edences in the central clearing-houses. And a heightening of one interest is very often accompanied by a general heightening and widening all round.

Compare the sleeping man and the fully vigilant. The Napoleons, the Goethes, and the Newtons, the men of the most intense interests, are commonly also the men with the most quick and varied simultaneous interests. The theory of the central reservoir is too crude. It reaches its highest absurdities in the hands of some psycho-analysts who are in the habit of asking where the *libido* has gone whenever an interest lapses. We can avoid these mistakes best by remembering that interest is not something additional to or behind activity, but just the activity itself.

Discrimination. Width, variety, and keenness of interests are marks of the superior mind because they are signs that in one respect at least the nervous system is well organized. But they may be accompanied by extreme stupidity. Sensitiveness as well as interest is necessary. Interest is a matter of the excitability of the centers concerned. Sensitiveness has to do with the delicacy and plasticity of their tuning. The sensitive man is he who discriminates when he is interested. The stupid man is he who does not; and discriminating is simply varying the response as the situation varies. Since it is essentially plasticity of tuning, it is closely connected with retention. The discriminating are those who retain the relevant effects of past experience. Too intense an interest seems often to hinder discrimination. We get 'excited,' as we say, and no longer know what we are doing.

The Initiation of Action. The arrangements by which activity in the nervous system is translated into bodily action through the outgoing (efferent) nerve paths are very similar to those by which impulses from the sense organs are sorted, co-ordinated, and associated in the incoming (afferent) path, and can be very briefly described. The association centers discharge into certain incito-motor centers which are among the best known regions of the cortex of the brain. These lie in a band roughly from ear to ear over the top of the head. If we give them a mild electric shock, as has been done by Dr. Harvey Cushing with the consent of a patient, the subject moves his limbs and does so with a full sense that he is voluntarily performing the action. This is quite different from the effect of stimulating the motor nerves in the spinal cord, or nearer still to the muscle. Then the patient merely feels his limb contract involuntarily. The bearing of these facts on the question of the Will is obvious.

The area in the cortex corresponding to separate groups of muscles varies, not with the number or size of the muscles, but with the variety and fineness of the movements they combine to produce; in other words, with the extent of co-ordination which is possible for them. Thus corresponding to the sensory co-ordination centers we have motor co-ordination centers, and these are at several levels. For familiar acquired movements, of which typewriting and swimming are examples, the impulse from the incito-motor center goes to a co-ordination center which discharges outwards a much more complicated pattern of impulses of a more stereotyped kind. These again probably have to be further elaborated and adjusted when they get to the spinal centers, whence they proceed along the final common path to the muscles. The analogy to a man playing a pianola is illuminating here. The incito-motor center selects the roll to be played and controls probably the tempo and expression; a mechanism relatively without initiative does the rest.

But even here the backwash effect, which we have noticed all through the working of the nervous system, comes in. In the muscles and their allied structures, the tendons and joints, are certain sense organs (known as the *proprioceptors*) whose business it is to keep the higher centers in touch with the movements of the limbs. The effect of the outgoing motor impulse which results in movement is immediately reported to the appropriate center. The headquarters [1] co-ordinating these impulses seems to be in the cerebellum (cf. Fig. II); and they have

[1] The elaborate researches of Magnus and Klejn (*Körperstellung*, 1924) on lower animals (and Walshe's work on similar reactions in Man) bring out the complicated nature of Postural Tone; through reflex action the movements not only of the head but of the limbs are co-ordinated into one system of postures, without necessary reference to cortical intervention. In his *Elementary Nervous System*, Collins has traced the nature of reflex action back to the very lowest animal life, in which a nervous system can hardly be posited. A systematic and co-ordinated study of the nervous processes in all animal life which lie behind action and response has been made by Herrick (*The Neurological Foundations of Animal Behavior*, 1924).

also for the most part to be adjusted with the impulses incessantly coming in from what is called the labyrinth—a set of organs in the ear which play the chief part in securing our balance. When we remember that every time we move an arm or turn the head when walking, hundreds of other muscles must make compensating movements or we shall fall over, it is easy to see that special co-ordinating arrangements are required. Even more complicated reflex co-ordinations maintain, whenever possible, our orientation.

The remaining transactions of the nervous system, notably those involved in pleasure and pain, in reasoning, and in the phenomena of deliberation, resolve, belief, prejudice, and suggestion will be discussed at a later stage when the introspective account of the mind is before us. Emotion will also be treated separately, and this account of the incomings and outgoings of the central nervous system is thus not complicated by a discussion of that other nervous system known as the involuntary or sympathetic (autonomic) which is essentially concerned with our vegetative life.

CHAPTER VI: THE GROWTH OF THE MIND IN ANIMALS

The Comparative Method. There are two ways of tracing the growth of the mind. We can take a series of animals from various levels of the biological scale and compare their behavior, making cautious guesses at the kinds of experience which are likely to accompany it. Or we can study the development of behavior and experience in the child as he grows up to manhood, supplementing this by comparisons between individuals who more or less perfectly achieve maturity. Both methods are instructive and the first naturally leads on to the second, since the most accomplished animals—chimpanzees and gorillas for example—seem, except as regards language, to reach and to stop short at about the stage at which a bright three-year-old child begins. Moreover, by studying animal behavior we are likely to avoid some of the errors which a too exclusive preoccupation with the child's mental life, as seen through its effects upon that of the adult, may introduce. The theories of psycho-analysis are peculiarly exposed to this danger.

Much of the difficulty of psychology has in fact arisen through studying mind in its most complex form in man. The minds of animals are much simpler than those of men, and, though more difficult to observe, are more easily understood when once satisfactory observations have been made. Even very lowly organisms such as *Amœba* display behavior which to some has seemed to indicate a rudimentary mind. But in animals with a nervous system we are on firmer ground, and it would be strange if a study of their behavior did not throw light upon our own. Man has developed certain of their capacities to an incomparable height, but though his activities are more complicated, they are still the same in essence.

The Nature of Instincts. Ants and bees have always been recognized as offering supreme examples of instinctive behavior, and the notion of an instinct is fundamental to psychology. To understand what an instinct is we need the notion of heredity. Every living creature begins life with a definite congenital make-up, a set of innate arrangements for coping with the situations in which it finds itself. In the insects, which usually have to fend for themselves from the first, these arrangements include innate neural tunings (dispositions as they are called) through which a particular situation, a particular set of stimuli, leads to a particular kind of response, sometimes extraordinarily definite, complex, and appropriate. This activity, which needs no learning and has no previous history, is said to be instinctive. And each well-marked kind of response corresponding to a well-marked kind of need and situation is called an *instinct*. There is no reason to suppose that instincts differ in any respect from other non-instinctive activities, except in being due to innate arrangements in the nervous system and not to arrangements which have been formed in the course of the vicissitudes of the individual's life. It is important not to regard an instinct as a peculiar kind of supernatural force or wisdom. It is no more mysterious, though no less, than any other of the animal's activities.

Instincts are not necessarily immutable. The nervous arrangements on which they depend are modifiable in greater or less degree. Different species and different individuals even of the same species vary in their capacity to modify their behavior.

Thus wasps, for example, will enlarge the entrance to their nests when trial has shown that a spider cannot be dragged in, and ants which have been tricked into leaping from an eminence into vinegar refuse in the future, for a while at least, to take similar leaps. That is to say, they show evidence of having 'learned by experience.' Their behavior, instead of being governed solely by innate arrangements in their nervous systems, is modified by their own individual experience. It becomes a blend, in other words, of instinctive and 'intelligent' behavior. But if we pass from the insects to the vertebrates we find that this new factor of 'intelligence' increases immensely. It is comparatively powerless in the insect and its effects are brief. The cockroach, as we saw, forgets its lessons in half an hour, the elderly ant and the youthful behave in a very similar fashion, but for the young chicken, the puppy, and the young chimpanzee life has much to teach which is learned with great readiness.

Instinct and Intelligence. This distinction between instinct and intelligence is sometimes difficult to grasp, largely because 'intelligence' is an ambiguous word. As opposed to 'instinct' it means only that the behavior which shows it is due in part to the *individual* past history, the *acquired* experience of the animal. Intelligent behavior, in other words, depends upon *retention*, and retention we studied in the last chapter. Instinctive behavior, by contrast, is due to innate congenital factors. All behavior, even that of the genius among men, is a blend of the two, though the relative importance of *congenital* and *acquired* factors varies enormously. But there is another sense of 'intelligence' which confuses this distinction. This refers to the comparative aptness of the behavior. Acquired behavior is usually, though not always, more appropriate, more successful, more useful, than instinctive. Compared with even the chicken, not a marvelously intelligent animal, the insect often seems stupid. The fatuous performance of a 'blue-bottle' on a windowpane is a good example. Revelant circumstances have changed, but the fly's behavior remains the same. Hence we tend to judge the 'intelligence' of a performance by its appropriateness. But we should remember that some purely instinctive conduct is extraordinarily apt, and that intelligence can lead to disastrous follies. The essential distinction lies in the extent to which congenital and acquired factors are governing the behavior.

The Process of Learning. Almost all behavior, we have said, is a blend of the two. How exactly do these two factors co-operate? And are we right in regarding them as separate factors? Let us consider a simple case. A newly hatched chick begins very early to peck at and swallow small objects. This is instinctive behavior. At first it may get one in five of the objects pecked at; after ten days it gets four out of five, which seems to be the best it can do. The improvement is partly due to learning and partly to maturation. As it grows older its instinctive arrangements work better, but exercise assists this maturation. So far as learning is at work, intelligence, in its lowliest form, is showing itself. The same thing happens with the flight of even the young swallow. It improves. But before long the chicken pecks at something, orange peel, for example, which is distasteful. The peel is at once rejected. Now note what occurs after a few of these distressing experiences. In the normal case, even though hungry, it refrains entirely from pecking. Something has been acquired which modifies its behavior. The sight of the peel no longer prompts the natural instinctive response. What exactly has happened? This process, known as 'acquirement of meaning,' is so important and psychologists are so at variance upon the account to be given, that a close study is very desirable. It leads us straight to the central principle involved in the growth of the mind.

The observable facts are not disputed, but only the interpretation to be placed upon them. Undoubtedly the chick shows on the second occasion that it has learned something through the first occasion. The most illuminating controversy arises over the apparently pedantic point as to whether this learning takes place on the first occasion or on the second. Let us state first the view which our account of retention in the preceding chapter suggests, and then see how far it escapes the objections which are usually brought against such views by those who do not regard retention as a sufficient explanation. The problem is quite clear and definite. How does the chicken learn not to peck at an orange peel?

The Modification of Responses. On the first occasion congenital arrangements in the chicken's brain cause it first to peck at and then to reject the peel. The situation 'spying the peel' touches off an innate disposition, which we have seen reason to regard as a persistent state of tuning among the neurones of a co-ordination center. This disposition causes pecking and seizing which would ordinarily be followed by swallowing. *But* when the peel is seized its disagreeable taste touches off, in an allied co-ordination center, another disposition causing rejection, a set of movements incompatible with swallowing. Thus the pecking-seizing-swallowing sequence is upset. And the co-ordination center which responded to the situation by setting this sequence in action is left just as in the case of Pavlov's dog, in a new state of tuning due to the backwash influence of the rejection-response or of the taste. Which it is does not matter; probably both are involved. This new state of tuning disconnects the peel situation from its former response. Next time the peel is spied the center is not discharged. The chicken passes the peel by. And its behavior is entirely explained by the working of retention; what is retained being not the former set of responses nor the former experience but a new tuning, a new modification of the disposition.

Now it has very commonly been supposed by psychologists that what is retained must be either the experience itself or the set of responses. And this for two reasons. First because the kind of retention with which we are most familiar in our own case, or at least which we can most easily observe, involves imagery. An image does seem to be a case of an experience being itself retained. Actually it is a *repetition* of an experience depending upon a disposition, which is all that is retained; but it is easy to overlook this fact. The attempt to explain the chick's actions in terms of imaging breaks down ultimately because it would leave its marked limitations as a thinker unexplained. No psychologist nowadays would seriously consider such an account.

The reason for thinking that it is responses which are retained is due to the conspicuousness of habits. When we repeat an action frequently it gets more and more confirmed and fixed. This is a very obvious effect of retention. Thus we tend to think of retention as primarily a stamping in of responses. On the principle that we notice what happens much more readily than what does not happen, we come to overlook the fundamental fact that retention works much more by knocking out responses than by stamping them in. As we have already seen, and as we shall see again, it is the *result* of the response which knocks it out or stamps it in, and more responses on the whole are unsuccessful than successful. The young hopeful begins by pecking at all small objects; the experienced bird rarely pecks at anything which does not agree with it.

Retention and Foresight. If we are not clear as to what it is that is retained, supposing it to be the actual experience or the response itself, or if we regard retention as merely a deepening of the neural paths actually traversed by an impulse, it is easy to refute a theory of learning which reduces it to retention. For what should happen on such a theory is simply a repetition with increased vigor of the original response, pecking-seizing-rejection, or perhaps a muddled combination of them instead of a bland ignoring of the peel.[1] And this argument has been used by many psychologists against the retention theory, and with justice so far as inadequate conceptions of retention are concerned. But a different moral has been drawn. Professor Stout,[2] for example, after arguing that mere revival or reproduction of past experience through an acquired trace

[1] When the retention is lapsing as it may in time, we get tentative and hesitating behavior. The chick seems doubtful.

[2] G. F. Stout, "Instinct and Intelligence," *British Journal of Psychology*, vol. iii, pp. 237 ff.

cannot make the required difference, draws the odd conclusion that the original experience must have been intelligent. But this is only a step towards a renunciation of all explanation. A reference to the future, he continues, seems to be involved in all intelligent behavior. The animal 'seeks' certain future results. But mere reproduction of the past will not give this reference to the future. Hence this reference must have been present from the first. And "such a power can in the last resource only be accounted for as involved in the fundamental nature of that relation between mind and reality, or between reality and mind, which we call knowledge."

This is giving up the problem in the grand style. But Stout is perfectly correct in saying that the transaction which is henceforth to make the difference takes place on the first occasion; it is the jar involved in the first response which retunes the center so far as impulses due to orange peel are concerned. And he is correct in stressing the importance of the reference to a future result, but not in regarding it as inexplicable. As we have seen, the intelligent response appears to take into account and be controlled by what would happen. Actually it is being controlled by what happened on former occasions; and this foresight and reference to the future, all-important as they are throughout behavior, can be explained without the need of any mysterious factors.

In order that past experience shall assist in controlling present behavior with a view (as it appears) to the future, it is not in the least necessary that it should be revived in the form of memory. The chick need not *remember* that the peel tasted unpleasant. It need not, in fact, be conscious at all, though there are fairly good reasons based on general analogies for supposing that it has some kind of simple consciousness. Probably the peel simply looks unattractive to it. Such arguments as are valid on this point largely depend on analogy from our own experience. When we refuse a dish we commonly feel just disinclined to partake of it; we do not, as a rule, remember former occasions on which it disagreed with us. Some people do, but only as a result of giving a kind of attention to their food which it is very unlikely that the chick can give. When by a judicious wriggle we avoid falling off a bicycle we do not need to remember former falls. As we shall see later, far more of our behavior is ordinarily governed by such *unconscious* action of the traces of the past than by conscious recollection, revival, deliberation, and decision.

This temptation to suppose that the only way in which we can learn by experience is by remembering it, and by bringing our memories to bear upon the present circumstances, is responsible for most of the trouble which the theory of instinct has caused the psychologist. At present it is causing great difficulties to psycho-analysis. If we realize from the outset that incidents of our past constantly and continuously affect our present behavior without our having any consciousness of them, we shall be spared much bewilderment when we come to consider what *the unconscious* may be and how to conceive it. We shall avoid also attributing too much consciousness to animals and in particular endowing them with conscious prevision or foresight of the ends which they seek and achieve. We are much less conscious and less prescient ourselves than we suppose.

Intelligence and instinct are not, we have seen, rival or opposed forces. Intelligence is the means by which, through experience, we refine and elaborate the play of the instincts.

Trial and Error. Now that the not very interesting chicken has served its purpose, we can pass to more elaborate forms of animal behavior, in experiments on trial and error. Let us consider that ingenious contraption, the puzzle-box. A cat with a need for fish is placed in a box from which it can only escape to gain access to the fish by pulling a string. The times taken on a number of successive attempts are recorded. It is found that they tend to grow less and less. The number of random movements which the cat makes decreases, not smoothly, but as a general tendency. Finally the cat learns to make the required kind of movement immediately. Often this learning takes place with remarkable suddenness. Now suppose that after the cat has learned to pull the string at once when it is hanging as a loop in one corner of the cage, we arrange the loop to hang in the middle of the box. What does the cat do? A bright cat is not found to repeat the whole series of random scratchings and clawings which originally led to its learning how to escape. Instead, after perhaps a claw or two at the place where the loop used to hang, it finds the loop in its new position and pulls it at once. This shows that it has 'grasped the connection,' as we are tempted to say, between pulling the loop and escape. The problem is to discover what this 'grasping of the connection' consists in. Is it a matter of 'insight' by the cat, or can it be accounted for merely by the stamping in of acquired responses?

It is important to realize how difficult the problem really is, and the best way to do this is to consider some of the theories which have been put forward and how far they succeed or fail as explanations.

The accepted view of learning held until recently by most experimenters in animal psychology (Thorndike has been the initiator of most of these investigations) was in broad outline this. Three laws were supposed to co-operate: the Law of Effect, the Law of Recency, the Law of Exercise. Different authorities have stressed these laws in different degrees. We are already familiar with them all. The Law of Effect is that, other things being equal, success leads to the repetition of a response, failure to its elimination. The Law of Recency is that, other things being equal, the last response is the one which has the best chance of recurring. The Law of Exercise is simply that repetition of any response tends to confirm it. By these three laws the response actually retained was supposed to be picked out of an original infinitely varied range of possible random instinctive responses, all equally likely to be made.

The selection was supposed to be a 'blind' selection not guided by any observation. "The cat learns to get out by getting out, not by seeing how to get out,"[1] is Woodworth's summary of this view.

One difficulty will probably have occurred to the reader. The theory might work if the movement finally made by the cat was always *exactly* the same. But in actual fact it is a certain *kind* of movement, not a perfectly specific movement, which is in the end adopted. The objection gets still more force when we find that the cat *transfers* the learned response to a different situation, pulling the loop at a different level and from a new angle. Quite different movements may then be required, prompted by quite different views of the loop. So that we cannot be content with any theory which deals with this kind of learning purely in terms of movements and stimuli. For the movements and stimuli are never exactly repeated. Learning, therefore, cannot be an establishment of firm connections between particular stimuli and particular movements. None the less, as a reaction to the older, anthropomorphic views which supposed the cat to reason the matter out, to act, in fact, just as we should if we were remarkably stupid, this theory was a great advance in the right direction.

Perception in Cats. We are forced back, then, to the question, What is a response? What is it that is learned? And to answer this we must take stock anew of the whole situation. There is the cat boxed

[1] R. S. Woodworth, *Psychology*, p. 310.

up, consumed by a lust for fish; and generally in an unsettled condition. Its whole activity must be regarded as the elaborate way in which this disturbance settles down. It bites the bars, pushes at them, claws and scratches, these all being either ways by which it has formerly escaped from somewhat similar situations or, if it is a very inexperienced cat, innate, instinctive activities. Finally it pulls the loop and escapes. All this happens again and again; it escapes at the end, sometimes of one series of scratchings, sometimes of another. In some way plainly the actual experience of the cat while pulling the loop, the particular state it is in at that moment, is the thing which matters. The problem is to work out what that particular moment of experience consists of.

A natural suggestion is that at least an important part of it is the sight of the loop. But we must not suppose that the cat sees it as a loop or perceives it in the same fashion as ourselves. For if it did it would also act more as we do. The proper inference is that the cat, which at first, perhaps, does not perceive the loop at all, comes gradually with repetition to perceive it in some sort of way. Little by little, out of the whole vague perception of obstacles everywhere, the loop gets more distinctness, not as a loop, but, as Koffka puts it, as "something to be pulled," and it is this perception of "something to be pulled" which is in time, through the pulling, connected with escaping, and so comes to be the link of transition between the boxed-up situation and the escape.

To see how this happens we may recall our account of the working of the brain. The cat's co-ordination centers are under strain, thanks to its need to escape. The release of strain which follows escape tends to fix, in the co-ordination centers, the pattern which immediately precedes it. In the case of the cat, *when in so unusual and difficult a situation as this*, a number of repetitions are required for this pattern to become fairly fixed. It is a new type of pattern for the cat, and thus easily evanesces. The cat makes no such to-do about getting through the door which is opened by the pull, or about going to the fish and eating it once the escape is effected.

This account, by which not a particular movement, but a *perception*, a sighting of the loop as 'something to be pulled,' is the heart of the response, gets over the main difficulty we found in the accepted theory. The cat learns not to make a certain movement, but to pull the loop. What is acquired is not a particular response, but a disposition, just as we saw must be the case with the chicken and the peel; in this case a disposition to perceive the loop as 'something to be pulled' and as the beginning of a transition towards escape. But let us consider this perception more closely. How far does it involve an insight by the cat into the situation as a whole? Only to a very slight extent. Only to the extent that, as opposed to the view of the Thorndike school, the learning is not merely a new connection, between a given situation and a given response, built up out of the cat's pre-existing repertory of reactions. The cat's world does now contain a new kind of thing. Its receptive centers are capable of handling a new pattern—and this, but nothing more than this is what is meant by insight.

The Gestalt Theory of Perception. The line of argument which we have been following is due to Koffka and Köhler, the leaders of what is known as the *Gestalt* School in Psychology. This is a vigorous movement, which has had the great merit of galvanizing into new life an immense number of problems which showed signs of congealment in a kind of semi-solution. The watchword of the school, the *Gestalt*, is peculiarly hard either to translate or to define. Words which have been suggested as equivalents in English are 'form,' 'shape,' 'configuration,' 'pattern,' 'unitary structure,' and 'functional disposition,' but none of them is very illuminating.

We have to gather what kind of thing a *Gestalt* is chiefly from the instances which we are given. The cat's new perception of 'something to be pulled' in this case is such an instance; the chicken's pecking-seizing-swallowing instinct is another; so is the tune whose recognition we studied in the preceding chapter. Or more accurately, in all these cases the states of tuning in virtue of which the cat perceives the loop, the chicken gets its food, and we recognize the tune are instances of *Gestalts*. A *Gestalt* in psychology, in other words, is a disposition, conceived not as a fixed pathway among neurones, but as a system which has a certain end-state, a certain poise to which it tends under a given set of conditions.

Gestalts, however, are not confined to psychological phenomena; they are to be found throughout nature. Koffka, quoting Köhler, illustrates the conception of a *Gestalt* by reference to an experiment with soap-films originally due to Van der Mensbrugghe. A loop of fine silk is taken which is tied inside a wire ring. The whole is then dipped in soap solution so as to produce a film. The loop A floats in the film, and can be moved into any shape we please

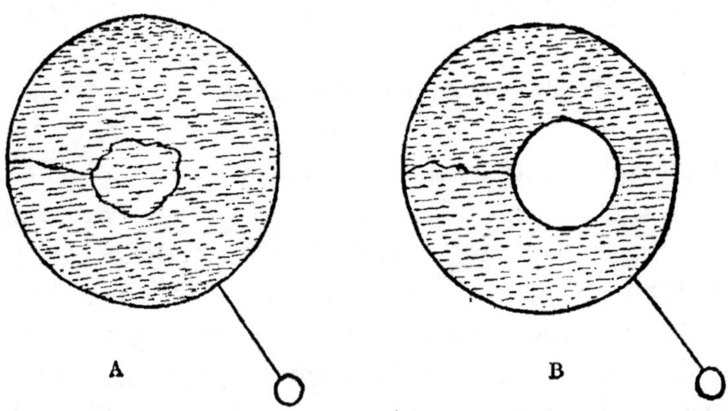

Fig. VII

(Fig. VII). The film inside the loop is now broken by touching it with a piece of filter paper cut into a fine point. At once the loop is drawn into a circle by the tension of the film surrounding it (B), and can be felt to resist attempts to change its shape.

"In this example," Koffka writes, "we can conceive of circularity as the 'end-situation,' puncturing the film as the stimulus releasing the movement, and the movement itself as the 'transitional situation.' The same procedure holds good for all events and especially for those that issue in the nervous system."[1]

A compass needle which comes to rest pointing north and south, or an atmospheric depression which comes to rest over the British Isles, might equally well be instanced. A *Gestalt*, then, is a system with an end-state to which it tends to return when disturbed. A new *Gestalt* is either a new system or a new end-state for an old system. Imagine a compass needle swung among a number of electro-magnets. Every change now in any of these magnets will produce a new end-state, a new position of rest for the compass needle. The point is the dependence of the 'transitional' situation, the activity which we observe, upon the end-state as well as upon the stimulus which sets it moving. How this dependence comes about and especially the part played in it by retention we have already considered. The weakness of the doctrine at present is in the vagueness with which the relations between *Gestalts* are treated. The cat's escape involves many *Gestalts* themselves combining into a larger inclusive *Gestalt*. What we most need to know is how these various *Gestalts* deal with one another. But this is a point which only further research can elicit.

[1] K. Koffka, *The Growth of the Mind* (1924), p. 106.

CHAPTER VII: THE MENTALITY OF APES

Köhler's Apes. We can now pass to the study of the animals which are the nearest relatives of man, and it is to Wolfgang Köhler that we are indebted for a study of the mind of the chimpanzee which is already a landmark in the history of animal psychology.

The great advantage of Köhler's experiments is that they set problems which, if insight or understanding occurs in apes, they might be expected to solve by this means—by the formation, that is to say, of new configurations, new *Gestalts*. The cat could not well be expected to master the mechanical construction of its box, since essential parts of it were quite hidden. But Köhler's apes, being given much simpler tasks, had an opportunity of really showing what they could do.

We will take what was perhaps the cleverest performance of Sultan, the most intelligent of Köhler's apes. Apes vary in intelligence almost as men do. All the animals easily mastered the use of sticks in dragging fruit placed outside the cage within reach. And from the very start they would place the stick correctly behind the fruit in order to draw it forward. There were no random movements. If the stick to be used lay so that both stick and fruit were visible together, there was, as a rule, no delay, but if they were widely separated, difficulties arose at first. The stick did not easily enter into the situation. It remained indifferent to the animal, 'something to bite upon' or 'something to jump with' or 'to throw,' not 'something to fetch fruit with.' In other words, the stick has to be perceived in a special way before it can be used; it has to be seen as a tool, as a step or link in the transition by which the end-state of securing the fruit is gained.

A chimpanzee who is not very excited or careless will rarely use implements not large enough for his purpose. He often brings them along, but at the decisive moment his whole behavior changes and his energy flags. He may poke once or throw a too short stick at the fruit; "but an observer with any experience will have been able to indicate at once the moment when the fresh hue of determination faded; the rest, then, is not a practical endeavor, but merely the expression of discouraged desire."[1]

The Construction of Tools. The elaborate experiments of Nadie Kohts in Moscow (1914-16) were chiefly devoted to showing that vision plays a predominant rôle in the perceptions of the chimpanzee, and Köhler's observations in Tenerife are particularly interesting on this point. Two sticks are often put together so that they *look* like one long stick, and the ape will then try to use them as such, regardless of the fact that they do not stay together and are *practically* useless. But are the two sticks ever combined so as to become technically useful? Sultan was the first to solve the problem. For more than

[1] W. Köhler, *The Mentality of Apes* (1924), p. 127.

an hour he failed, poking about in various ways, but although he several times put one stick exactly to the opening of the other he made no attempt to fit them together. Even a suggestion from the observer who put one finger into the opening of the stick under the animal's nose (without pointing to the other stick at all) was of no assistance. A little later, when sitting with his back to the fruit, Sultan happened to find himself holding one rod in either hand so that they were in a straight line; he pushed the thinner one a little way into the opening of the thicker, jumped up, ran immediately towards the railings, and began to draw a banana towards him with the double stick. Though the sticks fell apart, Sultan at once replaced them, and proceeded with the greatest assurance to rake fruit towards him, replacing the sticks whenever they slipped asunder. The proceeding so pleased him that he continued, without stopping to eat any of the fruit, to rake into his cage everything that he could reach.

The Process of Discovery. The contrast of this mode of discovery with the supposed blind random scratchings of the cat in the puzzle-box is very striking. And the contrast between Köhler's subtle, sympathetic, but not in the least anthropomorphic way of regarding his apes with the mere collection and analysis of 'performance-times' is equally noticeable. In fact, it has been suggested that some students of animal psychology show less intelligence with their problem than Sultan did with his. We see, however, that the learning here is not merely a matter of a stamping in of an accidental response through laws of Exercise, Recency, and Effect. Exercise comes in, it is true, at a later stage. The following day Sultan did not at once fit the sticks together, but did so as soon as other methods had been tried in vain. Later on he came to fit them together when necessary as his first procedure. We shall notice another less favorable effect of Exercise on a later page. Recency and Effect which are really aspects of one and the same law come in only if we regard them as concerned with the *fixation* of the new pattern by which the two inadequately short sticks are now *seen* as 'things to be fitted together.' They do not explain the formation of this pattern. They are laws of memory, not of first *achievement*, to use Koffka's term.

We need to make a considerable imaginative effort to understand how the achievement in such a case as this comes about. It plainly depends to a very great extent upon retention, upon the animal's previous acquirements in the way of perceptive configurations or, still to use Köhler's own term, *Gestalts*. Sultan already possessed dispositions enabling him to drag in fruit with sticks and to see two sticks touching one another end to end as one stick. What had to be formed was a new unity, by which both the perception of two bamboos as of different sizes and the act of fitting them together might be welded into the larger conative trend which is already causing him to seek a longer stick with which to drag in the fruit. The new structure forms as a *bridge* by which the larger, already operative system, thrown out of equilibrium by the sight of the too distant fruit, passes to its end-state. It closes the circuit and fills the gap in the activity which is going on. The initial step was no doubt due to chance, or to an activity which had nothing essentially to do with the rest of the proceedings. Sultan was playing [1] with the sticks, an operation run by quite a different set of co-ordination and association centers and by different needs, when he first fitted the sticks together. We must not suppose that he was trying then deliberately to fix them together with a view to getting a longer stick. Chance in this sense provided the means required; but it was not chance which caused the means to be used to bridge the gap. Sultan's intelligence is shown by the fact that the gap seized at once on the means and so filled itself in.

The most remarkable thing about the whole discovery is perhaps the extent to which the new perception worked in with, and brought into play with it, the animal's other acquired dispositions. He was given a bamboo, for example, and a stick which was just too large to fit into it. Köhler's account of the methods by which Sultan dealt with this situation is astonishing. He bit off a long splinter from one end of the bamboo and then surprisingly tried to fit the splinter into the other end. It would not go in. He then set to work to bite away enough

[1] Köhler remarks: "Play looks quite different. I have never seen a chimpanzee play while he was showing himself distinctly intent upon his ultimate purpose" (p. 113).

of the end of the solid stick. After a while he got it just to go in, but not deep enough; the sticks fell apart when he used them. After a while he tired of this biting (the wood was chosen to be especially hard) and set to work on the splinter, finally fixing it firmly in the sound end of the bamboo.

Consider the number of possible points at which he might have gone wrong, by spoiling both ends of the bamboo, for example, or working now at one end, now at the other, of the wooden stick. As Köhler remarks, "Sultan evidently had a bright day." Again when the end of the larger bamboo was partially closed by a plug, Sultan seized the tubes, looked for a moment at the block in the hole, tried to squeeze the thinner tube into the narrow opening between the block and the side of the tube, failed, and straightway pulled out the stopper, threw it aside, and connected the tubes.

From these examples we see that the new perception of 'tubes to be fitted into one another', itself demanded by the 'food to be dragged in' perception, in its turn demands other perceptions such as 'stick to be sharpened' or 'plug to be pulled out.'

Some other of these apes' activities will help to bring out further peculiarities of intelligence. It sometimes happened that when an ape had been practicing one activity for some time and was then asked to tackle a quite different problem, it would, if in difficulties, fall back upon the old technique. It would bring up a box which had been used in building, for example, when what was required was joining two sticks, or would open a door when what was needed was a jumping-pole performance. This is plainly a lingering effect of the Law of Exercise,—the old technique having fallen to the rank of habit. "Processes originally very valuable have a disagreeable tendency to sink to a lower rank with constant repetition. This . . . is usually supposed to bring about a great saving and it may be so both in man and anthropoid apes. But one must never forget what a startling resemblance there is between these crude stupidities of the chimpanzees arising from habit, and certain empty and meaningless repetitions of moral, political, and other principles in men."[1] Köhler notes that drowsiness, exhaustion, colds, or even excitement favor such mistakes.

Building Experiments. The building performances of the apes are especially interesting because of the resemblance they show to the young child's performances with his bricks. Bananas would be hung up so that the ape had to pile one box upon another to reach them. Dragging a box to the right place and standing on it for a leap was easily learned. So even was the placing in some fashion of another box on top of it. The same suddenness of the discovery was noticed here as in the case of the double stick. Sultan when he failed would seize a box and gallop all round the room with it, showing every sign of annoyance; not in order to use the box in building,

[1] Köhler, *Op. cit.*, p. 205.

but to give vent to his temper. This suggests that a good many of the cat's supposed random movements in the puzzle-box may have really nothing to do with escape, but be merely the cat's way of resenting the situation.

The ape's chief difficulty in building is not to see that one box can be put upon another; it is to see how to put it so that it will stay there. And this difficulty the chimpanzee apparently cannot completely solve any more than the child at a certain stage in its play with bricks can solve it. "*There are practically no statics to be noted in the chimpanzee.* Almost everything arising as 'a question of statics' he does not solve by insight, but by trying around blindly" (p. 154). He will poise one box cornerwise upon another, trying meanwhile "with concentrated gravity to ascend the pinnacle. With an amazing stubbornness and minute care Grande repeated this masterly mistake for years" (p. 163). Often her extraordinary gifts as an equilibrist lead to triumph. Grande in the photograph (Plate I) is retaining her painfully constructed edifice in equilibrium only through a careful distribution of her own weight. Unfortunately everything depends upon her not letting go of the bananas or pulling them down. A catastrophe occurred immediately after the photograph was taken. The other ape is the genius Sultan, who has been forbidden to take part in the building; the sympathetic participation shown in his left hand should be especially noticed.

After Köhler

PLATE I

Needs and Instincts. So far we have paid attention chiefly to the development of intelligence; this of course is only one aspect of the animal's mental growth, though it is the aspect which has been most studied. We have seen, however, that the animal's intelligent acts are all prompted by some definite need or set of needs, though we have kept somewhat monotonously to manifestations of one need only, the need for food. The reason is that this is the motive most convenient to the experimenter. But the animal's needs are various and the question naturally arises, How do the chimpanzee's needs compare with those of man, and what light do his presumably simpler needs throw upon our own, upon our desires, and the working of our passions in general?

We must distinguish between the animal's innate needs and its acquired needs. Most of man's needs and many of those of the higher animals, especially the domesticated animals, are acquired; they are, as it were, grafted as primitive needs in the manner described in Chapter V. The chimpanzee needs no boxes or fishing rods in its wild condition, and if we consider only congenital needs our question plainly is the one which has been so often asked, namely, How many instincts are there? To this, different answers have been given corresponding to the psychologist's purpose in raising the question. Thus Freud, having in view as simple and fundamental a classification of human instincts as possible, classifies them into two groups, ego-instincts and sex-instincts; while Thorndike, wishing to keep close to the facts, is content to list an indefinite number of specific situations with the instinctive responses which they elicit.

The Classification of Instincts. Another kind of answer is McDougall's, based definitely upon a theory of the relation of instinct to emotion. Emotion for McDougall is "a mode of experience which accompanies the working within us of instinctive impulses," and each instinct, "no matter how brought into play, is accompanied by its own peculiar quality of experience which may be called a primary emotion."[1] This clue followed out by McDougall with great industry and acumen has yielded very interesting results, although the metaphysical hypotheses by which he supports and recommends his scheme are unfortunately not of equal value and have discredited it in many quarters. The similarity between McDougall's formulation and that of Gall[2] suggests, moreover, that 'instincts' if treated as more than convenient popular terms, have all the disadvantages of the old-fashioned 'faculties.'

---

[1] W. McDougall, *An Outline of Psychology* (1923), p. 128.

[2] Illustrated by Dr. Bernard Hollander in "McDougall's Social Psychology Anticipated" (*Ethological Journal*, vol. ix, no. 4, 1924). Cf. C. D. Broad, *The Mind and Its Place in Nature* (1925). "I cannot pretend to believe that the psychologists of instinct, such as McDougall, have accomplished anything save to revive the faculty-psychology in an extreme form and with an amusingly pretentious parade of 'science'"; also Watson, *Behaviorism* (1925), p. 78.

McDougall's list of instincts is as follows:

Instincts	*Emotional Qualities*
1. Instinct of escape (of self-preservation, of avoidance, danger instinct)	Fear (terror, fright, alarm, trepidation).
2. Instinct of combat (aggression, pugnacity)	Anger (rage, fury, annoyance, irritation, displeasure).
3. Repulsion (repugnance)	Disgust (nausea, loathing, repugnance).
4. Parental (protective)	Tender emotion (love, tenderness, tender feeling).
5. Appeal	Distress (feeling of helplessness).
6. Pairing (mating, reproduction, sexual)	Lust (sexual emotion or excitement, sometimes called love —an unfortunate and confusing usage).
7. Curiosity (inquiry, discovery, investigation)	Curiosity (feeling of mystery, of strangeness, of the unknown, wonder).
8. Submission (self-abasement)	Feeling of subjection (of inferiority, of devotion, of humility, of attachment, of submission, negative self-feeling).
9. Assertion (self-display)	Elation (feeling of superiority, of masterfulness, of pride, of domination, positive self-feeling).
10. Social or gregarious instinct	Feeling of loneliness, of isolation, nostalgia.
11. Food-seeking (hunting)	Appetite or craving in narrower sense (gusto).
12. Acquisition (hoarding instinct)	Feeling of ownership, of possession (protectivity, feeling).

Instincts	Emotional Qualities
13. Construction	Feeling of creativeness, of making, of productivity.
14. Laughter	Amusement (jollity, carelessness, relaxation).

Besides the emotions here mentioned McDougall also recognizes blended and secondary emotions (such as horror, awe, gratitude, and scorn) and derived emotions (such as joy, sorrow, surprise, anxiety, hope, and despair). The last spring from the facilitation or obstruction of desires. But even with the addition of such further complexities it is difficult to see why the particular emotional qualities in the list should be chosen rather than these, as the accompaniment of the instinct. Thus loneliness only occurs when we are deprived of social activities, and is replaced by feelings of hilarity and affability; and similarly in the final stage of successful foraging craving gives place to an expansive feeling of content. But allowing for derived emotions in both cases, the difference between affability and digestive well-being is not reducible to a difference between loneliness and hunger. Hence each of McDougall's instincts seems to have not a single primary emotion attached to it, but a cycle of distinctive emotions.

A More Fundamental Division. For the purposes of scientific anthropology something more fundamental is clearly required; and a classification based on the primary and derivative needs discussed in Chapter V will provide the essentials. Thus pairing and food-seeking, together with what McDougall describes as the 'minor instincts' of urination and defecation, occur cyclically as a result of internal needs—like sleeping and waking, and organic processes such as breathing and digestion; whereas escape, combat (except perhaps in Irishmen), and repugnance only occur in connection with fairly specific external situations. In other words, instinctive responses of internal origin correspond to the primitive organic needs which we have been discussing above. These can legitimately be called drives, while the others are of the nature of readjustments arising through the obstruction or complication of such prior activities. Such an adjustment repeated frequently enough (cf. Chapter V) may become a derivative drive. Thus escape is a development of the much more primitive impulse to remove the skin from stimuli which threaten to destroy tissue; and flight from a loud noise is to be explained in terms of pre-human conditioning. The social instincts arise partly from sex and partly from the need to co-operate in hunting or housing problems.

Laughter. The case of laughter with its allied problems (the smile, tickling and the grin of gratification) will give the reader a good idea of the still undecided difficulties with which McDougall as a pioneer has been wrestling.[1] In 1908, in his *Social*

[1] The latest general survey of the problem will be found in Gregory's *The Nature of Laughter* (1924). To Max Eastman's *The Sense of Humor* (1921) must be attributed McDougall's inclusion of Laughter in his 1923 list. McDougall's article in *Psyche*, vol. ii, N. S. no. 4, April, 1922, explains his reasons for the inclusion on the lines of his 1913 British Association paper. Other useful studies of Laughter are those of Sully, *An Essay on Laughter* (1902), and Bergson, *Laughter* (E. T. 1910).

Psychology (p. 82), he spoke of seven instincts as being sufficient to account for "almost all the affective states that are popularly recognized as emotions." Others, such as the instinct of reproduction, then played "but a minor part in the genesis of the emotions." In 1923, the list of thirteen instincts all "common to most of the mammals, and the constituents of human nature," could hardly, in view of the work of Freud, put Reproduction on a less important plane than (say) Self-abasement. Accordingly, it is now included, along with five more, all on much the same level as the original seven, while laughter is somewhat reluctantly admitted as the one *possible* guest to avoid the unlucky number. As a problem picture we include a photograph of a chimpanzee which seems to have a more direct bearing on the still disputed occurrence of genuine amusement in an animal than any hitherto published.

The Value of McDougall's Scheme. Apart from theoretical considerations, McDougall's scheme, being in accord with popular language, gives us a rough-and-ready means of comparing different animal species in their responses to similar general situations, and of comparing the behavior of the animal in varying situations. If the reader will try to analyze the behavior of his dog, or that of his friends, by asking which of these instincts on various occasions are primarily concerned, he will soon discover that the list is very serviceable. McDougall's own use of it often throws light upon problems of behavior, though his descriptions of instinct itself

After Kohts

PLATE II.—CHIMPANZEE LAUGHING
(or not?)

for the most part are in terms of a hypothetical vitalism. "We have to recognize," he says, "that the instincts of an animal are, as it were, its very essence and central core, all its bodily organs and functions being merely servants of the instincts." And again: "The evolution of the animal world may properly be conceived as primarily and essentially the differentiation of instinctive tendencies from some primordial undifferentiated capacity to strive. It is this undifferentiated capacity to strive, this primordial energy, which M. Bergson has named *l'élan vital*, which others (notably Dr. C. G. Jung) speak of as the *libido*, and which perhaps is best named vital energy. We may regard the instincts as so many differentiated channels through which the vital energy pours itself into or through the organism."[1]

This is very far from a useful way of regarding the instincts. For the organism, after all, is what we know and can observe, and an instinct is something which we postulate for its convenience in allowing us to describe what we do observe, namely, the organism's behavior and, in our own case, its experience.

The Dangers of Anthropomorphism. One other temptation must be resisted before such a scheme can be used for the investigation of animal behavior. We must be chary of lending the animal, when it behaves much as we might do, mental processes similar in all respects to our own. Some apparently highly altruistic animal behavior, for example, is,

[1]McDougall, *op. cit. An Outline of Psychology*, pp. 112-113.

when closely examined, found to be very much simpler in its motives. As M. Giard has shown in his *Les origines de l'amour maternel*, the broody hen sits on her eggs not through any passion of maternal love, but to allay a local inflammation; and a capon suitably irritated with pepper can be turned into a most devoted foster-mother. Kirkman, with the black-headed gull, found that the bird does not resent the removal of her eggs, and would sit for the full incubating period on any object that is not too uncomfortable, such as a small square or circular box, or a golf-ball.[1]

Our own emotions are the clue to any scheme of instincts in so far as they allow us to classify our main activities, and the main kinds of situations which call them forth. We then look for similar activities and situations in animal behavior. But we do not, or should not, suppose that the emotions of animals very different in development from ourselves need have much in common with our own.

With this very necessary precaution in mind we can briefly consider some of the main features of animal behavior which are significant for human psychology.

Naturally the nearer we come to man in the biological tree the more significant is the behavior. The passions of the ant, of the cuttlefish, or of the crocodile, could we divine them, would tell us little about our own; but with the chimpanzee the case is altogether different. We can both conjecture them with

---

[1] *In lit.* To appear in his forthcoming *The Expression of Emotion in Birds.*

After Kohts

PLATE III.—CHIMPANZEE MATCHING COLORS

some probability and draw comparisons with profit; but the experiments of Nadie Kohts to which reference has already been made, and one of which is illustrated in Plate III, suggest that more depends on the skill and understanding of the human observer than has usually been supposed.

The Social Life of Apes. Group phenomena are among the most interesting in this respect, for the chimpanzee's strongest and most varied emotions arise through his membership of a group. As Professor Köhler points out, "A chimpanzee kept in solitude is not a real chimpanzee at all." An ape separated from his fellows will risk his very life to get back to them. The group, however, shows less interest in the separated one. He will stretch his arms imploringly towards them, howling and whimpering, and if they do not come to comfort him, will wave sticks towards them, and even throw things towards them, not out of anger, but in order to do something, no matter what, in their direction as a relief to his feelings. This tendency to do something in the direction of whatever is the object of the emotion is very general. And what is done is not necessarily at all useful.

The return of the lost one is the occasion for general rejoicings: "The whole group becomes very lively; they put their arms round him, even beat him a little for pleasure. . . . The oldest animal, who occupied a special position in the life of the community, was, on any such occasion, greeted by a universal welcome, such as was not accorded to the others" (p. 295).

An attack upon one member in the presence of the group often produces an extraordinary disturbance. The whole group sets up a howl,[1] as if with one voice. There seems no doubt that one chimpanzee will genuinely defend another, and not in his own interest. But they differ amazingly in this respect as in other points of character. Thus some chimpanzees rarely intentionally incite the others to mass-attack, but the gifted Sultan, always inclined to pose as a martyr, continually did so. He seems, in fact, to have borne a remarkable resemblance to many human geniuses; for instance, in his dislike of uninteresting jobs. "Once it was demanded of him, in the evening after all the animals had been fed, to collect the fruit skins which were lying about and put them in a basket. He quickly grasped what was wanted of him and did it—but only for two days. On the third day he had to be told every minute to go on; on the fourth he had to be ordered from one banana skin to the next, and on the fifth and following days his limbs had to be moved for every movement, seizing, picking up, walking, holding the skins over the basket, letting them drop, and so on, because they stopped dead at

[1] "Although the young chimpanzee uses significant sounds in considerable number and variety, it does not," write Yerkes and Learned, "in the ordinary and proper meaning of the term, speak" (*Chimpanzee Intelligence and its Vocal Expressions*, 1925). The whole question of animal speech, however, requires further careful investigation.

whatever place he had come to, or to which he had been led. The animal behaved like a run-down clock, or like certain types of mentally deficient persons, in whom similar things occur."

The actual sight of suffering will prompt behavior which looks in the highest degree solicitous and maternal, but with chimpanzees 'out of sight is out of mind.' *The ape seems to have practically no power of imagining.* Expressions of emotion which have no connection with the animal's material advantage are common. When punished, an imperious desire for forgiveness may be shown; the animal will make up to his human companion, with apish protests of friendship. Chimpanzees instantly take to little children and infants.

Animal Friendships. Marked and enduring friendships are found. One day Köhler noticed in Chica a 'disquieted hopping' which he recognized as usually a sign of guilt, but he could not discover any offense she had committed. "Thus made attentive, I became aware that her friend Tercera was missing, or rather, that a piece of her black fur kept on disappearing behind a box each time I came round the other side of it." Tercera was the guilty one.

The study of the sexual life of chimpanzees has still to be carried out in detail. It is likely to have a bearing upon the vexed question of the Freudian theory of infantile sexuality. But even so far as they go at present Köhler's observations are of great interest. "It seems to me," he writes, "that among these creatures sexual excitement is less specific and less differentiated from any other kind of excitement than among human beings. We may almost say that any strong emotion, and thus any strong external stimulus, tends to react directly upon both the colon and the genitals, but not so as to give the impression of exaggerated and concentrated sexuality, but rather of an inner vehemence and interdependence of all vivid inner processes." Again, "Even the strongest expressions of sexual behavior gave a very naïve impression, and the drive can under normal conditions merge constantly into the rest of the 'social,' or communal, life of the group. The sexuality of the chimpanzee is, as it were, less sexual than that of the civilized human being. Often when two chimpanzees meet one another, they seem to 'sketch' or indicate movements, which can hardly be classed definitely under either the category of joyous and cordial welcome, or sexual intimacy. . . . Thus chimpanzees embrace each other, with all degrees of emphasis and fervor, partly as a reassurance of their social cohesion, but also as a consolation in moments of terror and anxiety, and again 'just because life is so jolly.' In moments of special cordiality they fall over each other to the ground" (pp. 314-316). The general significance of this description for the psychology of childhood we shall make clear later.

Terror and Curiosity. When in doubt chimpanzees scratch their heads. When surprised or apprehensive or startled they display entirely human gestures. When frightened they fly or cling together; it is an intriguing fact that they were most terrified by certain small stuffed toys, cloth donkeys with black buttons for eyes. "One day I entered their room with one of these toys under my arm. Their reaction times may be very short; for in a moment a black cluster, consisting of the whole group of chimpanzees, hung suspended from the farthest corner of the wire roofing; each individual tried to thrust the other aside and bury his head deep in among them" (p. 333). It is tempting to connect this peculiar terror with the influence which effigies so mysteriously exert in the lives of primitive people.

Finally, for we must pass on to study these same activities in the child and in man, the chimpanzees recognized objects in photographs and, having been introduced to mirrors, thenceforward would spend hours studying reflections of themselves and of other things in pools, bright pieces of tin, and tiny splinters of glass. "What strange beings," as Köhler remarks, "to be permanently attracted by the contemplation of such phenomena, which can bring them not the least tangible or 'practical' benefit!"

CHAPTER VIII: MENTAL GROWTH IN MAN

THAT apish cousin of the chimpanzee from whom we descend probably differed from him in two important respects as well as in matters of degree. One was that he developed free images, and the other that he took to using speech.

The Development and Uses of Imagery. The power to form images corresponding to the things we have perceived is one of the most mysterious, as it is one of the most obvious, of our talents. It is an entirely open question whether images may not occur in the mental processes of even lowly animals. The point is extraordinarily difficult to decide, since, as Huxley put it, "nothing short of being a crayfish would give us positive assurance that such an animal possesses consciousness" (*The Crayfish*, p. 89). The line of argument is simple. If we find in our own behavior certain performances which never occur without consciousness in the form of images, and if for similar performances in the animal we can find no reason to suppose that they are carried out otherwise than in ourselves, then we are entitled with fair probability to suppose images to occur in the animal. But these Ifs are not at all easy to settle. To take the first only. We commonly do use images in certain situations—in planning a house, for example; but we can also dispense with them, or at least some people can.

The other premise is just as shaky. How are we to be certain that an animal's act is similar to one of our own? Dogmatism would be very rash in the matter, but the probable view on the whole is that if images do occur in the crayfish they are only exceptional and isolated events. Anything like a *train* of images is unlikely. For otherwise the animal would behave differently and show more intelligence. The same argument applies even to the chimpanzee. He fails in ways which trains of images would be likely to prevent.

But the child by the time he reaches the story-telling age (about four), beyond all doubt makes extensive use of images, and in two fashions. He uses them for practical purposes, in solving problems, and he uses them for emotional gratification, in fantasy or daydreaming, as part of the absorbing activity of play.

An image (see Chapter III) is essentially a perception taking place without the normal stimulation, without the incoming impulses from the sense-organs which perception demands. It is usual to divide images up into types—visual, auditory, kinæsthetic, etc.—corresponding to the sense organs, which would have to be stimulated for the corresponding perceptions. But this classification is somewhat artificial. We shall see later (Chapter XII) that most perceptions are very complicated, including commonly a variety of sensory factors. We perceive a table not only with our eyes, but through the effects of past handlings of it, for example. Correspondingly, an image of a table is rarely a purely visual affair, but more complicated. Sometimes, of course, one aspect will be more prominent than another. A few individuals appear to be entirely without imagery. For most people their power of imaging varies with their physiological state, being notably increased with the onset of sleep. Those much engaged in abstract thought are believed to have their normal imaging-power impaired. These differences sometimes make psychology unduly mysterious to beginners who happen to differ in their natural imagery from the authors they read. On the other hand, since a man's imagery is the part or aspect of his mind which he himself can most easily investigate, images have tended to take too prominent a position in psychology ever since the time of Locke, whose 'way of ideas' made images the foundation stone of the theory of the mind. Actually, however, images are not simple, primitive, or ultimate, but highly complex products arising at a late stage of development.

In the child the first appearance of free images is difficult to trace, just as in the ape. There is, further, reason to think that the distinction between actual perceiving and imaging is not, at an early age, nearly so clear cut as it is in adults. This sharp separation of the actual from the imaged is one of the many differences between the adult's world and the child's.

The uses of images are fairly evident; we shall discuss them, together with certain disadvantages, later (see also Chapter XIII). It is enough here to notice that their appearance in the free form of trains of ideas, more or less under the control of purpose and design, is a very important landmark in the history of the mind. Our present problem is to trace some of the probable steps in the development of imagery.

Imagery and Desire. One clue to this is the marked connection of images with emotion and desire. Compared with imaging, merely thinking of an object, an enemy, for example, tends to be unemotional. Another clue lies in one of the characteristics of images as opposed to perceptions. An image is always comparatively loose and devoid of connections. Every actual adult perception is fixed fast in a setting; all the rest of our contemporary stimulation gives it background and body; it has to maintain itself in relation to all this. But an image is, as it were, exempted from such rivalry. It floats relatively untroubled, hardly in time or space, and if subject to forces which control it, at least these forces are not the same as with the percept.

We can make this last point more precise by asking, Why does an image occur at all? A perception comes out of the interplay of a need and a situation. It is, we saw in the last chapter, a bridge by which the situation is used to satisfy a need. With an image there is, strictly speaking, no stimulus-situation, there is only the need, and such circumstances as amount to an absence of any stimulation which can be used to serve it. The image arises as a substitute for the missing situation. This is why the simplest imagining takes the form of 'wish-fulfillment.' The notion of 'wish-fulfillment' is of importance in practical psychology, in the psychology of every-day life. We shall return to it in Chapter XV. The name 'wish-fulfillment' is not very happy, since under wishes must be included both aversion and appetition. The essential point is that in wish-fulfillment the daydream or the cinema is substituted for the situation demanded by the need.

The wish may or may not be conscious; this remains true whichever sense we choose for the equivocal term 'consciousness.' The wish is merely activity prompted by the need; it may take the form of *desire*, an explicitly conscious striving, it may take the form of fear; or it may be ignored or disowned by whatever parts of the mind might be aware of its working. For the moment which of these happens does not matter.

Extensive use of imagery in practical affairs seems likely to be a development subsequent to this use of it as a direct though bodiless and illusory satisfier of needs. For wide experience and a very considerable plasticity are necessary before imagery becomes of real practical service. We commonly think of our imagery as guiding our action. We imagine what we are going to do, and then do it, so runs the traditional account. But ninety-nine times out of a hundred—as anyone who watches himself at all closely will agree—we actually do something else when the moment comes. Circumstances must govern our perceptions and guide us to the satisfaction of our needs; our preliminary imaginings prompted by our needs alone, cannot. Imagining, in fact, if it gets out of hand is a great danger. An enormous number of the catastrophes of the mind can be traced to just this, to phantasy which is blocking the ways of perception and substituting an illusory satisfaction for an actual solution of the problem.

But if images are not as directly useful as we often suppose, imagining, none the less, has an indirect value as an exercise of our powers of perception. Through much imagining (if not too stereotyped) the mind may become more plastic, more able to form new perceptions, when the occasion demands it.

Memory in the Child. "Imaging plays a conspicuous part in child life before much personal reminiscence begins."[1] Indeed, the late development of memory in the full sense is one of the most astonishing features of child life. It begins in a rudimentary form early in the second year, but remains very indefinite for a long while. "Even for a four-year-old child a definite remembrance of yesterday is difficult, and one of the day before impossible. At this age there exists a vague impression of happenings long past, likewise a rough distinction between before and after, and occasionally one between to-day and not to-day."[2]

---

[1] James Ward, *Psychological Principles*, p. 179.

[2] K. Koffka, *The Growth of the Mind*, p. 244. This may be the reason why we find it is difficult to recall infantile experiences. An-

Play. This vagueness and indeterminateness of memory in the child is probably connected with the predominance of play in its life. We shall never understand play—the most extensive activity of the most important period of our lives—either in general or in its particularities, unless we realize that the child's world is almost entirely unlike ours. All his perceptions differ from ours, not only in definiteness, but in kind. The description and analysis of this difference is a very valuable achievement of modern psychology, not only because an unsympathetic failure to realize it on the part of parents and others is bad for the child, but also because the common alternative, sentimental nonsense about it, is even worse.

The child's world differs from the adult's because his interests are different. The majority of the adult's interests do not yet exist for him, and therefore, the ways of perceiving which are going later to serve those interests do not exist either. Pre-eminently that way of perceiving things which springs from the endeavor to see them as they are, does not yet exist. It is true that adults differ among themselves in this respect, but their differences, however important, are slight if we compare them with

other reason is repression (cf. Chapter XIII). A third may be the slight extent to which a child verbalizes his experience (cf. Watson, *Behaviorism* (1925), p. 209), and a fourth is probably to be found in the fact that, since the child's world is so unlike ours, memories of it would be of little use to us, and would involve regression (cf. Ch. XV). When we have mastered a subject it is peculiarly difficult to recall our first crude conceptions of it.

the child. The young child perceives things *only* in their relation to his own needs and desires, and his world is a reflection of his own inner activities.

To understand what this implies we must consider the peculiar, the unique helplessness of the infant. The young guinea-pig is independent of its mother in three days' time, the young white rat in thirty; the young human being is still very dependent after three thousand days. This long subordination is, as has often been remarked, the secret of man's superiority, but it is also the clue to much which is less satisfactory in him. As we shall see, it has consequences which he must eliminate when he finally grows up, as well as consequences which he must retain.

Infantile Perception. The helpless dependence of the infant upon those who tend him affects his perceptions from the beginning. His first differentiated reactions to sounds are aroused by the human voice. He takes an interest in faces as early as his twenty-fifth day; even in the second month of his life the face and voice of his mother may cause him to laugh. After three months the recognition has developed in differentiation, and thereafter the child behaves quite differently towards familiar persons and to strangers.[1] Facial expressions influence him by the time he is six months old. But what *we* should regard as simple forms are not distinguished until much later. The letter O, for example, not till the

[1] W. Stern, *The Psychology of Early Childhood*, p. 108.

end of a year. These, if we consider them, are very remarkable facts. They imply that the infant is building up a view of the world very unlike that which at first sight we should suppose it to be forming. Unless we are careful we tend to think that the infant's world begins for him as a multitudinous chaos of lights and contacts and noises, "a big buzzing blooming confusion," as James put it, out of which he collects elements together and gradually combines them into groups which become for him separate things. His mother's face on this view would be a combination of countless sensations, and its various expressions indescribably complex distributions of light and shade. But in fact nothing of the kind is going on. The infant does not proceed from the simple to the complex; he begins with what biologically matters for him, and this in nearly all cases is complex.

The recognition of expressions is instructive. Few adults have exact ideas as to what precise contortions of a human visage express pleasure, friendliness, hostility, or pain. Unless they are artists or have especially studied the matter, they could usually give no accurate account of them, yet they constantly respond to them without error, and the chimpanzees do likewise. If the experimenter suddenly shows signs of extreme terror and stares at a particular spot as though possessed, all the chimpanzees will start as if struck by lightning and stare at the same spot, even though there is nothing of any significance there. The chimpanzees respond to what matters to them and so does the child. Nothing matters so much to him as expressions, and though we know expressions to be highly complex things, to him they are quite simple.[1]

Thus the infant's early outfit consists of perceptions, not perceptions of colors, spots, sounds, and touches as such, but of expressions, of patterns which favor or thwart his activities; and on this basis of perceptions he continues to build up his world, for it is a fundamental law of the mind that so long as it can it will use perceptions already acquired rather than form new ones. The child who calls a badger the first time it sees one a 'bow-wow' and the philosopher who tries to bring new facts under his old headings are obvious instances. Conversely, the child's comparatively undeveloped power of recognition and discrimination are due to its lack of experience of the ways in which signs change from situation to situation.

Primitive Mentality. The world of the child continues for a long while to be modeled for him on these patterns; to be therefore informed with intention towards him. Not that he explicitly supposes it to be alive or to be thinking and willing about him. To do this would imply that he made a distinction between the conscious and the unconscious, which in

[1] The reader who is familiar with the accounts given either by the Association Psychologists or by the Behaviorists may perhaps find this view paradoxical. But it is not in conflict with the theory that recognition of expression is conditioned.

fact he cannot yet make. He simply has only one way of regarding it. In this respect his world resembles that of primitive man, and the comparison between the child's mind and that of certain people of rude culture is illuminating.

All over the world, in Australia, in Africa, in Melanesia, and in the Arctic Circle, are to be found peoples for whom the idea of a mere accident in serious affairs even in the most obvious cases does not arise. When a man falls from a tree through trusting to a rotten branch, or when he is snapped up by a crocodile, or dies of a snake bite, or has his head cut open in battle, the view taken is that some enemy, not his own carelessness, or the branch, or the crocodile, the snake, or even necessarily the opposing swordsman, is ultimately responsible. Even his death through old age is put down to sorcery, and this view is arrived at not, as we might suppose, through elaborate and muddled ratiocination based upon a few misleading instances, but simply because the idea of an important happening undirected by some intention is too difficult for them to form. Their only way of perceiving serious events is to regard them as caused by some intention. Thus, a sorcerer by his magic must have made the man fall, or entered into the crocodile or the snake, or deprived the warrior of his accustomed skill in guarding his head. The primitive thinker, in fact, will only ask questions which begin with 'why.'[1] Mere matter

[1] Cf. J. Piaget, *Language and Thought of the Child*, 1926, for a masterly analysis of the questions asked by a child of seven.

of 'how' seem to him trivial. He will point out that the crocodile snapped up one man rather than another, or snapped him up to-day, but not yesterday, and he is not content with any explanation which does not reduce this to somebody's intention; so he continues to bathe just as before in crocodile-infested waters, confident that the saurians will not harm him unless charged thereto by the malice of some sorcerer. What he regards as the practical step is to seek out and slaughter the sorcerer; for a mere slaughter of crocodiles would only lead to his choosing some other means whereby to wreak his malice. This behavior will seem to us unbelievably obtuse unless we realize the mental peculiarity in which it is rooted. It is a consequence of the primitive's way of perceiving events; his set of perceptions takes no account of events which are not directed at somebody by somebody else. But to understand how this way of perceiving accidents comes to be so preposterously fixed, we have to notice another characteristic of primitive mentality, namely the prodigious influence of society upon it. In any group in which no difference of opinion exists it is almost impossible for an individual to dissent from the common doctrine. We shall shortly have to consider again this influence of society, of the common doctrine and the common practice, on the individual mind. Even in the most highly civilized communities it is still overwhelmingly powerful. But our present task is to describe the world of the child.

The Play World and the Real World. His world, we have said, is the reflection of his interests, and since these interests are simpler than the adult's, his is a different world. But besides being simpler they are more separate. For the adult and in the degree to which he differs from a child, nearly all his activities are linked together and mutually influence one another. What he does in the morning is influenced by what he is going to do in the afternoon and so on. In other words, his various interests are integrated, though never perfectly. In the child this integration has hardly begun. And this probably explains the tardy development of systematic memory in him. His life is a multitude of pieces rather than a fabric, and his world corresponds. Thus a shift of interest has an effect upon his world which to the adult is difficult to comprehend. The block which ten minutes ago was an automobile suddenly becomes something to throw about, and the next moment may turn into a tree. How are we to picture these changes in the child's way of perceiving it?

In the first place we must be clear that there is no question of any actual illusion. If the block could be actually turned by magic into a tree or an automobile, the child would be as surprised as we should. On the other hand, his perceptions of it are certainly more plastic than ours, because they are less definite, and so at the same time are his perceptions of a tree and of an automobile. We regard the block consistently as a wooden cube, but to the child it is only something which favors now one and now another of his interests. We can, if we like, get him to see it as we see it, but only by giving him an interest in so doing. We can use his desire to please us or be flattered by us, for example. Similarly with trees and automobiles. They are not to him the intricate objects which they are to us, but only things which excite him in different ways, and these excitements are still easily detachable from their objects. For in us a block and an automobile are each inextricably fixed in extensive and conflicting systems of interests. But the child's interests do not yet ramify and are still fluid. We get nearest to his condition sometimes in our dreams when we treat one thing as though it was another without any difficulty or doubt, but at the same time without any illusion.

This plasticity of the child's world is gradually broken into by the demands which adults make upon him. A certain number of his activities are allowed free course, others are controlled, so a separation grows up between the world of adults and his own world. The adult's world hangs together and has a consistency from which his own world is free. But it is, therefore, a world full of opposition, constantly denying possibilities which his own world can realize. Thus a struggle may arise between the two worlds, the world of reality, as we may call it, and the world of desire or make-believe; and the outcome of this struggle is often decisive for the individual's character and personality.

The Conflict with Reality. The two worlds interact curiously. Little by little the distinctions and interconnections forced on the child by the actual world get taken over into his play world. And as the division between them grows clearer to him, the attractions of the play world increase. In the play world he is master; in the other world of the adult he is constantly being coerced. But as more and more of the consistent patterns of the actual world get taken over into play, freedom here becomes more difficult. The crisis comes when the play world through this limitation—through the degree in which it has taken over patterns from the actual world—begins to offer difficulties to the child. Two paths are open to him. He may break up these patterns again and so lapse back into a freer, more 'unreal' kind of activity, or he may be driven by these difficulties in the direction of an increased mastery of the actual world.

To speak of this as a crisis is perhaps misleading; it is not a single event; it is a struggle which always lasts many years and may last a whole lifetime, and it arises not over one difficulty, but at innumerable points. It may be decided in one way for some clashes, and in the opposite way for others. To take a typical example: though schoolmasters for good and obvious reasons encourage the confusion, play and games are really entirely different activities.[1]

[1] It is astonishing to find many admirable psychologists confusing them. The distinction between pure play and games arises at every stage of human development. Thus private conversation among intimates is often play; but public debate, at a philosophical congress, for example, is characteristically a game. The non-competitive

Most people can remember something of the process of transition, and perhaps, too, something of the resentment the child feels when the grown-up first attempts this particular interference with his play. An afternoon spent with a bat and a ball, and perhaps one or two friends (though these are not strictly necessary) who really participate in the activity, every stroke being a performance only to be equalled by a Babe Ruth, a Lenglen, or a Jack Hobbs, is one thing. A tense and humiliating endeavor to rival the *actual* performances of older and more skilled companions, or to escape their derision, is quite another. It is not play at all, but actual life in one of its most searching forms. Games, in fact, are one of the chief instruments by which the play world is broken down.

The result of this and innumerable similar conflicts is a certain balance between the amount and kind of energy which the individual devotes to actual affairs (including games) and the amount and kind devoted to genuine play which little by little becomes fantasy or daydreaming. Most people have one or two lines, often unknown to anyone, along which they continue all their lives to play—that is, to dream, not to act; offshoots as it were of the original dream-world which have never been drawn into the larger unity of coherent waking purposes. These are a common cause of mental troubles; for, as we shall see, they lead to the setting up of unreal

sports, camping, climbing, fishing, hunting (when genuinely non-competitive), are play. Competitive sports are games.

standards, of ideals which can never be attained in the actual world. The dreamer remains in a state of constant dissatisfaction with any substitute offered for his dream-image, or unconsciously takes refuge in illness to evade the test of public achievement.

CHAPTER IX: MAN'S LINGUISTIC HERITAGE

Speech. The chief social influences exerted on the child come about through *speech.* The importance of speech in human psychology is even yet generally underestimated. It is not too much to say that our minds differ from those of the animals because of speech. Its discovery was probably the origin of man. He came about as a distinct genus through it. As the comparative anatomist points out, "The localized expansion of the acoustic territory which is revealed in the most primitive members of the human family, must imply that the biological significance of hearing was suddenly enhanced at the time of the emergence of the human family. In fact, it seems a legitimate inference from the facts to assume that the acquisition of the power of communicating ideas and the fruits of experience from one individual to another by means of articulate speech may have been one of the factors, if not the fundamental factor, in converting an ape into a human being."[1] Thus it behooves us to consider this acquisition in some detail.

Expressions and Names. Even in the chimpanzee, as we have seen, and in many far lower animals, a rudimentary form of speech is found. The dog

[1] G. Elliot Smith, "The Evolution of Intelligence," in *Problems of Personality, Studies in Honor of Dr. Morton Prince,* pp. 6-7.

barks and whines, the frog croaks, and the cat's virtuosity is well known, but it is better to give these prehuman manifestations of vocal powers another name. We must regard them as *expressions* of the animal's activities; in most cases they will be expressions of fairly well marked emotions, and this merely expressive use of sounds must be clearly distinguished from their use in *naming*, though of course many sounds have both functions.

The difference, though simple, is very fundamental. A merely expressive cry arises directly from the animal's need, his want, his desire, his joy or fear, his interest in general and *it varies with this activity*. But a naming cry arises from the perception of a given state of affairs and *varies with this state of affairs*. Briefly we express ourselves alike because *we* are alike; we name things alike because *they* are alike. Plainly naming cannot arise until the animal can respond to situations not merely as eliciting this or that activity, but as possessing this or that character. But we must look rather closely in order to understand what exactly this distinction amounts to.

All the animal's activity and also all that of man, as we have insisted in Chapters III and IV, arises in the course of meeting needs. Every perception, even, arises only as a link or bridge in a larger activity directed to the satisfaction of some need. This principle seems to destroy the distinction we have just attempted to make between expressive vocal activity and naming; for naming is also an expression of a need. This is true; all use of speech involves expression; but some vocal activity involves more than this, involves what is known technically as *objective reference*, and it is this further use of speech which is man's peculiar achievement. Our problem is to see just how this achievement comes about.

The clue is to remember that the higher use of speech has developed out of the lower. Even in the earliest animal cries there is a rudiment of this 'objective reference.' The cry is a part of the animal's emotional reaction and the reaction is very definitely set off only by a certain kind of situation. The nightingale's song and the frog's croak are parts of their mating performances. "Speech in its origin," as Malinowski puts it,[1] "is a *mode of action*, not a *countersign of thought*," and this is still true even in much later performances. "Children, savages, and civilized adults alike react with vocal expressions to certain situations, whether these arouse bodily pain or mental anguish, fear or passion, intense curiosity or powerful joy." We can see this particularly clearly in the case of children. "To the child, words are not only a means of expression, but an efficient mode of action. The name of a person uttered aloud in a piteous voice possesses the power of materializing this person. Food has to be called for and it appears in the majority of cases."[1] We

[1] Bronislaw Malinowski, "The Problem of Meaning in Primitive Languages," in op. cit., *The Meaning of Meaning*, p. 451.

may compare Sultan's trick alluded to in Chapter VII, of inciting the rest of the apes to mutiny. In neither case need we suppose any explicit thought. Both are more simple responses than, for example, using a stick to drag in fruit.

Early Stages of Communication. None the less a considerable degree of communion is possible even at this stage, as the ape's social behavior shows. Since the sounds uttered vary with the situation, one ape is able to cause the others to respond appropriately even when they are not themselves yet in the situation. In social animals the cry serves instead. It prompts to action; it acts in this purely *emotive* way long before any explicit reflection upon, or recognition of, the situation can have arisen. We must always remember, in considering language at any stage, that its use in reflection, as an instrument of thought, is a kind of diversion of it from its original uses.

It will help us to imagine some of the steps in this distinctively human 'misuse of language' [1] if we realize how confused (from our adult point of view) both the animal and the infant are. We make a distinction between our emotions, which are *in us*, and the things outside of us, which cause them, and between our thought of a thing and the thing itself. We distinguish between uttering a cry and hearing

[1] There is an influential school of Philosophy, that of Bergson, which would have us recur, as far as may be, to the more primitive use, to gain thereby a more intimate sense of reality. Cf. Karin Stephen, *The Misuse of Mind*, 1922, p. 42.

it as we utter it; between the noise a thing makes and the thing which makes it. But the animal and the infant draw none of these distinctions. To them the world is 'nice,' 'nasty,' 'horrible,' 'strange,' 'enraging,' or 'familiar,' not 'blue,' 'cold,' 'swift,' 'soft,' 'loud,' 'large,' or 'heavy.' In fact the mind's first classifications are emotional rather than objective, and the first classification of all is doubtless into 'satisfactory' and 'unsatisfactory'—in respect of particular needs. So when a social animal utters a danger cry the others take to flight merely because the situation has suddenly become 'fearful.' If we suppose any more complex mental goings-on in them we shall be misinterpreting their behavior. Similarly, when the infant hears its mother speaking kindly, the situation merely becomes 'comfortable,' and its bubbling reply is merely part of this comfortableness; just as the flight is part of the fearfulness. The contrast drawn by the adult between the situation and the response in such cases only arises much later, and for the animal perhaps never.

The danger and other social cries of animals can be regarded as primitive names, if we are careful to remember how unlike our own mental processes the animal's are. And what they name is not any specific feature of the situation but the whole thing. At the same time the animal does not regard the cry as a name, as a separate part even, of the situation. It is inextricably part of the whole state of affairs even when he utters it himself. This may help us to understand how it is that children, savages, and even men eminent in the world of scholarship, so strangely and so persistently proceed as though the name were part of the thing—a tendency which is still exerting an evil influence upon thought.[1]

The passage from this most primitive of all uses of names to the civilized adult's must have been a long and slow business in which increased discrimination between situations (the development of new perceptions as we traced it in the chimpanzee) and the use of expressive sounds as a means of socially manipulating these discriminations have gone together. The earlier stages are merely conjectural as yet. Probably some form of co-operative work played a large part. Apes only co-operate as it were by accident. Three apes each wishing to move a heavy box will move it together, when none of them could stir it alone. But their activities are not *concerted* in the stricter sense. None the less, from this to concerted action is not a large step, and such action, whether in building or in hunting, might easily lead to a further step in the use of sounds. Grunts actually the effect of efforts might become indicative of them, thus fixing and inciting socially this particular form of behavior, and so on. Upon the later stages of this co-operative use of language by primitive peoples Malinowski's account of a Trobriand fishing expedition is instructive.

The Child's Conquest of Speech. We gain firmer ground as we pass from speculations to the actual

[1] Cf. the author's *The Meaning of Meaning*, Chapter II, for much evidence of this tendency and this influence.

observable behavior of the savage and the child. The infant's first articulated words, his *mámá*, for example, should be regarded not as names, but more as single word sentences analogous to the adult's commands or appeals. They are specialized cries for help, and are entirely of an expressive character springing directly out of the infant's original needs. Thus they are not very far removed from the exiled chimpanzee's appeals to his companions. But, as a rule, about the middle of the second year of life, a change takes place. A sudden increase in vocabulary combines with a thirst for names. The child makes what the Sterns describe as "the most important discovery of his life," namely the discovery that things have names. Naturally he jumps to the conclusion that everything has a name, a conclusion which sometimes causes perplexity to his parents; and from this he goes on to treat his former appeal-words as names, to regard the name as part of the thing, to invent names for things on the ground of a resemblance between the thing as it appears to him and the name, to transfer names to other things which for him are similar, and to combine names already acquired into new names for new and more complex objects. Even general words such as 'this' or 'one' or 'make' get used freely at a very early age.

Imitation. In all this eager and triumphant activity in which the child achieves what often seems to be the greatest intellectual performance of his whole lifetime, we can see clearly the dominant need which is at work. It is his need to escape from his former state of helplessness and to extend his dominion over the world. His main method in this progressive conquest is imitation, and we may, perhaps, best consider here this important feature of behavior.

There is no necessity to invoke a special instinct for imitation. The connection between hearing a word, not as a mere noise, but as an articulate sound, and pronouncing it is very close. The nervous centers concerned are in intimate connection. Whenever the child utters a word, he immediately hears it, and, as we have suggested, it is doubtful whether the young infant makes any distinction between them. The closeness of this connection is shown also by the extraordinary precocity of some children in singing. Erwin Nyiregyházi, for example, began to imitate singing before he was one year old, and could correctly reproduce melodies before he could speak.[1] The same is reported of Handel. That the perception should be the key to the movements required to reproduce it and that the reproduction should often take place as a kind of completion of the whole process is not more mysterious than anything else that we do. At a later stage deliberate imitation arises, due to a conscious desire to repeat what has been done by others. This plays an essential part in the learning of speech and in most of the child's other acquisitions.

The Dominion of Society. It will be evident that the acquisition of language is not only an extension

[1] G. Révész, *The Psychology of a Musical Prodigy*, p. 7.

of the child's dominion over the world, but also an extension of society's dominion over him. He is forced thereby into closer conformity with already established ways of regarding the world, not only because the wishes of adults can now take a more intimate hold upon him, but because automatically his mind takes over the traditional naming patterns.

Man's dependence upon tradition and upon his membership of a society has led some psychologists to conceive of society as a power or force outside of man. If we pay sufficient attention to the ways in which parents and elders influence the child, through language and otherwise, and to the ways in which men influence one another, there is no occasion for such vague speculations. Group or social psychology is the psychology of men in groups or societies. Change a man's group and you change him, but a great deal of confusion reigns among psychologists upon this point. It is a common practice to write of the 'group mind' as though this were something analogous to the individual mind. But we should be clear that it is merely a handy term for a system of individual minds in more or less close interaction. To conceive of it as a 'super-soul,' floating outside all the individual minds of the members of the group, is a concession to mental laziness. At present the large and important French school of sociologists led by Durkheim is especially prone to this temptation.

The Virtues and Drawbacks of Language. We may regard our linguistic heritage both as an immense advantage and, on a smaller scale, as a calamity. When we consider how impotent any single mind would be to make for itself a picture of reality one thousandth part as adequate as that to which language leads us, we see the advantages. The discoverer of the auxiliary verb, of the preposition, and of the definite article should have their portraits, could they be painted, in every school. Needless to say, no such heroes ever existed; these mighty instruments arose much as our hands gradually became free for general purposes. Yet there is another side to this endowment. At many points language badly misrepresents the world as we know it. All current languages embody in their grammar and vocabulary an outlook upon the world which is passing away. The fact that we are forced to use nouns for what are essentially happenings rather than things (as when we say 'an emotion,' 'a perception,' 'a thought,' instead of an emotional, a perceptual or a ratiocinative event), is an example. The struggle which psychology is having now to rid itself of a false 'atomism' and to arrive at 'dynamic' conceptions is primarily a struggle against a bad legacy in language. Innumerable other examples could be given.

But language has still other drawbacks than this of smuggling inappropriate ideas into our minds while we are too young to protect ourselves. It is the vehicle of tradition in more than intellectual matters. Far too many of our moral attitudes come to us unscrutinized and without proper criticism through language alone. Consider those two prodigious engines of moral discipline, the simple words 'good' and 'bad.' Originally to the child they are equivalent to 'permitted' and 'not-permitted.' Little by little the problem, "By whom permitted?" may be faced; but in the end any such coherent interpretation of the words usually lapses, the higher reaches of the investigation being so obscure, and the mind is left simply with attitudes of acceptance and rejection which the words touch off. The individual has regressed, in other words, into an infantile or animal state; 'bad' has become once more merely a danger cry and 'good' a lure call. Hence when anything is generally alleged to be good or to be bad, the great majority of people in the great majority of their moments react without any view as to what it is that is being said. This nebulosity is a great obstacle in the many cases in which a revaluation of traditional attitudes is made necessary by changed circumstances and increased knowledge.

Many political watchwords, of which illustrations are not needed, are good examples of language which has lapsed unobserved into this infantile condition. It would not, perhaps, be an exaggeration to say that half of what passes for current thought on general affairs is not thought at all, but language operated at a merely emotional level.

There need be nothing surprising in this. Apart from his technical pursuits, his hunting, his building, etc., we have seen that primitive man's outlook is not governed by the facts of nature, but by what we regard as superstitious whimsies; and this level of mental activity has only been transcended at comparatively rare moments in human history, for example in Assyria under Assurbanipal. We have been living on the legacy of these early achievements ever since, as the Renaissance shows; and if we have carried the task rather further by the advance of science during the last three hundred years, this should not blind us to the precariousness of our hold upon high civilization. Great though the difference may be as regards 'seeing things as they are' between the educated adult and the child or the savage, from another point of view it is still too slight. We are still human, all-too-human as Nietzsche so insistently pointed out.

CHAPTER X: BEHAVIOR

The Historical Background of Behaviorism. During the last thirty years academic psychology has received a number of salutary shocks. The greatest of these has come from psycho-analysis. Here was a body of mixed observations and doctrine set forth by doctors who paid practically no attention at all to accepted views, who virtually ignored the fact that a science calling itself psychology was already in existence. The orthodox psychologists for some time retaliated by ignoring psycho-analysis. But however little of the *doctrines* of psycho-analysis become ultimately accepted, there can be no doubt that the shock has been salutary. A striking example is a confession of the late Dr. Rivers, an exceptionally active and well-informed psychologist. Just before the War he helped to draw up a syllabus for a course in psychological medicine. When he came to revise it just after the War he discovered to his astonishment that it included no mention of Instinct.[1] This change of view among orthodox psychologists was due more to the labors of Freud than to anything else.

But to-day the conception of instinct is itself being challenged by none more vigorously than by Watson and the Behaviorists whose work and views have given a fresh shock—more particularly to American

[1] W. H. R. Rivers, *Psychology and Politics*, p. 4.

psychology. Other countries have hitherto paid remarkably little attention, which at first sight is odd since American work in this field is for the most part closely followed.

One possible explanation of this neglect is that in Europe sides have already often been taken on what is regarded as in part a religious issue.[1]

The Nature of Observation. The doctrine of Behaviorism can be summed up briefly in two statements: (1) That psychology deals only with what can be observed. (2) That 'consciousness' is a meaningless term. It is worth while to consider each of these statements closely.

When the behaviorist speaks of *observation* he means something which can be done by a photographic film or a spring balance just as well as by a human being. What is observed is one event, the observation of it is another; and what happens is merely that the observed event under suitable conditions is accompanied by the observing event—which varies with it. Thus an observation is simply one form of what is called a 'causal sequence'[2] and any event succeeding and varying with another might, on a behaviorist account, be said to observe it. But the particular observations with which the behaviorist

[1] Cf. the controversies arising out of the doctrines of Hobbes, La Mettrie, Condillac, Bentham, Comte, and G. H. Lewes, for example, as dealt with in Lange's monumental work, *The History of Materialism*.

[2] For a clear discussion of modern views of causation Bertrand Russell's *The A B C of Relativity*, (1925) pp. 103-205 may be very profitably consulted.

is concerned are events in people, in human observers, which follow other events in other people or in themselves. Now it would appear at first sight that events in people and in ourselves could be divided into two kinds: those which are conscious, or are accompanied by consciousness—as when we hear a noise, have a tooth out, are frightened, lift a heavy weight or deliberately choose between actions; and those which are not conscious, not accompanied by consciousness—as when by a series of muscular contractions we pass food through the stomach, when we balance ourselves, dilate the pupil, or perform a habitual involuntary gesture. This difference which has nearly always been considered very striking, unmistakable, and fundamental, is denied by strict behaviorists. And this denial is the novel point in their doctrine.

The grounds for it are simple, as simple as the denial itself. If we observe some one else, Watson points out, the only difference that we can detect between what he would claim as a conscious event in him and an unconscious event is that the activities in his muscles and glands and the happenings in his nervous system which accompany them are different in the two cases. *We* never observe any of this consciousness he speaks of; all we observe is changes in his behavior, including the vocal movements by which he speaks of it to us, and if he observes us *he* will never observe any consciousness in us. This is very true and the contrary view has never been held. But Watson concludes that consciousness is "a plain assumption just as unprovable, just as unapproachable, as the old concept of the soul" (*Behaviorism*, p. 5).

Self-observation. Compare now the case in which we observe ourselves. Let us stand before a mirror and, not to choose too violent an experiment, let us gently tweak a tuft of hair. No more than before do we observe any consciousness in the movements which we see, either in the tweaks or in the facial contractions which may follow if they grow more vigorous. None the less, another series of changes is certainly taking place. Each tension of the skin is accompanied by these changes, as is each movement of the arm, and about these changes we are even more sure than about our actual movements. The problem, however, is whether these changes are known through *observation*, in the sense defined above.

If they are, we must admit that we do not yet know which events, by varying with which others, are 'observing' them. It is possible that conscious events only become conscious through causing other events which thus observe them—just as Watson's reactions observe an infant's reactions to a mouse—but by an inner observation. We do not yet know enough about the working of the brain to be certain that this does not happen. Yet it seems improbable that consciousness is a matter of observation in this sense. Conscious events certainly observe other events and are observed by them, *i.e.*, they have causes and effects, but it must be doubted whether this being observed has anything to do with their consciousness.

The first half of Behaviorism then, the contention that psychology deals only with what can be observed, excludes consciousness from its field of study, for we clearly cannot yet systematically observe it in this sense. And the behaviorists are left with a perfectly definite field for research, namely the observable responses which different situations excite and the history and interconnections of these situations and responses. Much valuable work is being done by them in this field. We shall consider some of their results later.

The Status of Consciousness. But the other half of Behaviorism is less successful. Fortunately it is much less important. That consciousness is a meaningless term, that it "is neither a definable nor a usable concept; that it is merely another word for the 'soul' of more ancient times" (*Behaviorism*, p. 3), and that it is a pure assumption—all this does not follow from its non-observable nature. We do not observe consciousness; we have it or are it, and in fact most of our observations of other things require it. In this respect the point of view of the behaviorist is not a point of view, but a mistake.

Yet this denial is plainly not due merely to a blunder;[1] it springs from much more interesting

[1] Logical muddles certainly do seem to haunt behavioristic literature. On this point Roback may be quoted: "So inured are we

sources. There is, in fact, something very unsatisfactory about introspection as a scientific method. It often produces conflicting evidence which is difficult to criticize, and it requires a technique which is not strictly analogous to the other techniques of science. In physics or in physiology any able man can be trained to be a moderately good investigator and any failings he may have (inaccuracy or clumsiness, for example) are easily detected. But in introspection the causes of discrepancies and the kind of training required to produce improvement are still very uncertain.[1] Thus men impatient of the slow task of clarifying problems, who like to see their work clear ahead of them in the form of definite questions to be answered by a definite technique, readily tend to despise introspection. This impatience rather than bad arguments is responsible for the negative side of Behaviorism. There is also the feeling that any adding in of 'conscious' factors which cannot be measured and do not obey the same laws as the rest of nature must play havoc with all

---

becoming to the sight of flagrant logical blunders that ludicrous statements are given a resemblance of significance and are treated in all seriousness. Thus if it be true that Watson '*from introspection* . . . insists that consciousness has no existence in man or in animals,' as we are told by Pillsbury, we should put him into the class of the brilliant individual who dreamt he was wide awake, which gave him such a shock that he woke up very briskly only to find himself sound asleep" (A. A. Roback, *Behaviorism and Psychology*, p. 8). The italics are ours.

[1] Cf. MacCurdy, *The Psychology of Emotion*, p. 59: "We all of us introspect to the advantage of our pet theories . . . the most valid material is to be derived from the experience of those who are not trained introspectionists."

hopes of satisfactory explanations; and this feeling is justified. An essentially physiological explanation ought not to be eked out by scraps of experience. It should remain physiology. But this is not—and here the Behaviorists made their mistake—the same thing as saying that there can be no study of consciousness or that the study may not provide valuable indications in working out a physiological theory of behavior. In point of fact, it constantly so serves.

What is valid in the doctrine is the insistence upon external observation of behavior, as an indispensable method in psychology. But this is hardly an innovation. The more novel point is the demand that this behavior should be conceived in terms of itself and that we should exclude from our interpretations of it any but a limited number of physiological ideas. This self-imposed limitation need not be, but is, commonly confused by the behaviorist with the quite different point of the occurrence of consciousness. It is one thing to say: "Let us try to describe and explain all human behavior entirely in terms of interaction between stimulus-situation and response," and quite another to say, "Let us try to persuade people that they have no consciousness." The first is of real value, and likely, if it can be carried rather further, to change our views on many points, and possibly to bring out the rôle of consciousness in a new light. The second is merely waste of time.

The Methods of Behaviorism. The methods and conceptions so far developed by Behaviorism are extremely simple. They derive very largely from

Pavlov's conditioned reflex methods which we have described in Chapter III. But in man stimuli often become conditioned after only one occurrence. And the situations in which human behavior takes place consist of uncountable numbers of different stimuli. Moreover, man's adjustment involves multitudes of responses, and the problem of strictly tracing out the process by which response depends upon situation is overwhelmingly complex. Even in Pavlov's laboratory, when the dog, a simpler animal, is shielded during the experiment in every possible way—sitting on a table in a dark sound-proof room entirely separated from the experimenter who sees him only through a periscope and gives him the stimuli and measures his responses by indirect electrical means—it is still often difficult to get trustworthy results; a fly, for example, which was fluttering in a corner of the dark chamber quite away from the dog was found on one occasion to be upsetting the whole experiment. When the experimenter is not separated from the dog, accidents in his manner quite beyond his control play a hopelessly disturbing part in producing the responses obtained.

It is not very surprising, then, that the experiments of behaviorists with human beings in a more or less ordinary mixed environment should seem in comparison crude and their results doubtful. The conditions are a little better with infants, and it is here that the best work has been done. It was work which very badly needed doing, since the behavior of the very young has been for fairly obvious reasons much neglected.

The Origins of Fear. One of Watson's most interesting observations was that the peculiar and recognizable response which is ordinarily known as fear, "a jump, a start, a respiratory pause followed by more rapid breathing with marked vasomotor changes" (changes in the blood flow, *e.g.* growing pale), sudden closure of the eye, clutching of hands, puckering of lips, is only elicited in 'new-borns' by two kinds of stimuli, loud noises, and being suddenly left without support. But as is well known, a normal three-year-old shows fear for a great number of other things. Here is a representative list from Watson: darkness, and all rabbits, rats, dogs, fish, frogs, insects, and mechanical animal toys. Watson's thesis is that all these fears arise because at some time the appearance of a dog, for example, has coincided with either a loud noise or being knocked over (loss of support). The dog later, when it merely approaches causes the fear, just as the note caused Pavlov's dog's mouth to water. This fear then gets transferred to other situations which the infant groups with it,[1] and so on. Evidently this view has no use for 'instincts' except in the sense of initial characteristic responses to characteristic situations. But these, as Watson points out, are shown

[1] Thus Albert B., eleven months old, who had an (experimentally) conditioned fear of a white rat, showed fear five days later of a rabbit, a dog, a fur coat, cotton wool, but not of bricks (*Behaviorism*, p. 128).

by a boomerang, which when properly thrown behaves quite unlike an ordinary stick. The child would be a very complicated kind of boomerang, and its instincts merely the result of its structure at birth.

Now this, it will be realized, is, if it is correct, an extremely important contribution. Watson finds in children who have not been emotionally conditioned no such fears of dogs or darkness, and if this is established, a prospect of a comparatively fearless humanity is opened up if only we can manage our nurseries aright. There is, however, the possibility that maturation may introduce complications. Even though loud noises and loss of support be the only stimuli which cause fear immediately after birth, it may be the case that later on other stimuli come to have the same effect merely through the infant's growth. Maturation certainly plays some part, and some very definite responses only appear at a very late age. The specific sexual responses appearing with adolescence are an obvious instance.

The Unconditioned Emotions. The exact truth in this matter will only be discovered by further experimental research and Watson is undoubtedly to be congratulated for the part he has played in furthering such experimentation. He has come to consider that the unlearned (unconditioned) beginnings of emotional reactions are three in number. Fear, elicited as above, Rage, elicited by hampering of bodily movements, and Love, elicited by stroking of the skin, tickling, gentle rocking, and patting. Love responses include "those popularly called 'affectionate,' 'good-natured,' 'kindly,' . . . as well as the responses we see in adults between the sexes. They all have a common origin" (*Behaviorism*, p. 123).

Watson further points out that since the same object (say a parent) may in one situation become a conditionad stimulus for fear, in another for rage and in another for love, these three original groups of responses can easily become complicated through experience. Only, he does not use the word 'experience.' To do so would be to link his labors up with those of more traditional psychologists. His extremely provoking attitude towards academic psychologists and towards psycho-analysts alike, amusing and inspiriting though it is when we realize that his work is likely to be of great assistance to them and is not in conflict with theirs, is to be regretted if it debars them, as it may, from taking due notice and advantage of it. They have already shown too often the natural tendency to reply in kind. It may be suggested that these very different views and methods are not irreconcilable. Nothing so readily gives a beginner in psychology a sense of helplessness and annoyance as the existence of violently opposed views which he more often than not suspects to be mere verbal variants. And indeed Watson's 'boomerang' analogy shows that he is not far removed from the position of Koffka as regards instinct (*The Growth of the Mind*, p. 106), while his account of the conditioning of the love-emotion brings him very near to the important group of psycho-analysts represented by Kempf and Frinck. The fundamental divisions among psychologists are often less serious than they appear.

CHAPTER XI: LOOKING INWARDS

Bouvard and Pécuchêt in the great novel by Flaubert resolved to take up psychology. The goal of psychology, they read, is to study the facts which take place "in the bosom of the self"; these are discovered by introspection. "And for a fortnight, after breakfast regularly, they hunted about at random in their minds, hoping to make notable discoveries, and made none and were much surprised."

The Elusiveness of Consciousness. They had reason to be surprised, for it is indeed odd that introspection tells us so little. If the old metaphysical view, that the known and the knower must be alike, were sound, our own minds should be the most certain objects of our knowledge. Yet they are to-day perhaps the least certain. The most mysterious thing in the universe to man is at present himself, his own mind and its nature. It has not always been so. In the ages of faith, the Dark Ages, as the historians have called them, the outside world seemed much more mysterious than man. Thus he tried to explain it in terms of himself. He either made it a stage on which the drama of his own life was enacted, a thing with no further interest of its own, or he pictured it as being animated and guided somewhat after the fashion of himself. The balance has changed since then. Nowadays his tendency is to conceive himself as far as possible in terms of his knowledge of the outer world.

It is curious to reflect that the things which man best understands are on the whole the things which least concern him. He can predict the movements of the planets, but not the weather, he has fathomed the deep sea, but cannot measure his own desires, he knows more about beer than about his blood . . . and at the heart of all his knowledge is a mystery, namely how he gets it. This last problem we shall discuss later. Here we have a simpler task, to describe *from within* what conscious life is like, basing our account upon the facts which are always accessible to everyone.

The reason why Bouvard and Pécuchêt made no discoveries was that they asked no definite questions. It is only by *interrogating* consciousness that we get any light upon it. It will be well to begin by drawing up a list of the principal questions we propose to raise in the order in which we shall raise them:

(1) What is the Self?
(2) Where is experience located?
(3) What kind of a thing is an experience?
(4) What are the essential aspects of experience?

The answers to these questions must inevitably be tentative. The value of studying them lies not in the answers which we obtain, but in the insight into our nature which results from the inquiry.

The Distorting Influence of Language. Throughout this undertaking we must beware of three allied dangers. In the first place, language was not developed with a view to this account. Not only is there a bad shortage of words for the task, but such words as we are compelled to use are ill fitted to it, and distort the account unless we watch them closely and do not take them too much at their face value. Language was developed to describe (at the common-sense level) what we see or hear, not to describe seeing or hearing. It is a distorting influence here not only as a vocabulary, but as a syntax. For example, it is natural to say 'I have a thought.' But that suggests a fact analogous to 'I have a penny,' whereas what it really stands for would be better put by saying "A thinking is happening in me"; but even here 'in' and 'me' are misleading. And when we talk of 'ideas,' 'sensations,' or 'pleasures' the case, as we shall see, is worse still. Language, in fact, is not only a means by which we hide our thoughts from other people; it is a veil which helps to hide our own lives from ourselves.

Hypotheses and Abstractions. The second danger is no less insidious. It comes from the great difficulty of distinguishing here between our hypotheses and the facts these hypotheses were introduced to explain. The Self, strange as it may appear, is such an hypothesis, so are, more evidently, the Will, the Memory, the Intelligence, the Instincts, and the Unconscious. And in fact most of the terms of psychology stand for hypotheses, not for facts. The facts are there all the while, they make up our lives, but it is impossible to weave them together into any intelligible system without some hypotheses. The trouble is that we easily mistake the hypotheses for the facts. When we reflect upon our experience they tend to come between us and the facts. Thus many accounts of introspection given by psychologists seem to a naïve reader to have nothing to do with anything he knows about; which is an absurd result. This is one of Bergson's most effective contentions; but, alas! it must be added that Bergson's own hypotheses are just as misleading on many points as the traditional ones.

The third danger is one on which Bergson has also insisted. When we analyze an experience theoretically we often find it convenient to suppose it built up out of certain elements in certain combinations. For example, much psychology has proceeded successfully on the assumption that *sensations* are the basic elements out of which all experience is compounded. An amazing amount of detailed information about our perception of nature has been achieved by the aid of this assumption. So that it comes as a shock to be forced to ask: "Do we ever have sensations?" None the less this question must not only be asked but be decided in the negative. We do not have sensations; they don't occur. They are products of abstraction. We shall see later, and in Chapter XII what this denial amounts to.

The Conscious Subject or Self. With these dangers in view we may proceed. What is the first obvious and overwhelming fact about our ordinary experience? It is that it seems *to belong to us*, to be the experience of a self. We do not find isolated bits of experience belonging to nobody. All experience seems to be attached to, to be part of, a system of experiences which we call a person or say belongs to a person. In fact, it is impossible to describe a complete concrete bit of experience without bringing in either a proper name or a personal pronoun. We find experience always organized into personal histories.

But let us not be too hasty. Is this really a fact or is it an hypothesis? Have we merely recorded what we find or have we added an interpretation, an assumption, in giving our account? If we look closely we shall discover an assumption, namely that there is something to be called a self, or person. How far is it well grounded?

First, a point about which there can be no doubt whatever. Experience is systematic; any moment of our normal lives has a peculiar systematic structure which is what we are pointing out when we say that it is *our* experience, or belongs to us. There may be certain exceptions, but if so they are abnormal and probably pathological. Certain occurrences in mediumistic trances suggest that it may be possible for detached fragments of experience to occur,[1] but these we need not here consider.

The main fact is clear; any moment of your life is *yours* in some very important sense, and, further, any two moments of your life are linked together in a peculiar way, through both belonging to you.

[1] Cf. C. D. Broad, *The Mind and Its Place in Nature*, p. 541.

By what hypothesis can we explain this cardinal fact. What, in other words, are you?

A traditional answer has been that there is something highly indescribable which persists throughout your whole history and is essentially you. Your experiences are either modifications of this something, as the varied-colored lights shining through a pane of glass might be regarded as modifications of the glass, or else they are either states of something else (*e.g.*, your body or your empirical ego) or trains of facts, which you, the indescribable something, the transcendental ego, apprehend. It is plain that this view, the simple 'Soul' view, can take various forms. It is on the whole less prominent in recent psychology than ever before. Its merit is simplicity; its chief demerit is that it is so difficult to see what evidence, other than Psychical Research, could possibly either overthrow it or establish it. It hangs in the air out of reach of investigation, and it is almost a duty for man in the present crisis of his career to prefer views which run the risk of refutation, since all his recent advances have come through damage done to cherished convictions. It is hard to admit that the beliefs we most cling to are usually in the long run the most dangerous. Let us see what other more risky views have been suggested.

We can obviously, if we please, put the body in the place of the soul, and say that an experience is yours because it is a happening in your body. This, as the view most exposed to danger, is perhaps the most to be recommended. We have discussed its other merits on a former page (Chapter II). But for our present purposes, the description not the explanation of our experience, this hypothesis is of importance only in one respect. We see which this is if we ask, *Where* does our experience seem to take place?

The Localization of Experience. Plainly for the most part in the head, though not exclusively. Nearly all thought of absent things or about abstract topics (some people with very vivid imagery are exceptions) seems to happen in the head. But emotions often seem to occupy large tracts of the body; a longing for company can sometimes be as definitely located in the stomach as a hunger. Feelings of touch normally seem to be at or near the point touched on the surface of the skin, though a different state of affairs can arise. For example, when a nerve which has been cut is regenerated, the outgrowing processes of the neurones may wander into quite different regions from those which knew them before. When this happens a touch, *e.g.*, on the thigh may be felt as a touch on the heel. What are known as referred pains are also curious examples. An affection of the liver may give rise to pain in the neck, and the pain of angina pectoris may first be felt in the left little finger. In these cases the intervention of reflexes is responsible for the illusion.

But, in general, experiences due to stimuli arising within the body are felt very nearly where they occur. It is different with what are known as the *distance receptors*—the eye and ear, for example. We locate the butterfly, whose flight we are following, out in the air, not in the eye, and very rightly. But where do we locate the seeing of it? Probably the answer should be—nowhere. Sometimes, when the eye is tired, we may think we feel the seeing in the eye. But with discrimination we discern that what we are feeling there is not strictly visual, but muscular, a strain in the eye muscles. If we compare the sight of the butterfly with the best image we can form of it with closed eyes the difference as to location of the two experiences is usually very marked, though individuals differ and differ from day to day. A moderate visualizer has a sense of activity with a definite orientation going on inside his skull and filling up most of its cavity which is quite absent in ordinary vision, for which it would plainly be a disadvantage. Whereas the apparent direction of imaginings inside the skull is a decided gain. Compare visualizing a monkey before you and behind, a bird in the sky and a beetle in the ground; a sense of strain in one direction or another is with most people an important part of the experience. We shall see later (Chapter XII) that movements of the eyes have much to do with this.

On the whole, then, experiences tend to be located roughly in the regions in which their neural counterparts occur, and when this is not the case good reasons can be found for the anomaly. And to this extent the hypothesis that the self, to which an experience belongs and which binds together the divers experiences of one history, is the body, is useful in describing experience.

The Self as a Mnemic Bundle. It has been suggested that it is unnecessary to suppose any one persistent thing whose states would be the experience of one person; that the total collection of these states would be itself sufficient. Memory might be the bond which united my experiences into one self and yours into a different self. My experiences are only revived in me, never in you. Every one of my experiences is dependent upon my past experience; it involves, as we have seen, a partial repetition of past experience; and, again, it arises in a setting of just previous experience of mine: it is either a continuation or a contrast to what has just been happening. It overlaps an experience which overlaps another, and so on. Experience, in other words, is sensibly continuous. The most sudden changes in it are at least *changes*. We do not have first one experience and then a totally new and different one. The new experience *grows out* of the old, and if we look closely we shall find them to have much in common. We are not like a single thread on which separate juxtaposed pearls of experience are strung. Our consciousness is an affair of many strands. A loud noise may seem to interrupt the whole stream of our thought, but if we look more closely we shall find, bridging the gulf between the two experiences, a swarm of undisturbed accompaniments. The feel of our feet thrusting against the ground, the continuous interplay of the poises of our body, the tensions and relaxations of our breathing, our other organic rhythms, numberless ordinarily unnoticed mental happenings contribute to supply a blended background to consciousness. This 'field of marginal attention,' this background of consciousness, has also been supposed by some [1] to be the self. It stands over against the interesting item of consciousness, the item which in some way has to be coped with; it is the subject that is aware of and concerned with this item as its correlative object.

This type of view is to be distinguished from the traditional view, the view which language favors. On that view experience is something which something else, not an experience at all, but an *experient*, has, enjoys, contemplates, or undergoes. On this view, there is only the experience; the apparent cleavage between experient and experience is due merely to unequal stability in the components of the total field of experience. The parts which, as we say, "need attention," the less stable parts about which something should be done, appear as objects, the rest play the part of an apparent self or subject.

The Dynamic View of the Mind. The reader need not resent this view as an attempt to dissolve him into thin air. All his observable characteristics remain as before. It is merely another way of describing the same facts. Most objections to it, however, probably derive from its seeming less favorable to a belief in survival of death than the more traditional view. Whether there is a self and what it is cannot

[1] Cf. H. R. Marshall, *Consciousness*, p. 535.

yet be decided, but it is possible to be rather more definite with regard to our third main question. What kind of a thing is an experience in general? It has become clear that experience is dynamic, not static; it is a stream of events, not merely a series of states. We can put this in another way. The mind is not a thing, but an activity.

We are so accustomed to thinking in terms of things like bricks, loaves, boots, atoms, and electrons, which, if they change at all, do so in such crude fashions and affect one another in such simple ways, that to conceive of experience as a system of energies whose changes bear very little analogy to the changes in such 'material objects' is difficult. Those possessing some slight acquaintance with, for example, elementary electrical theory will have an advantage here. For they will be less exposed to the danger of conceiving the matter too crudely.

A vocabulary of 'tensions,' 'stresses,' 'impulses,' 'currents,' 'tendencies,' and 'flows' is far more adequate in describing experiences than one of 'sensation,' 'percepts,' 'ideas,' 'concepts,' and 'images.' This is what the assertion that experience is dynamic, that the mind is an activity, amounts to. These traditional psychological terms are in fact a serious obstacle to a real understanding. They suggest too much that consciousness is a kind of shop window containing these various items in various arrangements with a mysterious factory in the background turning out the products displayed. But these images, ideas, etc., are not products, but *processes*.

What we observe when we introspect is the working of the factory itself. An image or an idea is a change, a redistribution of energies. Hence the peculiar fluidity of consciousness passing away from us always like a stream. And if we think of our experiences as like waves or eddies rather than like the flowing water or bits of stick passing down the stream, we shall come nearer to an adequate conception.

Disturbance and Recovery of Equilibrium. One further general character of experience must be noted before we go on to consider it in more detail. This concerns the way, in general, that these changes come about. We have already hinted that an experience only becomes an object for consciousness if it needs in some way to be dealt with. And we may take the subject to be the rest of the mind, which is called upon to deal with it. The important point here, important on any view of the self, is that experience is initiated through the need of the mind to deal with a situation—that is, to make a new adaption. Our everyday psychological language is full of phrases suggesting the importance of this fact. 'To attend to' something means ordinarily to try to put it right, or to put ourselves right with regard to it. To 'be concerned with' has a similar sense, and so has to 'be interested in' (literally, to interest is to make a difference).

If we ask ourselves why on any occasion we are having one kind of experience rather than another we find that it is because in this experience we are dealing with a situation, setting ourselves right with regard to it or setting it right with regard to us, or attempting to do so. This is true whether we take extensive and lengthy experiences (a courtship or legal action, for example) or brief and restricted experiences (a moment of introspection). In every case what is happening is essentially an attempt to restore equilibrium to a system of activities which has been disturbed. The disturbance may come from without, it may be due to a smell of burning which *disturbs our equanimity* as regards the safety of our dwelling. We sniff, set down our glass, get up, and take whatever steps we can think of to make sure all is well. Only thereby can the system of impulses which has been disturbed come to rest[1] again. Only so do we become, as we say, at ease again. Or the disturbance may come from within: we remember suddenly that we have not posted a letter, and the uneasy feeling that ensues drives us out to do so.

Let us take a more intricate situation. Why does anyone study psychology? There may be a thousand different reasons in different cases, but all these reasons, these motives, will be found to be disturbances, direct or indirect, of ways in which we have adjusted ourselves to our world. Let us consider two possible cases. A man may take up psychology for a very direct reason, namely because he becomes curious about the mind. He wonders what it is and how it works. Language and current ideas

---

[1] Not in the sense that nothing is happening, but that the happenings are not changing.

provide a means of dealing with questions about the mind which most people somehow find sufficient; if this man is curious it is because these current ways of handling the matter do not satisfy him, they do not enable him to meet the situation as it is to him, he is out of adjustment, and his curiosity and questionings are his attempts to gain a new adjustment. Every question is in fact what it feels like, a step on a path towards a state of affairs in which adjustment relieves tension. The path followed may or may not lead there.

But his reasons may be more complicated. He may be taking up psychology not out of any interest in the subject, but because it is scheduled as part of a course leading to a degree, and he may not desire the degree itself, but only wish to satisfy a parent or trustee who expects him to take it. This is perhaps a more typical instance than the last. His attitude towards his trustee, a very powerful group of interests, has acquired a certain adjustment which in turn involves a subordinate group, his degree-getting activities, and these in turn require a new group of impulses to be formed and ordered, those which will enable him to satisfy his examiners in psychology. Now every check in the formation of this new group throws the higher systems out of order and this can only be set straight again by further advance. He is driven on through his study of psychology by a series of disturbances of these major systems and his advances as a psychologist are steps towards the restoration of order in them.

This, of course, is a simplified account; other motives, of the same kind, however, will come into play. Short-circuiting occurs, and as a rule the internal equilibrium of the new system coming into being has considerable importance. The student will enjoy the subject if he understands it as far as he has gone, or thinks he does—both are conditions of equilibrium, of different order, however. Bewilderment and confusion, on the other hand, are conditions of disequilibrium, states of distress, in other words, and as such tend either to cause the student to make further efforts or to abandon the subject.

The Ultimate Modes of Consciousness. In this instance the threefold distinction which almost all psychologists have made between knowing, feeling, and striving (or cognition, affection, and conation, as they call them) can be easily made out. Nearly every experience, it has generally been agreed, presents these distinct irreducible aspects. It is a knowing of, or thinking about, something; it is pleasurable or unpleasant; and it is a striving towards something. And to consider their relative prominence in different cases and examine their mutual dependence upon one another is the best general method of analyzing an experience. We must beware, however, of the temptation to regard them as separable. Any one of them may lapse so as to be hardly, if at all, present, and there are perhaps states of mind in which they are not distinguishable; but we do not find processes which are purely cognitive, purely affective, or purely conative, any more than we find moving bodies which have no mass, or lines in nature which have no breadth. When the psychologist says that they are irreducible he means that none of them can be described in terms of the others. We must guard ourselves also against thinking of them only in their most highly developed forms. For example, we can be thinking of something even when we cannot say what it is we are thinking of. Ordinarily our awareness (thinking) is of this or that—a toothache, a sonata, space-time—but sometimes, as when we are just going to sleep, we may merely have a vague awareness of what not. Similarly with low degrees of pleasure and unpleasure. And there are relatively inert experiences in which we seem merely passive, but actually are feebly pursuing a course or feebly endeavoring to escape it.

Striving and Desire. Doubt has often been expressed as to whether we are actually *conscious* of striving, whether the fact that we strive is not merely an inference from our behavior. What we might suppose to be conscious striving, it has been urged, is simply *awareness* of some of the effects of striving. When we strive we tend to contract our muscles; it may be only the muscles of our jaws or scalp, as when we are thinking hard. What we supposed to be consciousness of striving would on this view be merely awareness of these contractions. Doubtless a great deal, which can easily be mistaken for striving itself, is really only awareness of these effects of striving. But after carefully distinguishing this awareness from striving, clear introspective evidence remains for striving itself as a component of consciousness. It is most clearly revealed in desire, which is striving directed towards an end, an idea of which is in consciousness. States of indecision in which a conflict of desires leads eventually to decision and resolve bring this striving aspect into special prominence. We must, however, beware of a common confusion here. It is misleading to speak of consciousness *of* striving, because this is equivalent to an unawareness of it. We are not ordinarily aware of striving; we merely consciously strive. Just as to have a feeling is not the same thing as to be aware of it (as in introspection), and to be aware of being spoken to is not the same thing as to be aware (introspectively) of our awareness itself, in the same way to strive is not the same thing as to be aware of it. We may become aware of it in introspection, but it is not an awareness itself, but a quite distinct component of consciousness.

The Unity of the Mind. It is extremely important to stress the close organic unity of these three components, because the natural temptation, once they have been distinguished, is to treat each of them in semi-independence of the others. To put them together again is then a difficult matter. In particular the separate treatment of cognition (awareness) has led to endless trouble. The doctrine of sensations and sense-data is a typical product of this tactical mistake. If we set aside the striving aspect of consciousness we easily fall into the trap of supposing that influences from the external world impress themselves somehow, through the sense organs and their nervous connections, upon a passive, merely receptive, 'mind.' The dynamic conception recedes into the background. Vision, for example, becomes the mere reception of a multitude of 'sense-data' which, by dragging up from a mental archive copies (images) of other sense-data formerly received, arrange themselves into percepts. Such a theory (known in the history of psychology as 'presentationism') is a mythology. Both sense-data and images in this use of the word are abstractions, as we shall see in the next chapter. For careful introspection knows nothing of sense-data (except perhaps in certain cases of pains and shocks which we shall consider in a moment) or of sensations (an older term for the same abstracta, abandoned by those who wish to make various distinctions between what is sensed and the sensing of it). The most simple and rudimentary awareness is from the beginning *perceiving*, an active process, that is to say, something that we do, not something that merely happens to us.

The importance of this point will be seen if we consider how sedulously philosophers have sought for data in experience upon which to construct their systems. One of the chief results which modern psychology has brought out is that this quest is vain, if by a datum we mean something simple, unanalyzable and ultimate which can safely be used as a foundation stone without asking any more about it. Experience does not provide such data. The simplest of our experiences is a highly complex *proc-*

ess; and this result is of fundamental consequence for our general speculative outlook on the world. To put it shortly, what have for centuries been regarded as the foundations of all our knowledge have given way, and no one is any the worse for it.

Shock. But what exactly is the difference between something which we do and something which merely happens to us? It is clear enough sometimes to introspection. Compare the experiences of looking at a picture with that of having a tooth drawn, or listening to music with being in a boiler factory, or stroking a kitten with being knocked on the head. The difference in these cases is that with the picture, the music, and the cat we are responding; our perceptions are steps we take as a result of stimulation, steps towards adjustment. If the adjustment is easy and smooth, but not so easy as to be automatic and stereotyped, we feel pleased: if it is difficult or fails, we feel displeasure. The whole conscious experience in either case is controlled by the precise condition of the new poise towards which we are tending. Consider the needle of a compass. There is a certain position at which the magnetic forces acting upon it are in equipoise. If we disturb it, there ensue wagglings, steps through which it returns to a position of rest. By a metaphor which is not too strained we can say that it is seeking this position. Now picture the needle geared up to a motor and driven round and round. This roughly represents what happens to us in the dentist's chair, the boiler factory, or under the sand-bag of the Apache. Instead of responding, according to the laws of our own structure, to the disturbance which has set us waggling, instead of dealing with the situation, the situation is dealing with us.

From this brief indication the reader will be able to see how a detailed account would run. The essential point is that in perception what happens is governed by the end-state of poise towards which we are tending, whereas in sensation, on the comparatively rare occasions on which it occurs, all possibility of tending to an equipoise is set aside by the violent, paralyzing shock of the occurrence.

But, it will be asked, is not there always a substratum of sensation in all perception? Granted that the finished perception is a response, is there not a purely receptive initial stage, the disturbance, namely, which sets the response in action? The reply is that this, except in the extreme instances of shock and pain, is not conscious, and even in these exceptional cases it is very arguable that consciousness entirely consists in baffled efforts to cope with the happening.

The Process of Introspection. Another case in which what seem to be sensations are unduly prominent occurs perhaps in introspection. We ought to realize throughout that what happens when we look inwards is different from what happens when we are not introspecting. Introspection is not simply an uncovering, a revealing of our ordinary experiences; it is a further and a different experience. What seem to be the 'data' of introspection do not occur at all when we are not looking inwards. In terms of a dynamic view of the mind, introspection itself is the result of a fresh disturbance of equipoise of quite a different order from those which govern the experiences which we introspect. A diagram of the situation (Fig. VIII) may make it clearer.

The original experience which is introspected and the introspection of it are separate systems of activity,

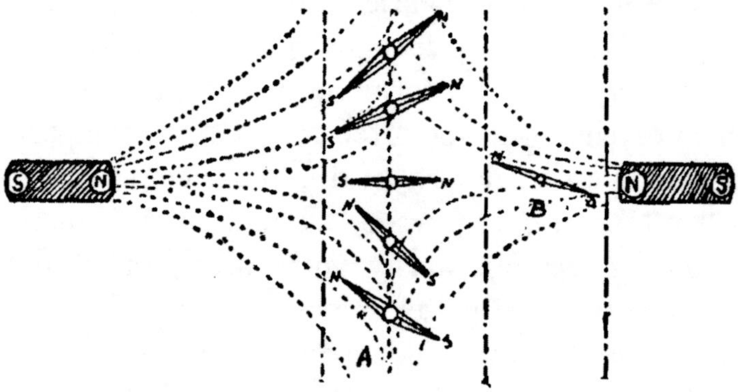

Fig. VIII

A. THE INTROSPECTED EXPERIENCE B. THE INTROSPECTION

[Here A is one system of tendencies, figured as a set of compass needles being disturbed by a magnet on the left (a stimulus). As they swing they disturb one another, but are finding a general state of equipoise. When this system is introspected another system, B, is following in a sense A's changes, but B is also being influenced by a magnet of its own on the right (an interest).]

the second is set in play and controlled in part by the first. But not altogether so controlled, for other factors, such as the question we are asking and our theory of the mind, also intervene. What we get in introspection is not Experience A revealed, but Experience A as it appears to Experience B. How far this is a reliable report of A depends upon how reliable it need be in order to satisfy the purpose for which we are introspecting. Thus the introspections which a man makes while grappling with a dangerous practical situation, for example those of a cragsman deciding whether he has balance enough to round a projection, are likely to be very faithful reports of his actual present experience. But those of a psychologist attempting to discover introspective grounds for one of his pet theories are not so trustworthy. And further we must distinguish our actual introspections from our verbal formulations of them—a point which psychologists too often forget when comparing the introspection reports of different people.

The Mental Masquerade. There is yet another reason for dealing warily with introspective 'data' whether these are 'sensations' or anything else. Events in the mind hide behind one another. A great deal happens that only appears in consciousness when translated into or disguised as other happenings. Our visual experience, for example, is so much more adequate, rich, and elaborate than our touch, our muscular, our kinesthetic experience, that these tend to be represented in consciousness by images and perceptions of a visual nature. It is only when something serious goes wrong with them that we can notice how much their absence matters to consciousness. Similarly, with the very important tributary of experience which goes by the name of the cœnæsthesia, our general organic sensibility due to the state of our body as a whole. It is always coloring our consciousness, but to take note of it in introspection is extraordinarily difficult. We are much more likely to describe it as a peculiar peacefulness or vividness about the landscape or a singular glare in the light or stuffiness in the air than to take it as what it really is in itself. As Wallon well remarks, "the data of introspection no more correspond to our actual psychic processes than they give an exact representation of the external world. They are only a group of signs, formulæ, and convenient interpretations for our relations with the whole situation."[1] These are not reasons for neglecting, much less for rejecting, introspection. We have obviously nothing to take its peculiar place. But we should remember that it does not give either a complete report of what is happening or one that must always be taken at its face value.

Pleasure-Unpleasure. Passing now to the pleasure-unpleasure aspect, the *affective* aspect as it is called, we may note first how central this seems in all experience. What James so finely described as the secret solicitancy of pleasure and repugnancy of pain often appear to introspection as the mainspring of the whole activity. Probably this is largely an illusion. Pleasure and unpleasure are products of our activities rather than their sources. Two questions arise for consideration: (1) Do pleasure and unpleasure make up the whole of the effective aspect? and (2) What exactly is their—evidently close—connection with striving? As to (1) it seems at first sight natural to bring emotional characters of experience under this heading. Fear, disgust, anger,

[1] In Dumas' *Traité de Psychologie*, vol. i, p. 223.

and love may seem at least to contain specific modifications of consciousness with as good a right to be classed among affective phenomena as pleasure or unpleasure. But when we look more closely these emotional characters turn out to be composite. We cannot reduce pleasure and unpleasure either to awareness or to striving or to a blend of the two; but we can reduce fear to a union of awareness, unpleasure and conscious striving, and its peculiar character is given it by what we are aware of, how we are striving, and, as a rule, unpleasure. Ghost-story fear and other pleasant fears ought strictly from the introspective point of view to be called by another name. What we know about emotions, not through introspection, but from other sources, supports this conclusion. They are composite experiences and get their character from their composition. (2) External observations also corroborate introspection as regards the second question. Pleasure and unpleasure are very intimately connected with the course of striving, with its progress towards a 'satisfactory' or 'unsatisfactory' stage. Success seems always to be pleasant, and failure unpleasant, but the success or failure may be local merely, as we need hardly point out; and a great success, though intensely pleasant, may be from the point of view of the whole organism, the whole history of the mind, a disaster. So it is with the ecstasies of the drug addict.

How intricate the interplay of pleasure and unpleasure may be is well shown in some introspective experiments undertaken by Wohlgemuth. Here is the report[1] of one of his subjects, a highly trained introspectionist when given a small bottle of heliotropine to sniff:

"Sensation at first unpleasant. The Unpleasure persisted for a brief period at the same intensity. Then it increased quite suddenly. A moment later I detected a pleasant component in the sensation. For a brief period the Pleasure and Unpleasure distinctly coexisted. The Unpleasure vanished from consciousness rather abruptly and for a short time the Pleasure was very considerable. It seemed to me of an exciting character which was accompanied by fairly widespread organic sensations of a typical kind. I noticed particularly a slight catch in the breath which occurred at the moment of greatest Pleasure. I think the sensations might be described as thrilling, or slightly vibratory, in character. I think they are similar in kind to those that I have sometimes experienced during incipient erotic excitation. This high degree of pleasure persisted only for a very short time. The olfactory sensation itself became then much less pleasant and the organic sensations died down. During expiration there was some slight discontent at the disappearance of the sensation. The absence of the sensation was uninteresting and there was a corresponding pleasure at its reappearance. This was quite distinct from the sensory pleasure itself."

[1] *Pleasure-Unpleasure*, 1919, p. 55.

Pains. Pains need a word of elucidation perhaps. They are usually unpleasant but not always; and some people enjoy playing with a not too sensitive tooth. It is best to distinguish them sharply from the unpleasure which ordinarily accompanies them and to regard them as a special class of perceptions, a class which has for obvious biological reasons a precedence normally over most other perceptions since they arise for the most part from what are called *nocuous* stimuli, stimuli likely to lead to damage of the tissues. But as our early example of the tree climber and the wasp will show, and as many surprising abnormal phenomena show, pain may lose this precedence. In hypnotic conditions, even major operations can be performed without the patient showing any signs of pain, and there is the classic story[1] of a cheerful and corpulent politician, who in an election crisis calmly bit off his damaged finger as though it were the most natural thing in the world to do.

Æsthetic Experiences. Our general analysis can be applied to every kind of experience. A response to Shakespeare's *Hamlet* differs from a response to Wohlgemuth's *Heliotropine* only by being a larger and much more finely organized unit. Its greater value is a consequence of its higher degree of organization. Here, as always, our experience is a stream of processes tending from an initial arousal or disturbance to an end-state of rest or acquiescence. A situation has arisen, it may be gradually as in *Hamlet*,

[1] Ribot, *The Psychology of the Emotions*, p. 33.

which is only met when the various systems aroused have found a new equipoise, an end-state in which we are readjusted to it. Usually this new poise involves many steps—in æsthetic experiences they are peculiarly elaborate—and the paths followed by the numerous impulses which have to be brought into a harmony may have to wind round obstacles. What we are aware of meanwhile are the factors supplied either from without (in perception) or from within (in emotion) which guide our response. Our awareness itself is our response as it develops. Our feeling, our pleasure or displeasure, is the free or baffled flowing of the response. Our hopes, regrets, doubts, hesitations are the eddies and backwashes of the stream. The states of enjoyment to which the term Beauty is probably best restricted show more clearly than any others the reconciliation of the most varied impulses in a balanced integral experience (synæsthesis).[1]

The Span of Attention. Usually, in ordinary life, we are not a single stream, but a welter of many semi-independent streams. We may be adding up figures, watching a neighbor, and thinking of what we shall do later on in the day simultaneously. Several separately disturbed systems are tending independently to their end-states. When there is only one such process going on we say we are *absorbed*

[1] For an analysis, by the author and others, of the many very different uses of the term Beauty and of their psychological basis, see *The Foundations of Æsthetics*, second edition, 1925, London and New York.

by what we are doing. When there are too many such separate disturbances or when the settlement of one interferes with that of the others we complain of distraction. In deep absorption, as is evident from the story of the Mysore mathematician who tied a cobra round his neck in mistake for a cravat, a change in the general situation which would ordinarily cause deep disturbance passes apparently unnoticed. What happens in such cases is difficult to decide. It is often alleged that such changes are *always* noticed, unconsciously. The possibility of sometimes recovering them from memory, by hypnosis or other special means, as in psycho-analysis, is the evidence for this view. It is not very strong evidence, however, for we more often never remember them and they have no observable effect upon us whatever. What we need to make this evidence satisfactory is some account of the differences between stimuli that are unconsciously noticed and can be recalled by appropriate means, and those that cannot be recalled although noticed.

The Limits of Consciousness. What probably happens in the majority of cases is that we do consciously notice the change, but, since for the moment it has no significance for us, we do nothing further about it. Thus our response to it is extremely brief and does not initiate further disturbances as it would if we were *attending*. For our deeper disturbances are always due to prior responses to shallower disturbances. When we recognize something this recognition (itself a response to a disturbance) may, like the fuse of a shell, throw much more important systems into turmoil. But in deep absorption the linkage between our systems of impulses is impaired, for all systems save those which are already active. In Chapter III we touched upon some possible physiological explanations of this fact of inhibition.

Attention, then, is essentially conscious interest, and interest is nothing else than the tendency of a disturbed system to regain equipoise. But the width of distribution of attention varies greatly in different experiences. We may have many simultaneous interests or only one single interest, yet the single interest may have many ramifications. Often, though the dominant interest is single, in other words though everything in the experience is implicated in the attainment of a single final equipoise which is the goal of the experience, the mutual relevance of the parts cannot be intellectually worked out. It is only shown by their final co-operation. Works of art are among the best instances of such experiences. Who can say quite how the metrical movement of 'Kubla Khan' is relevant to the sense of the lines? Yet it is an integral part of the whole poem, not merely appropriate, but essential.

Interests may be unconscious as well as conscious. As to why some are and others are not we know as yet very little. Sometimes an interest seems to be unconscious because consciousness of it would be unpleasant. Yet many unpleasant interests are conscious. This part of psychology, to which we return later (Chapter XIV), is as yet comparatively in its infancy. To consider it we have to pass outside the bounds of introspection, which are beginning to appear curiously and significantly restricted. Our minds certainly are far larger than our normal consciousness, but it may be remarked that this has been discovered chiefly through special means (hypnosis and psycho-analysis) which have enabled the bounds of introspection to be extended.

CHAPTER XII: LOOKING OUTWARDS

Our Knowledge of the External World. We are apt to regard our knowledge of the outside world as a matter of course, and to think that things can hardly help being much as we perceive them. But here again psychology is unsettling. We are not nearly in such close contact as we suppose with even the things we seem to know best—our chairs, our motorcycles, our friends. We have seen (Chapter III) how stimuli falling upon special sense organs at the surface of the body cause impulses to be volleyed in along the afferent neurones leading to reception and co-ordinating centers; and how they there compete for the discharge of these centers and thus for a share in still more intricate transactions of the association circuits. And in the chapters which followed we saw how far from passive we are in our perceptions, and the extent to which what we see depends upon our needs and interests. We have now to look rather more closely at all this with a view to discovering, if we may, how much of the world is really there before us as we ordinarily think it and how much of it is merely a reflection of ourselves.

A first point to settle is our use of the word *sensation*. Something was said about this in the preceding chapter, but we may here remind the reader that all sensations are perceptions, though sometimes humble ones. To quote Piéron:[1] "In reality any impression whatever implies a perception, of varying precision but undeniable. If I am touched on the right arm and I feel something, I can at least indicate the approximate region of the body involved, if not the exact place of the contact. I do not confuse the foot with the head and I am sure that it is a matter of a contact, not of an odor or light, even without being able to state the exact nature of this

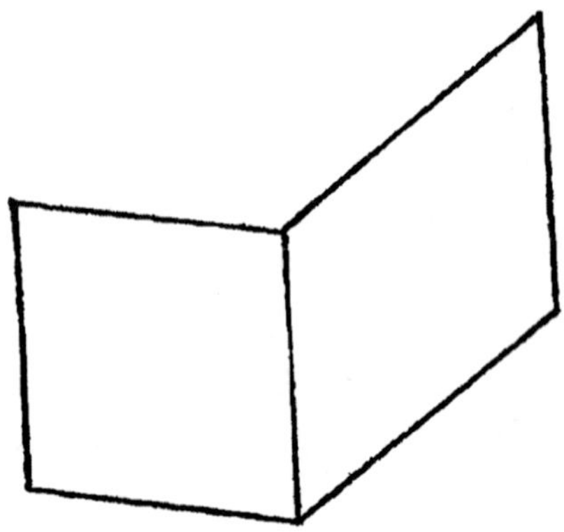

Fig. IX

contact. As soon as a sensation is definitely felt, an excitation received really is occasioning an associative reaction which includes the evocation of representations and verbal symbols, the taking of attitudes, and, if necessary, motor reactions. But when we speak of perceptive function we are referring to high degrees of this function of elementary thought, which have become delicate and exact, as distinguished from the crude manifestations which are never absent if there is really a definite sensation."

[1] *Thought and the Brain* (1926), part ii, chap. ii, §3.

None the less, a great deal of valuable work upon our perceptions has been done on the contrary assumption that sensations are independent elements. Up to a certain point these hypothetical abstractions work well enough; beyond that point they make perception incomprehensible. Philosophic doctrines based on sensations (they are usually rechristened 'sense-data,' after much discussion of the distinction between sensing and what is sensed) are built upon a very insecure foundation.

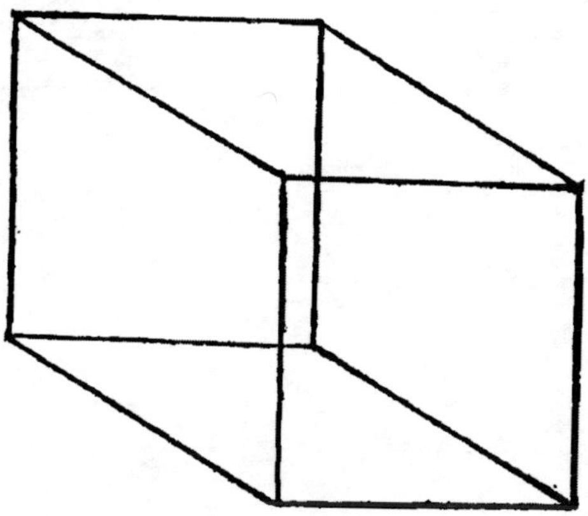

FIG. X.

Illusions of Sight and Touch. Certain well-known illusions show clearly how complex our perceptual processes are even when they seem simple. Bend a visiting card or a small piece of smooth paper so that it will stand upright like a half-open book upon the tablecloth (Fig. IX), and gaze at it with one eye. You can see it either as if opening towards you or away from you. (Notice also the ways in which the colors tend to become more noticeable in the

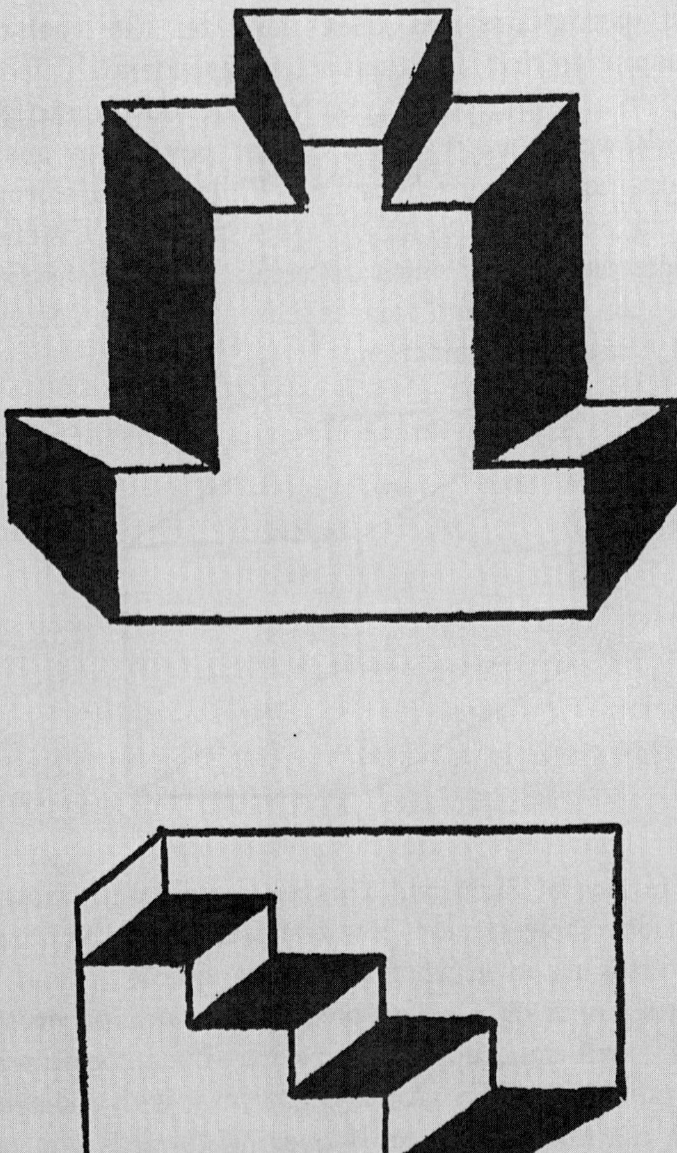

Fig. XI

'unreal' position.) Or look with both eyes at Fig. X. It can be seen either as one cube or as another, or as a series of boxes with the tops or the sides off, or as a flat design.

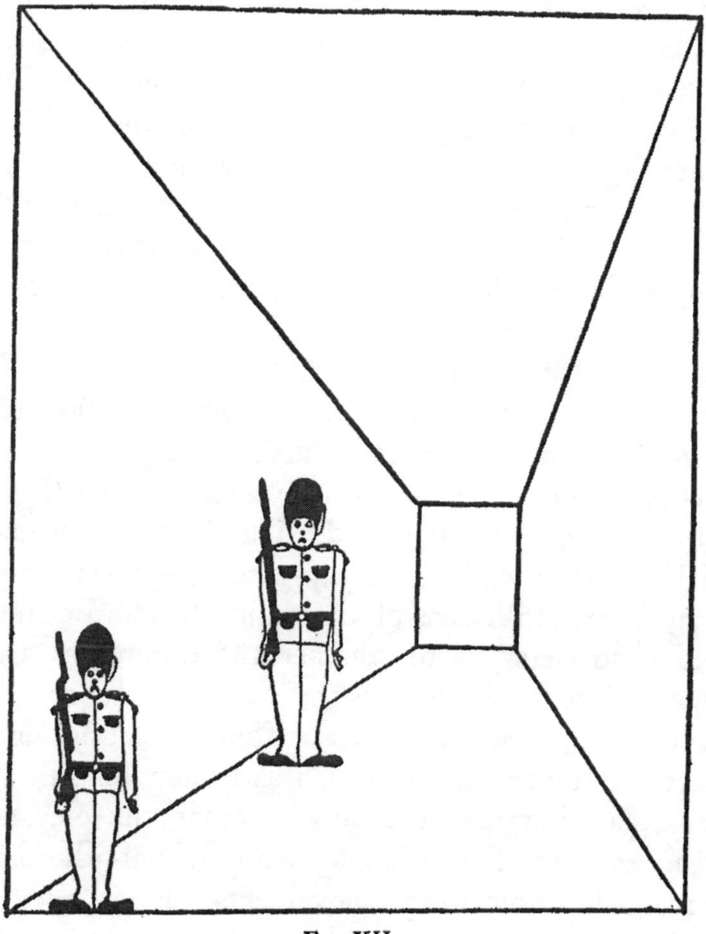

Fig. XII

The Monument-Gateway ambiguity (Fig. XI) is still more striking. By gazing steadily it can be seen either as a solid or as an opening; while the staircase below it can also be seen as an overhanging cornice. In Figure XII the warriors, though drawn the same size, appear, through the illusion of perspective, to be one taller than the other. The alternating relief is related to the Traube-Hering wave phenomenon of blood pressure, whereas the perspective illusion is probably due to the expectation of ocular convergence which produces a giant in the middle distance. To take a different sense, try to hold a walking-stick vertically with your eyes shut and your head bent well over to one side, or cross two fingers and touch them with a pencil placed between them.

In these ways it is not difficult to convince oneself that a great deal more than a mere reception of stimuli by the sense organs occurs in perception. The detail of the processes responsible for some of these illusions is not yet established. The rhythmic fluctuations which attention is always undergoing certainly play a part in illusions of alternating form. But the old controversy as to whether the differences are due to different judgments about the same sensations or to different sensations has shifted to a much more subtle and adequate discussion as to how central, at what stage inwards from the sense organ, the relevant changes are. For example, many visual illusions have been traced to eye-movements. Even in such an apparently simple matter as the comparison of vertical and horizontal lines an illusion is found. We over-estimate vertical lines; and this was thought to be due to the greater difficulty of raising the eyes as compared with shifting them sideways. But by showing the lines to be compared only for a moment, this effect of eye-movements is cut out, yet the vertical line is still over-estimated. The conclusion drawn is that though actual eye-movements may be originally involved, once visual space-perception has been acquired, more central processes can do their work for them.

Eye-movements. It will repay us to consider eye-movements a little more closely. Without the experimental work and without the neurological evidence, we should never have realized what an astonishing amount they do for us, and how much of our world depends upon them.

Consider dizziness, for example. This seems to us merely an odd and unpleasant experience to be avoided when possible. Yet it is but the exaggerated or disturbed working of a mechanism without which we should never know where we are or where anything else is. Whenever we turn about, a small apparatus within the ears, containing a fluid resembling sea water,[1] very like a set of spirit-levels and known as the semicircular canals, takes note of it much as a half-emptied flask in our pocket would. But this agitation in itself tells us nothing. It does not *directly* give rise to perceptions; the semicircular canals have no direct connections with the cortex of the cerebrum. And yet our sense of orientation, our knowledge of which way we are facing, and our

[1] This, together with the salinity of our blood-plasma, is part of the evidence for man's aquatic existence in the remote past.

whole left-and-right-turn consciousness, undoubtedly do depend upon what happens in these semicircular canals. They tell us indirectly by a reflex provocation of turning movements of the eyes to right and left. It is these eye-movements which tell us when we turn,[1] and without them we have no sense of turning. The dizzy man, when he shuts his eyes, feels as though *he* was turning; if he opens them the things he sees seem to spin round, but the other way.

This extraordinary indirectness with which we perceive what is happening is paralleled almost everywhere in perception. Consider how we locate sounds. For low notes it is easy. The tympanic membranes in the two ears are in different phases of vibration; but once again this difference does not of itself give rise to direct perception of where the sound is. Here again, reflexes involving eye-movements come in, and it is the same in the more difficult matter of locating high notes and noises. Notice, moreover, a very curious fact. Attention directed to two sounds with a view to distinguishing them fails when the difference between them is decreased to a certain minimum. But the differences made use of in locating sounds are far less than this. In other words, the differential threshold for the reflex by which location is effected is lower than that for the sensation.[2]

---

[1] This, of course, applies to passive turning. Muscular perceptions obviously come in when we twist our trunk or limbs.

[2] It has been suggested that water-diviners who perceive the presence of a spring or stream deep under the surface of the earth by the movement in their hands of the divining rod are showing a

If we place two suitably chosen sources of sound at different distances from the 'subject' of an experiment we can get him to localize them as one source. Where he imagines it to be depends upon the sounds. Now if we vary the frequency of one of the sources, he perceives this change as a movement of the imaginary source, *before* he perceives it as a change in the sound.

The same indirectness turns up even in the way in which we locate touches on the skin. A pinch or a stab with a pin might seem to be given directly just where it is; but not so. It has to be found, so to speak, and its localization depends upon the reflexes which it sets up; if these are deranged it becomes misplaced.

Recognition. But these are mere superficial complexities in the mechanism of perception. Let us go a step deeper. Consider how we perceive forms which are familiar to us. Something is put into our hand; we perceive it instantly to be a key without any process of exploring it with the fingers. Certain injuries to the brain make this impossible, but we may still be able by exploratory movements to make out its shape and form without being able to recognize it *as* a key. And other injuries produce the converse effect. We can tell that it is a key, yet cannot work out what the shape is. This last is the really puzzling instance. We can find many parallels in normal life. There are people, there are expres-

similar capacity. If so, the auditory threshold for the reflex must be very low indeed.

sions, there are situations which we recognize instantly, yet if we try to work out what it is that distinguishes them from other people, expressions, or situations, we fail altogether to get a satisfactory explanation. Of course in such cases we may make mistakes, and probably far more often than we suppose. Yet how a chair seen from a new angle is recognized at once as that same chair, is the fundamental question in perception.

It is natural to suppose that something, its color or some detail of shape, is the cause of the identification; and this no doubt is usually the case. But the detail itself may be presented to us at an angle from which we have never before perceived it. The more difficult problem is how this *new* aspect may be instantly responded to, in spite of its difference from all the aspects which we have formerly beheld. It seems clear that the mind (or a co-ordination center in the brain, if we prefer so to put it) responds not only to stimuli which it has already received, but thereafter to a certain range of stimuli. When these other stimuli closely resemble the original, this is not surprising. But in many cases the set of aspects by which we instantly recognize a thing are extraordinarily varied. A coin seen with the rim or the flat side showing is very different. Yet we recognize even unfamiliar things from new aspects without difficulty.

Sign-interpretation. This fact, that we recognize what we have never seen, is not difficult to explain if we take account of the ways in which our outlook upon the world has developed. The child, as we saw in Chapter VIII, is comparatively deficient in this power. But the adult has been watching things move and studying their systematic transformations of shape most of his life. Thus as regards most objects a very wide range of shapes have become equivalent for him; they are aspects of one object. When he sees a new object, the trace or disposition left in him is not a single isolated pattern of the sensory stimulation, but a setting, ready if need be to respond to an immense variety of patterns—most of those, in fact, into which this pattern can be transformed by movements of the object. It is this disposition, the product not only of the original sight of the object, but of all his former experience with somewhat similar objects, that enables him to interpret aright the new aspect, when it comes. This influence of experience explains why the expert—the entomologist or the seaman, for example—is so much more quick and accurate than the amateur in interpreting professional signs.

Most recognition is an extremely complicated performance. We have seen already how interest affects it. But innumerable other factors also play a part. The whole situation must be taken into account if we are to understand recognition. For example, a stimulus which in war-time we should interpret rightly as a sign of an air raid we may equally rightly after the cessation of hostilities interpret as an earthquake. Yet in neither case need we make any conscious reference to the international situation. The general circumstances bar out all but a relatively small number of the possibilities and our recognition is a choice between those responses which are left. Sufficient attention is rarely given to these wider factors in interpretation by those who concentrate on the elementary problems of recognition.

General Consequences. But on any possible view of recognition in the light of the facts and analyses now at our disposal our account of interpretation in the wider sense, the sense in which it is relevant to current speculation on the reality of the external world, must make psychology the key to the riddle of the universe. To some, indeed, psychological study seems to yield conclusive evidence that our curiosity as to the nature of things must forever remain unsatisfied. "We can never solve the so-called world-riddle because what seem riddles to us are merely the contradictions we have ourselves created," says Havelock Ellis. "We make our own world; when we have made it awry we can remake it approximately truer. . . . Man lives by imagination." And Vaihinger has urged that the contradictions which thought endeavors to resolve are actually essential to its successful operation. In any case, he holds, we can never free ourselves from psychological accretions; for just as the digestive system breaks up the matter which it receives, mixes it with its own juices and so makes it suitable for assimilation in the practical interests of the organism, "so the psyche envelops the thing perceived with categories which it has developed out of itself."

The Psychology of Fictions. Our intellectual chyme and chyle would, for those who accept this approximately Kantian account, be no guide whatever to the physical happenings outside our skin, since perception is not even a process of assimilation on the causal view; nothing of the external stimulus (usually a form of vibration) is actually taken in by the receptors. "Our sensations produce within the psyche itself purely subjective processes to which, in the modern view, nothing in reality—picture it as we will—can correspond"; and the explanation of the way in which we distort reality and yet successfully cope with it "is to be sought in the nature of thought itself." In other words, the only field open to the metaphysically inclined would be the study of the mental processes to which external stimuli give rise. The interest—and the intricacy—of the study would, of course, be further enhanced by the allied study of the behavior and distortions of the various symbol-systems by which analytic and reflective ('discursive') thought is supported; of the languages, that is to say, in which knowledge is enshrined.

Fictions in Modern Physics. This insistence on the psychological foundations of our theories of the external world receives frequent support from the utterances of the most respected modern physicists.

For some, the tendency of the mind (on which Bergson and Wallon have laid much stress) to select only the permanent, reinforced as it is by the analytic influence of language, has seemed of necessity to render any scientific account of the universe arbitrary. And apart from this selection of the primary entities from which physics is able to construct a self-contained system by virtue of cyclic definition, the theory of relativity has much to say about the mental factor in scientific explanation. "All through the physical world," according to Professor Eddington, "runs an unknown content, which must really be the stuff of our consciousness. . . . We have found that where science has progressed the farthest, the mind has but regained from nature that which the mind has put into nature. We have found a strange footprint on the shores of the unknown. We have devised profound theories, one after another, to account for its origin. At last we have succeeded in reconstructing the creature that made the footprint. And lo! it is our own."[1] Of particular interest is the suggestion that 'time,' the whole 'historical' conception of things, is a mental contribution; that events do not 'happen,' but we happen to come across them—and might under certain circumstances know the past from the future instead of the future from the past! And it was Einstein himself who, in a speech in honor of Planck in 1918, spoke of the ideal of physics as the attainment of a world-picture, and of the motives which impel men "to seek a simplified synoptic view of the world conformable to their own

[1] *Space, Time, and Gravitation* (1922), pp. 200-201. This view of the mental factor in science is further elaborated in Professor Eddington's essay on "The Domain of Physical Science" in *Science, Religion and Reality*, 1925 (by ten authors).

nature, overcoming the world by replacing it with this picture."

Moreover, it is not sufficiently stressed by historians of philosophy that on a systematic reclassification of the subject-matter of the sciences not only 'solipsists'[1] (Lat. *solus, ipse*=alone, myself) but the majority of those who in the past have called themselves Idealists, maintaining that to be known is to be "in the mind" or an "invention of the mind," have in reality still further extended the scope of a possible psychology, though without themselves actually embarking on its details.

New World Vistas. It is as though soon after the return of Columbus general opinion in Europe, while admitting the existence of a land in the West which might profitably be further explored, was unable to realize the significance of the discovery. The appeals of pioneers for support in further exploration meet, let us suppose, with undue apathy, even with a certain skepticism; El Dorado, it is replied, is in all probability altogether elsewhere; this so-called America seems to contain dangerous and not altogether respectable inmates, and in any case there is no reason to suppose that the land discovered is not part of China—which has already been largely explored by Polo and other reliable observers. Our

[1] Cf. N. R. Campbell, *Physics: The Elements* (Cambridge, 1920), part i, p. 264: "Ultimately the conclusion cannot be avoided that other persons (if any one cares to express it so) are merely inventions of my own mind." It is worth recording, however, that the rest of Dr. Campbell's work is a valuable and level-headed discussion of material objects and other people.

far-sighted travelers, however, are insistent: for is not what they have already seen sufficient to satisfy anyone that the Old World must eventually suffer eclipse? They appeal to respected authorities: and call to their aid historical research—which reveals that the wisest and the most speculative alike have located in the States the possible source of all that is least understood and most essential to the future of humanity; the nest of the great auk, the lost Atlantis, the spot to which flies go in winter, Fundamentalism, the most Humorous Stories, Ford Cars, and Untold Natural Resources. Their case is undoubtedly stronger. If but a few of the prophets and sages are justified in their attributions, the importance of this America cannot, they urge, be denied. In due course the invasion of Stratford-on-Avon occurs.[1]

So it may be with Psychology.

The Human Equation. The general question, therefore, raised at the beginning of this chapter—How far do our ways of perceiving the world really tell us what it is like and how far do they only tell us what we are like?—is one which the psychologist will ultimately be called upon to answer. It may be that the physicist, in reacting against an uncritical account of 'matter,' will be found to have gone too far. But in any case the sort of difficulties we have been considering are essential preliminaries to that

[1] For the more subtle influences of America on the psychology of Europeans, *New World Vistas*, by James Wood (Kegan Paul, 1926), should be read.

answer, remote though the issue may have appeared to those who approach the subject for the first time. The reorientations and revaluations which have given rise to psychology as a serious branch of science have occurred in the lifetime of many who are still engaged in its development. It is still premature to speak of final conclusions when we are only beginning to learn to think.

It is surprising how little the psychology of imagination has as yet been utilized in the service of physics. Our powers of conceiving the world in other aspects than those suggested by foraging and engineering have hardly been explored at all. Writers like Lewis Carroll, Fournier d'Albe, Helen Keller, Nicod, and Wells have, in different ways, no less than the physicists we have mentioned, made a remarkable beginning. But the windows which might be opened on the world by a full study of animal, primitive, and abnormal psychology (cf. Chapter XVII) are still for the most part darkened by prejudice and ignorance. At any rate, it is clear that for some time to come a chief task of psychology is that of demarcation; for, as we shall see when dealing with emotion, we constantly project our feelings as well as our constructions into the outer world. Psychology can point to the difference between the infant and the trained observer in all branches of natural knowledge, and it can describe this difference fairly definitely. The child, as we saw, fails comparatively to separate the factors in perception introduced by his desires from the factors which the external situation supplies. The pursuit of truth is the slow weeding out of the desire factors. One of the chief ways in which it is done is through the distinction between means and ends. To remain unbiased in the manipulation of means is often indispensable if we are to attain the ends desired. Thus the scientist learns not to cook his evidence if he wishes to prove his conclusion. Even the astronomer has a 'personal equation' to eliminate, before he regards his observations as objective.

When all desire has been discounted we may still, as Vaihinger maintains, be left in our view of nature with a distortion due to the instrument (the mind) which is viewing it. For this distortion the only possible correction is an exact knowledge of how the mind works. In other words, psychology must criticize itself. Our account of the mind must at least be such that the mind could know about itself. And probably the desire-bias of which we have spoken is stronger in psychology than in any other science. We may well be such as we should hate to think we are. For some of these biases, however, we are learning to allow, chiefly as a result of the discoveries of the psycho-analysts. But we shall be more ready to discuss their findings when we have considered how we think and the nature of our emotions.

CHAPTER XIII: HOW WE THINK

Ideas. Thinking, according to Babbitt, would consist in getting hold of, getting rid of, arranging, and working out ideas; but just what ideas are is a point which he leaves vague. It is this point which we have now to consider.

One account which is of great historical significance regards ideas as images. Ideas obviously *represent* in some way the things that they are *of*; and since images are the mental events which most plainly represent things, this view had much in its favor. But it breaks down if we have to admit that many people think without images, that even when images occur they may be quite irrelevant and accidental, and that they tend to appear chiefly after the thinking has got into difficulties.

The most thorough work on this point has been done by the group of psychologists known as the Würzburg School. Their method looks simple, but actually is very difficult and laborious. An experimenter sits down with his subject and sets him a series of problems carefully chosen beforehand. For instance, he asks him, "Can you calculate the velocity of a freely falling body?" or, "Does evolution involve progress?" The subject replies 'yes' or 'no' as soon as he has made up his mind. The time taken is noted and then the subject dictates as full an account as he can of what has been happening in his mind, the experimenter meanwhile carefully studying the way in which this account is given, the subject's hesitations, degree of certainty, and so forth. After a great deal of careful practice it becomes much more easy to notice what happens than the reader may suppose.

Images. The result of the best of these studies is to show that images are not the essential ingredients of thinking, and the same conclusion applies also to words, the other definite and easily recognizable entities which have been suggested as what we are really talking about when we speak of ideas. Quite often the thinking is finished before any words have come into the mind and a definite search for suitable words follows. But a failure to understand may give rise to a need for words in order to formulate the difficulty more clearly. And the same applies to images when the problem concerns concrete things that we are accustomed to handle and look at. Briefly, words and images are invaluable *helps* in thinking; they are not necessary to it.

It is important to realize that individuals differ enormously in the type of image they employ. One man will use predominantly visual images (though many who think they are visualizers are really making use of eye-movements); another, auditory; another, kinæsthetic—*i.e.*, images of movements of the limbs and trunk. Indeed, every sensation may have its corresponding imagery, and organic sensations, which, as we shall see, play a great part in emotion, may also be represented. What are sometimes referred to as verbal images are of course only images of words and not a special type of image; they may be of three kinds, visual (as when we see a printed or written word in the mind's eye), auditory (as when we hear an imagined voice), or motor (as when we have an image corresponding to the sensations which accompany speech). It is found in aphasia that injuries to the brain may sometimes cause grave disabilities in one form of verbal imagery, though not in the others. Some people are reported to have no images at all. The usual case is for one type to be predominant, though not to the exclusion of the others. The point is of practical importance, since it is of little use to appeal to a person of a primarily auditory type by means of diagrams or metaphors deriving from vision. All forms of imagery tend to be heightened at the onset of sleep, and this may be connected with the fact that vivid imagery is more frequent in childhood. The vividness of dream images may be a result of regression or a return to the state of our early years (cf. Chapters VIII and XV).

Attitudes. But the rest of the conscious happenings which take place in thinking are far less easy to describe: a sense of the end to be reached, a sense of the direction in which the thought is moving, a sense of orientation, of our whereabouts, senses of novelty and familiarity and of reality, of ease and difficulty, of the relations between our thoughts, and a variety of attitudes towards the stages of the thinking, towards the problem and the answer. These and many more such things are reported. We can recognize them easily enough in most of our thinking. Some of them belong rather to the conative and affective aspects of experience than to the cognitive (cf. Chapter XI). But to understand what kind of thing they are is not easy. As Binet wrote: "Further researches have chiefly brought into evidence our ignorance," and at present from the standpoint of introspection we can but humbly accept this conclusion.

This incurable elusiveness of thinking is the reason why so many have fallen back upon imagery, the least slippery of introspective data, as the key to the matter. Thinking somehow is a mode of manipulating representations of the world. Perhaps we use images even when we can't detect them? But plainly, such a suggestion can only be considered in the last resort.

Representation. It is worth while looking more closely at what representation involves. It is tempting to suppose that the only way in which one thing (a mental event, for example) can represent another (a lobster, perhaps) is by resembling it. Accordingly, many philosophers have made resemblance, identity of structure, fundamental for the explanation of how our ideas come to be *of* things. "We make for ourselves pictures of facts," says Wittgenstein in his famous *Tractatus Logico-Philosophicus*. "The picture is a model of reality." But is this resemblance really necessary? The instances we gave in the last chapter of the indirect ways in which we take cognizance of space are enough to make it very doubtful. The movement of a klaxon down the street and the reflexes through which we notice it seem to have no very obvious identity of structure. And in fact the more closely we study the processes by which we perceive things the less plausible is it to suppose that they are necessarily reflections or models of the things. Yet in some sense they represent these things. What is this sense? The answer seems to be that our mental events represent things not through being models or reflections of them, but by being the effects in us of contact with them.

The point at issue may appear a little obscure, but the question is really very simple and, like many simple questions, it is of fundamental importance. What is the link between our minds and the world in virtue of which our thoughts are about the world, are thoughts *of* things, not merely isolated happenings in our minds? In other words, *what is knowing?* If we can answer this question, the rest of our account of thinking is an easier matter. For thinking is merely the testing and manipulation of knowledge in the service of our purposes.

Until recently, views on this basic problem have usually been minor varieties of one opinion. And this has amounted to saying that the problem is insoluble, or that it is not a psychological problem. The relation of our thoughts to the things they are of has been said to be an unique and ultimate relation. It has been called the 'subject-object relation,' it has been named 'awareness,' 'cognition,' or 'apprehension'; or the thing has been said to be 'presented' to the mind. But this is merely to name the problem, not to attack it. A reader opening most of the standard classical works on psychology for the first time will experience unnecessary bewilderment and disappointment when he looks for an answer to this question. And yet some sort of an answer may reasonably be expected. After all, we are thinking about things most of our lives. We ought to be able to give some account of how we do it.

The simplest form of thinking about things is perceiving them, and this we have already described above. The next most obvious form is imagining them, through reproducing the mental events which occurred in perception. In both these forms of thinking the significant relation between the mental event (the perceiving or the imagining) and the thing perceived or imagined is that the thing is the principal cause, in a way which we can trace, of the mental event. The thought is of *this* thing rather than *that* because it is *caused* by this thing, not by that. Because it is a *response* to this thing, not to that. A flash of lightning causes in us an experience. How it does so we know in outline. The view which is gaining ground is that this causal connection between the flash and the perceiving of it *is* the knowing relation itself. But it has often been held that the causal connection is only the *condition* of the knowing, that when it holds another relation of quite a different kind mysteriously arises, namely, the presentation of the flash to the mind. If something further could be said about this alleged relation, the case for it would be stronger. It may be suspected that such accounts are due to a disguised persistence of the view, common in children and primitive peoples, that to think of something is in some way to direct an influence upon it; partly also perhaps to presumptuous man's reluctance to accept the operations of the mind as natural facts, to his preference for regarding the mind as in some sense outside nature. It is one of the merits of Behaviorism, of the psychology of 'stimulus and response,' that it has helped greatly to stress the causal view of knowing.

We have seen how, through retention (Chapters III and IV), we come to react to situations which are not present. Thinking about absent things is essentially reacting as though they were not absent. As Rignano[1] rightly says, thinking is experimentation. It is a process of experimenting not with things, but with their mental representatives. And these representatives are ideas. Ideas will include images as a special sub-class, and also words in some cases, when we are dealing with topics very familiar to us, for instance; in such cases, if only the words are occurring, Watson's account of thinking as sub-vocal talking would clearly appiy.[2] But as a rule

[1] *The Psychology of Reasoning* (1923). Rignano lays great stress upon *imaginary* experiments; and, with the proviso that actual images need not be involved in them, his account is very clear and helpful.

[2] Two questions must always be distinguished: (1) What are the happenings in us when we think? and (2) What is the link between these happenings and the things which they are of? We should

words only represent things through other ideas. The majority of the processes in our minds which represent things, and so are ideas, are probably neither images nor words.

Emotional Representation. In some cases, with certain types, though rarely with those engaged in intellectual activities, the representing idea may be an emotion, a feeling, or a mood. Primitive men, and probably animals, classify and distinguish between objects less by means of representations of them in the strict sense than by revivals of emotions to which they have given rise. These emotive classifications are the germ of all thought and we tend constantly to fall back upon them, in what, for example, are known as 'intuitive' judgments of people's personalities. We often judge a new acquaintance to be 'sly,' less from any namable characters of his appearance or behavior than through the emotion which he arouses. We use the emotion as a sign, overlooking, as far as consciousness goes, the signs which were of course, necessary for the emotion to arise. We shall see in the next chapter, in connection with the autonomic nervous system, how these very subtle intuitive responses are brought about. Similarly we often think of absent persons in terms of the feeling we have for them. It is hardly necessary to point out that such thinking, apart from the fact that it

---

remember that this link is as a rule very indirect. A good deal of mathematics is a way of thinking by means of symbols about operations with symbols that stand only for general aspects of things with which ordinary observation deals, of course less successfully, in other ways.

cannot be developed by means of verbal symbols, is highly elusive and variable, though often capable of great delicacy and penetration.

Association. We may now go back to Mr. Babbitt and his account, correct so far as it goes of what we do with our ideas when we think. First as to how we get them together. This is what is known as the *association* of ideas. The classical doctrine was that the ruling principle here is contiguity. If two ideas have occurred together in the past, or if the sources of them, our contacts with the things which they represent, were originally together, then the one will tend to be accompanied again by the other. This is the obvious consequence of retention as we studied it in Chapter III, and it admittedly plays a great part. Other things being equal, contiguity rules; but, as later work has shown, other things never are equal. Contiguity operates only subject to the guidance of interest. If we are thinking about golf, the ideas which are associated with the idea of grass will be quite different from those which will gather if we are thinking about Nebuchadnezzar. The governing principle in association is the direction of interest, and contiguity only works inside this principle. Clearness and consecutiveness of thinking, in other words, depends primarily upon clearness in our interests. Perhaps most of the blunders of thought are due to confused and mixed interests. The extraordinary views of many demented persons can be traced to eccentricities of their interests.

We may consider two typical failures in thinking

from this point of view, the undue persistence of an irrelevant set of ideas and the failure to hit on the relevant idea even when it ought to be obvious. The first usually springs from an intrusion of interests which have nothing to do with the situation; the second either from a weakness of the relevant interest or from the same kind of cause as the first. For whatever we may be thinking about on any occasion it is fairly certain that our interests will be far more mixed than we suppose. Now each of our interests acts in a twofold way. It facilitates some processes and inhibits others. And stupidity in the form of overlooking the obvious key-idea of the situation, that distressing but familiar complaint from which we all suffer so constantly, is chiefly a matter of the inhibition of this key-idea by some interest which may be influencing us quite unawares.

Some of the phenomena of forgetting names are illuminating here. We shall understand them better when we have discussed in Chapter XV how the mind goes wrong, but it will be helpful to allude to them now. We often find ourselves forgetting one name out of a group, it may even be the name we are most familiar with among them. This seems inexplicable until perhaps we notice, after looking it up, that a minute or two later we are slightly depressed and going over in our minds irksome thoughts of things not done or of occasions when we made fools of ourselves. Then we notice, perhaps, that the name is similar in sound to the name of a central figure in these irksome reflections.

These bizarre twists illustrate the very indirect ways in which our interests can interfere with one another. And a great many of our more puzzling momentary and localized stupidities may be put down to this cause. People very commonly refuse to form new ideas rather owing to the discomfort the ideas would produce than through any real intellectual difficulty. But general stupidity, like forgetting, has wider sources. Apart from gross physiological causes—fever, fatigue, and the like—it may come from insufficient experience and familiarity with the right kinds of situation. We handle our ideas of things much as we handle the things themselves, and no one can be expected to work out in thought what is wrong with a car if he has never had much to do with cars.

Concepts. In addition to the thinking that is a recapitulation, as it were, of the concrete handling of things, there is another, a higher order of thinking, abstract or conceptual thinking as it may be called; and individuals differ in this even more than they do in the simpler kind of thinking.

We saw in the preceding chapter that we can recognize a chair even when it is seen from an unfamiliar angle. There must be a structure in the mind by which it recognizes not this or that particular sensory pattern, but any one of a vast range of patterns which are indifferently taken for the chair. Similarly going a stage higher, we have structures which recognize not this or that chair, but any chair; and, higher still, a piece of furniture as such.

This hierarchy of higher and higher co-ordinating perceptual structures is paralleled in thinking. Our particular *ideas* of individual cars stand to our general idea or 'concept' of a car just as the particular sensory patterns which the chair may present stand to our recognition of it as the chair. The concept is a higher level co-ordinating structure which responds indifferently to any one of an indefinitely large range of particular representations. And it may in abstract thinking operate in conjunction with other concepts without the aid of any *particular* representations at all. When this abstract thinking gets into difficulties we fall back upon particular representations, often in the form of images, in order to see where we are going wrong, just as we look again at the chair if for any reason our first recognition of it seems to be misleading us. We climb down from our higher level, so to speak.

People differ enormously in the level at which they think most successfully and in the degree to which they develop these higher structures and can get ahead without constant recourse to particular representations. Great practical success, as with many business men, engineers, and doctors, is possible without abstract ideas or concepts. For success in the wider understanding of things, however, they are indispensable and they offer innumerable short cuts even in the most practical matters. But, as is well known, short cuts have their dangers and the theorist who cannot climb down and get back to facts and instances soon becomes a lost man.

The Influence of Language on Thought. Most abstract thinking tends easily to wander. Thus a concrete record, plan, or scheme of its steps is invaluable to it. This it is one of the main functions of language to provide, though not, as we have seen (Chapter IX), its primary or original function. Words strung together give a kind of mechanical model of thinking. In the case of mathematics, which by starting from the simplest aspects of things has become the most developed form of abstract thinking, the words, the symbolism, employed to represent the steps and stages of the thinking have become nearly perfect. But ordinary language is a comparatively crude representation of thinking. This is partly because it has other simultaneous jobs to do as well. It reflects the thinker's attitudes to things as well as his thoughts about them, and it is bent and twisted throughout in the interests of communication. For language, in addition to serving the thinker himself, is used in order to make other people go through the same thinking processes. The troubles which this entails are unending.[1] The moral for all discussion is that we should not mistake the verbal formulation for the thought itself, and should remember that it is always at best an imperfect representation of it.

There is another aspect of this influence of language upon thought which should be mentioned.

[1] For a discussion of these aspects of language see the author's *The Meaning of Meaning*, pp. 358-360; also Richards, *Principles of Literary Criticism*, p. 261.

It is often said[1] that we get many of our concepts given us ready-made by language. We should notice that this is only a loose and superficial way of talking. We get the words, but the thoughts in connection with which we use them are our own achievement, helped, of course, immensely by intercourse with others. A very great number of our words and forms of speech we use without any corresponding concepts. We make a purely conventional use of them, uttering them on the same sorts of occasions as other people do, and without thought. But when we do think with them our thinking is the product of our own experience carried up to one level or another; and thus the thoughts of people using the same words may be, as we are always painfully discovering, very different. It would be convenient if concepts could be acquired ready-made in this fashion, but actually they have to be arrived at by more arduous means. Educators in particular should never forget that to give the language is one thing and to cause corresponding concepts to be developed is quite another.

Thinking is often described in terms of beliefs, judgments, propositions, assumptions, hypotheses, and arguments.[2] A belief would by many schools be

---

[1] *E.g.*, H. Delacroix, "La plus grand partie de nos concepts nous arrive toute formée par le langage," in *Traité de Psychologie*, ii, p. 127.

[2] How psychology may be treated by the very acute thinkers who have favored the logical and mathematical approaches will be gathered from the work of Meinong, *Über Annahmen*, part i, chap. i, (cf. Urban, *Valuation*), or from Professor Moore's *Philosophical Studies*, chap. ii.

described as a group of ideas united by an act of judgment which predicates some of these ideas of others, thus forming a proposition, which as a whole is asserted. The stringing together of such assertions would constitute argument or discursive thought. This type of analysis is usually encountered in the introductory chapters of treatises on logic. It has a long and distinguished history, since the discussion of the thought processes in a narrow sense and in almost complete separation from the other aspects of mental activity, made up until comparatively recently the major part of psychology. For some of the logician's special purposes it has its advantages, but it presents an essentially artificial view of thinking. As so often in psychology, the distinctions which are convenient for one purpose are misleading, unless they can be reinterpreted, for another. We have refused throughout these pages to regard ideas, images, or perceptions as entities independent of the activities in the course of which they arise. We must treat judgments, beliefs, propositions and hypotheses in the same fashion. The difference then between a belief or a proposition which is accepted and asserted and one which is merely entertained, supposed, or assumed, is, apart from differences in the belief feelings which we discuss in the next chapter, a difference in the way in which we use them. They are groups of ideas which are formed in the service of our interests. They are ways in which our interests are working themselves out. A settled belief is an arrangement of ideas which in a certain field of occasions is going to be used to control action. Provisional beliefs, hypotheses, and assumptions are arrangements which are being experimented with, on a large or on a small scale. The difference is paralleled exactly in our handling of objects, even in cases where no reflection and no consciousness intervene. We handle liquids and solids, for example, quite differently; and our most settled beliefs are those which correspond to such routines of daily experience and behavior.

Any such functional group of ideas as a belief or a proposition has, of course, an intricate internal structure: these units of thought may take all the forms which experience suggests and, in mathematics, for example, new forms which only prolonged experimentation could have evolved. Many of these patterns of thought are indirectly represented in grammar. Compare 'He will come' with 'He may come.' But grammar is nearly always ambiguous. The difference here may be in the group of ideas itself, a looser structure in the second example; or it may lie not in the group of ideas, but in our attitude to it as a whole, to 'his coming' as a unit, the same in both cases. To take another pair of examples. Much controversy has raged round the question whether the 'time-element' in 'He fell' and 'He will fall' is in the 'proposition' (i.e., in psychological language, the group of ideas) or in our attitude to it. It is possible to be extraordinarily subtle over the point in the language of 'propositions' and 'propositional functions'—the language of mathematical logic—but it seems unlikely on general grounds that the mind is incapable of handling the difference in both ways. In all such problems of analysis everything depends, of course, upon our purpose and the context in which we make the assertion.

The logical analysis of thinking, then, is neither a rival to nor in conflict with the psychological, though it may often seem to be so. Here, as constantly in psychology, we have to deal with what amounts to a double or triple staffing of the system—if we may compare the ideas by which we think about mental happenings with the personnel which directs a railway. It would be very inconvenient to have two or more staffs looking after the same branch line if their aims were, as here, divergent, and it seems reasonable that the special interests and conceptions of the logicians should give way to the more general claims of psychology. They will in the end lose nothing by so doing.

We must now turn to consider the emotional side of life. As we have suggested, much of the difficulty and confusion of thinking is only explicable when we take account of this other aspect of our mental activities.

CHAPTER XIV: EMOTION AND CHARACTER

Our emotions are the most obscure part of our lives, and, as might be expected, the theory of emotion is the most backward part of psychology. This is the reason for postponing detailed consideration of it to so late a stage, not any minor or secondary importance of the emotional aspect of experience and behavior. On the contrary, the history of a life is a history of interests rather than of ideas; and, if we could follow it closely enough, we should find that an understanding of the emotional situation was at every turn the key to the rest. Moreover, it is on his emotional organization that a man's character essentially depends.

Emotional Reverberation. A surprising amount is known already about the phenomena of emotion and the difficulty is less due to a lack of data than to indecision as to what is to be called cause and what effect among these phenomena. Let us examine first the theory around which most recent discussion has revolved. This is the celebrated Lange-James hypothesis of organic resonance, so called after the two adherents who first brought it into prominence.

In fear, the perception of an alarming object, or of an alarming change in the situation, is followed not only by characteristic action, but by an extensive agitation all through the body. Changes take place in the digestive, respiratory, glandular, and circulatory organs. Our hair stands on end, we blush or grow pale, we sweat, our pupils dilate, our digestive canal is paralyzed, our pulse quickens, and so forth. Most of these changes are brought about through the agency of the sympathetic nervous system. This is a part of what is known as the 'involuntary' or 'autonomic' nervous system, which looks after our vegetative life and sees to the co-ordinations required in order that our internal organs shall work together. It is partially independent of the central or 'voluntary' nervous system which we discussed in Chapters III-V; but the degree of this independence is disputed. The supplementary diagram in Figure II shows the relationship between the spinal roots and the sympathetic chain.

The Sympathetic System. The involuntary system is composed of three sections. There is a 'cranial' section whence a nerve supply is distributed to the heart, lungs, stomach, and intestines, to the arteries of the salivary glands, to the muscles which contract the pupil of the eye and to the tear glands. Parallel to part of the spinal cord there are two chains of ganglia (one of these chains appears in Fig. II) running down parallel with the spinal cord, and distributing a nerve supply to these same organs; to the liver, spleen etc.; to visceral and peripheral arteries; to the smooth muscles which move the hairs; to the adrenal glands; perhaps to the skeletal muscles; and also to the colon, the bladder, the arteries of the external genitals, and the internal genitals:

this nervous organization makes up the 'sympathetic' system. Thirdly, there is the 'sacral' section which supplies more directly this last set (colon, etc.). The cranial and sacral sections together are as a rule antagonistic to the sympathetic in their effects; their positive influence is spoken of as 'vagotonic', while that of the sympathetic is called 'sympatheticotonic.' Thus "the cranial supply to the eye contracts the pupil, the sympathetic dilates it; the cranial slows the heart, the sympathetic accelerates it; the sacral contracts the lower part of the large intestine, the sympathetic relaxes it; the sacral relaxes the exit from the bladder, the sympathetic contracts it."[1] The relation between the two is thus somewhat similar to that between the nerve supplies to antagonistic muscles, flexors and extensors in the leg, for example, and there are probably arrangements for reciprocal inhibition in the brain. But the sympathetic usually wins in a struggle between them. The cranial and sacral sections in general promote fairly specific reactions in the organs they serve; their neurones go directly to ganglia in or near to these organs: but the sympathetic system promotes very diffused and widespread reactions; the neurones which leave the spinal cord go to ganglia close to it whence diverge other ('post-ganglionic') fibers in all directions.

One further point should be mentioned to make this sketch sufficiently complete for our purposes. Among the organs supplied by the sympathetic system alone are two small bodies in front of the kidneys,

[1] Cannon, *Bodily Changes in Pain, Hunger, Fear, and Rage*, p. 34.

the adrenal glands to which reference was made above. These secrete and discharge into the blood-stream a substance known as adrenalin which, in extraordinarily minute amounts, has, when carried by the blood to organs innervated by the sympathetic, precisely the same effect as if they were receiving nervous impulses from the sympathetic. By this mechanism the power of the sympathetic is enormously increased. But adrenalin produces other effects as well, of which the most important is a facilitation of the supply of fuel to the muscles and of the rebuilding of chemical compounds broken down in muscular work. Thus this liberation of adrenalin through the action of the sympathetic explains both the increased exertion possible in emotional excitement and the reduction of fatigue.

We rarely appreciate the extent and complexity of the autonomic reactions that are constantly occurring in our normal daily life. In sudden emotional shocks, they are fairly evident; but it is not easy to realize that our internal organic economy undergoes marked variations as our gaze wanders from the clouds to the daisies on the lawn. If the subject be suitably connected with a galvanometer it is found that his resistance varies with changes in his affective condition. This gives us a new and very delicate method of exploring his emotional reactions.[1] The emotional effects of colors and musical notes, so dif-

[1] See Whately Smith, *The Measurement of Emotion* (1922), for a recent discussion of the problems raised by this 'psycho-galvanic reflex,' based on 45,000 observations.

ficult to explain, must probably be traced to these reflex organic resonances. In fact, as the subtler, less easily described effects of our surroundings upon consciousness show, this ever-present background of organic sensibilty (the cœnæsthesia, as it is called) is one of the most important factors in our lives. It is the basis of our feelings of familiarity and strangeness, and plays a great part in orientating us in all our daily affairs. Violent disturbances of it, due to gross physiological causes, seem to have much to do with some forms of insanity, in which the patient may complain, for example, that he is made of glass or full of frogs, and spend much time endeavoring to explain his strange state by many extravagant suppositions and beliefs. It has been suggested further—for example, by Smith Ely Jelliffe—that electrical, climatic, or other influences may act directly upon the autonomic system, so that it can be regarded as a "receptor and transformer of cosmic energy." [1]

Criticism of the Theory of Organic Resonance. We can now return to the Lange-James hypothesis. This was that the emotions, at least the coarser of them, were made up of the effects in consciousness of these changes in the working of the organs brought about by the involuntary nervous system and principally by the sympathetic. The perception of the

[1] Dr. Crookshank comments upon this: "His suggestion is a bold, valuable, and illuminating one. It gives us a physiological link between man and the universe," apart from the ordinary senses. *Influenza*, Essays by Several Authors, p. 505.

alarming object, in the case of fear, activates the sympathetic through its connections with the central nervous system; and the resultant changes reported through the afferent channels of the central voluntary system in the form of organic sensations were supposed to make up the body of the emotion.

It must be acknowledged that these organic sensations do make up a good deal of our experience in emotion. On the other hand, there are reasons for denying that they form the whole emotion or that the differences between our various emotions can be traced to differences in these organic reverberations. In the first place, the organic changes taking place in all violent emotions are very similar. Rage and fear have similar organic conditions, and these again are hardly distinguishable from those elicited by intense pain. Yet as experiences the three are markedly different, though less so as they grow more intense. James himself limited his theory to these coarser emotions. The subtler, more intellectual emotions "affect us with a pleasure that seems ingrained in the very form of the representation itself, and to borrow nothing from any reverberation surging up from the parts below the brain."[1] He considered, however, that they might gain a reinforcement, an added brilliance and solidity, from these secondary sources.

But there is, even for the coarser emotions, some evidence against organic sensations as the essential constituents. This comes from two sources: experi-

[1] *Principles of Psychology*, vol. ii, p. 468.

mental physiology and clinical observation. A puppy only nine weeks old continues to show signs of emotional excitement even after its brain is disconnected from all the body except the head and shoulders.[1] In older dogs we might suppose that images or other cerebral representations of visceral changes were in action, but in so young a puppy this seems improbable. On the other hand, we have no proof that the puppy feels any emotion; we only know that it acts as though it does. But it might well do so without any consciousness at all. The other evidence is that human patients whose spinal cords have been divided so that their bodies are completely paralyzed and insensitive, may retain their whole emotional range and show no abnormalities.[2] But here representations of former visceral reverberations may well be sufficient. Neither kind of evidence, then, is conclusive.

The result of this discussion is that the distinctive features which make an emotional experience so totally unlike any non-emotional experience are probably due to organic reverberations, and to representations of the effects of such reverberations in the past. We can feel an emotion without any visceral disturbance, but this is only because we have formerly undergone these disturbances; and the subtler emotions may differ from the coarser in being composed of imagery rather than sensations. So far, then, the Lange-James hypothesis may be ac-

[1] Cannon, *op. cit.*, p. 281.
[2] J. MacCurdy, *The Psychology of Emotion* (1925), p. 51.

cepted, but we should not conclude that these organic disturbances and representations of them are the whole story of an emotion. There is much more to be added.

The Disguise of the Organic Response. One important addition is fairly obvious. In an emotion the organic disturbance is not necessarily recognized for what it is. Or to put it the other way round, when it is recognized the emotion is changed and, it may be, dissipated. Most people have noticed the brusque transition from an emotion to a neutral awareness of gooseflesh, trembling, sickness, breathlessness, and so on, which sometimes happens. It is a commonplace that we can show all the signs of fear without actually experiencing fear, the emotion. We may note the signs ourselves and say: "How curious! I seem to be afraid, but I am not." A good instance is a sudden 'appalling' noise which we recognize instantly as nothing that we need bother about. Shortly afterwards the whole organic reaction ensues, with its leaping pulse, its shivers down the backbone, and the rest of it. But *then* these phenomena appear as what they are and have no tinge of the genuine thrill of fear. Certain bad actors and actresses in particular can cause us violent visceral perturbations, yet we remain *emotionally* quite unmoved.

Projection. A great deal of our experience undergoes, as it occurs, a peculiar and very important transformation. Instead of seeming to be where its neural counterpart is, it appears from the first to be out in the external world whence the stimulus to which it is due originates. Visual objects and ordinary sounds, for example, we irresistibly locate outside us. This process is known as *projection.* But very low or very shrill noises may seem in comparison to be in the ear, and the pain of a pin-prick is very definitely in us, not in the pin. No projection takes place. Intermediate cases occur with perceptions of warmth and cold. Sometimes it is we who are hot, sometimes the sun. An especially interesting case is that of movements. A dizzy man with eyes open sees the world revolving, with eyes shut he himself revolves. Now it has been pointed out, by Lipps and others, that very much of our perception of forms, notably of architectural forms, involves projection either of slight movements of our own or of images of such movements. Thus a mountain rises and a steeple soars. Actually we do not doubt that it remains stationary, but our projected movements lend it a curious and important appearance of life and movement. This special form of projection is known as Empathy or Einfühlung.

The difference, then, between an emotion and a mere organic disturbance is in part in the degree of projection. Chimpanzees, we saw, when in emotion, tend to do *something*, no matter what, in the direction of the object which has moved them. It is reasonable to take this as a sign of projection. In ourselves, emotions are nearly always projected. We think of the emotion which a picture causes us as a character of it, namely its beauty, much as we assume the perception of red which it may cause in us to be a redness in some part of it. In the same way we tend, unless very sophisticated, to regard all the objects of our emotions as possessing qualities which, when we look more closely into the matter, we find to be merely projections of our own reactions. Such qualities are nobility, splendor, niceness, ugliness, and rhythm. Sometimes, as in these cases, we have independent names for them. Sometimes we use names which derive from the names of our reactions —pleasant, disgusting, charming, hateful, appalling. In both cases the fact of projection makes an immense difference to our response, not only as an organic reverberation, but in the ways in which we behave towards the object.

Incipient Action. Besides the organic discharge, or the representation of it, there is in every emotion another set of effects. The perception which gives rise to the emotion instigates a process of preparation for action. We have only to watch a baseball crowd to see how at every crisis the spectators more or less unwittingly get ready themselves to do what they hope will be done. And even when we cannot actually observe these preliminary settings of the muscles for action there is reason to suppose that very extensive processes of preparation take place at higher levels. These higher level settings, totally different in the case of fear and rage, for example, seem very largely to make the difference between the emotions; for they govern our responses and, when we do not go so far as overt action, they are our response. Thus the difference between being frightened and being made merely to quiver may be largely a matter of the extent to which our response develops.

Conflict and Emotion. But here we come across a striking fact which again shows how complex emotional phenomena must be. When our response is complete, instantaneous and unimpeded, we have no emotional experience at all. We step out of the way of a car without a qualm. When we know what to do and can do it at once we feel nothing. And this is so even when the chances of destruction remain very high. So long as there is something definite to be done we are free from fear. And to a large extent this is so with all the emotions. The lover's agitation takes on a much more moderate tone as soon as he is assured of acceptance. The Corsican bandit in the bush sights his piece at an enemy with a dispassionate eye, being assured both of escape and of approbation. It seems certain that some degree of conflict between rival tendencies, rival responses to the situation, is required for the full development of emotion. The experience of all who are familiar with dangerous situations, notably the experience of the soldier, is conclusive as regards fear. So that McDougall is not quite correct in dismissing, as merely "a curious dogma,"[1] the opinion that a conflict of tendencies is involved in all emotion.

Pathological emotions strongly support this conclusion. Most people have known fears, angers, attractions, feelings of tenderness, of wonder, of be-

[1] *An Outline of Psychology* (1923), p. 329.

wilderment, and of gaiety, which seemed quite ungrounded and inexplicable in view of the facts of the situation. And though some of these emotional *moods* are more easily accounted for, as due, for example, to the weather or to an oncoming attack of influenza, the extreme emotional aberrations of neurotics can often only be explained as due to such mental conflicts; and frequently these conflicts can actually be discovered. A striking example can be taken from Morton Prince's celebrated case of alternating personality or co-consciousness, 'Miss Beauchamp.' The patient had a number of separate personalities, two of which concern us here, B I and B IV.

"An emotion," writes Prince, "apparently paradoxical, would be aroused in B IV in connection with a strange person or place. . . . The memories of the experiences to which these emotions belonged were a part of B I's life and could easily be recalled by her when the personalities again alternated and B I came into existence."[1] But B I showed less emotion than B IV in connection with these experiences. Innumerable other cases might be instanced in which a morbid fear, due not to the actual present situation, but to forgotten experiences, is lessened or removed entirely when these experiences are brought to mind. Now what does this bringing to mind involve?

The Unconscious. Here we are confronted by the problem of the unconscious. We have seen, however, that of all the processes which are occurring in our

[1] *The Unconscious*, p. 385.

brains at any moment, only a small part is accompanied by consciousness; and it seems but a natural supposal that the unconscious consists of the rest. There seem, further, to be no good reasons for thinking that these unconscious processes differ very greatly in themselves from those which are conscious. There must, of course, be some very important difference, but what it is there is no means at present of knowing. Perhaps the best suggestion is that it is a difference, not in the nature of the processes, but in their systematic relationships.

In these cases of pathological forgetting, when a hidden activity seems to be interfering with the main stream, notably by causing groundless emotion, and yet cannot be readily made conscious, the unconscious activity is said to be *repressed.* We shall discuss repression in the following chapter. Here we need only note that the repressing agent is probably the successful activity itself; though it is not necessarily aware that it is repressing anything. Repression is the inhibition or partial inhibition of one activity by another. The repressed activity is inhibited either because it is now, or has been at some past time, incompatible with the inhibiting activity. If it were allowed free access to the final common paths we should be behaving differently. Our actual behavior cuts it out, but often the inhibition is incomplete; the repressed activity in part gets through, characteristically as groundless emotion, and if we are right in tracing emotion to a conflict of tendencies, it is not surprising that the emotion due to repressed tendencies is often intense. But the emotional effects of the interplay of incompatible tendencies are far more varied than this account so far would suggest. The baffled tendency does not necessarily give consciousness the emotional tinge which it would evoke if allowed more freedom. A 'forbidden' activity which, if it were successful, would cause a predominantly pleasant emotion, may, when defeated, lead to an emotion of anxiety. It is as though the danger which it offers to the triumphant activities were the source of the emotion. And in fact these activities are, in the measure in which the repressed tendency is strong, in a state of insecurity. We may often misinterpret this sense of anxiety, supposing, for example, that it is due to the dangers of modern traffic when actually it springs from the partial success of Potiphar's wife.

The causes of our emotions are, it follows, not always so obvious as they often appear. It is a commonplace that joys spring from the temporary rout of distresses, and there is reason to suppose that this is true in a deeper sense. For the normal condition of the mind is one of strain, a great number of tendencies being with difficulty repressed. The characteristic condition of elation is one in which either a very complete momentary triumph of some group of impulses has taken place—possibly after a sudden resolve which may lead either to a conversion or to a debauch—or in which there has been a reorganization of the mind which gives hitherto repressed tendencies a new means of co-operating with their former opponents. In the one case a swing of the pendulum is taking place; in the other the pendulum has been rehung.

Belief and Doubt. It remains to discuss two other topics which less evidently come under the heading of emotional phenomena. One of these includes belief, doubt, prejudice, and so forth; the other, deliberation, resolve, and the fluctuations of the will. As experiences all these are essentially emotional. We often say that a man holds such and such beliefs, is skeptical in such and such matters, or that he is bigoted, determined, irresolute, or changeable, when we do not thereby intend to describe his experience, but merely to indicate his typical ways of behaving. In these cases we are referring to the more or less permanent dispositions which determine what he will do, and these dispositions may operate without any awareness on his part. Many beliefs in this sense are formed without any feeling accompaniment. We saw in Chapter XI that cognition, feeling, and conation are not separable aspects of experience. Similarly, a disposition must be regarded as having the same three aspects, though which aspect is most prominent will, of course, vary with the whole state of mind. Some psychologists speak of conative dispositions and cognitive dispositions as though they were quite independent facts of structure. This is a confusing usage due to the effects of an artificial and obsolete schematization.

As dispositions our beliefs are unconscious, and since they may operate without our awareness we find that many doubts and decisions are also unconscious. But when we analyze the states of consciousness known by these names we find that the distinctive character of a crisis of belief or doubt is a feeling, of the same general kind as joy, for example, or fear, though unique in flavor. Expectation, bare assent, and familiarity are examples of such belief-feelings. They are generally less intense than emotions, although pathological forms of doubt and ecstatic belief are not infrequent. Both seem able to occur in cases where there is nothing definite which is either doubted or believed. In the nitrous oxide and mescal exaltations, for example, anything can be believed to a degree of intensity which quite overshadows waking conviction;[1] and in doubting manias everything can be doubted. The patient may sometimes even doubt whether he exists.

It may be added that the intensity of the belief-feeling is no criterion of the permanence of the disposition which it leaves behind. Many people who experience the most intense beliefs are also the most changeable and instable in their convictions. As a rule in such cases and in normal life, the belief or doubt feelings are very subtly interwoven with the other emotions. We rarely believe strongly unless some emotion—it may be joy or fear, pride or humility—is reinforcing the belief. And doubt, more evidently, perhaps, is commonly dependent upon a prior clash of interests and a resultant emotion.

---

[1] Cf. Leuba, *The Psychology of Religious Mysticism* (1925), pp. 27, 274-275.

But if these intellectual feelings spring from other emotions they also give rise to them, since they modify so fundamentally the course of our responses. Strong belief is almost always the sign of the triumph of some important interest. It may be a grounded triumph in the case of a Galileo and his pendulum, or an ungrounded triumph as with an inebriate and his lamp-post. Even skepticism is for many people a source of infinite ironic delight.

Deliberation and Resolve. The experiences of deliberation and resolve are plainly very similar to beliefs and doubts. Doubt is a special form of irresolution. We may, it is true, 'make up our minds' and form a resolve without any definite belief, either that we are following the best course or that the situation requires it; but supporting beliefs very commonly develop. And such beliefs, when they are due to our being already involved in a line of action with a certain amount of our energy and time invested in it, rather than to evidence, are typical prejudices. As we shall see in the next chapter, the majority of our prejudices are unconscious; whence the notorious difficulty of proving to anyone that he is prejudiced.

The Sentiments. The majority of adult emotions arise only in connection with what are known technically as the sentiments. A sentiment is a group of interests organized around a set of objects or ideas. Typical instances are friendships, antipathies, the self-regarding sentiment, and the sentiment of patriotism. The interests making up a sentiment may be very varied and thus the result of any promise or threat to one of them will not be uniform, but will depend upon the momentary condition of the others. The sentiments are for the most part made up of the conscious interests. The others are unconscious because they have failed to fit in with any of our avowed sentiments—do not help, as it were, to form a sentimental *gestalt*. Hence the unconscious interests tend to be isolated and comparatively chaotic. Sometimes, however, a conflict between sentiments, common in childhood, may occur. Then, if the rivalry cannot be solved by a reorganization of one or other or both of them, a whole group of interests may be repressed. Such repressed sentiments, and sentiments which in general are out of accord with the main body of sentiments which makes up the character, are known as *complexes*. With these we shall be more concerned in the following chapter.

CHAPTER XV: HOW THE MIND GOES WRONG

Character and the Unconscious. By a man's 'character' at any time we may mean either his dominant sentiments and beliefs or the whole system of all his sentiments and complexes, conscious and unconscious alike, the entire organization of his dispositions. This last is perhaps better named his personality.[1] Obviously in both senses character changes, but in the narrower sense the changes are apt to be particularly sudden and bewildering. Change a man's social environment and he will often behave like another man.

It is clearly impossible to describe or even to mention all the multitudinous strands which make up a character. Yet by taking only one of the main strands and studying its origins and vicissitudes we can gain an insight into the ways in which the whole vastly more complex system develops. And for this purpose we may take with advantage the most important set of trends in human personality, the sexual interests. They are also the interests about which in recent years most has been learned.

Sudden advances in knowledge usually have their

[1] A discussion which brings out the physiological and psychical bases of character particularly well will be found in *Personality*, by Dr. R. G. Gordon (1925). It contains also one of the least biased accounts of the varieties of psycho-analytic theory which have yet appeared.

dangers. A new principle of explanation for a time throws older hypotheses into shadow. It is not surprising, then, if certain psycho-analysts have rather overworked their explanations, which, although developed chiefly in connection with morbid conditions of mind, have succeeded none the less in revealing a great deal about human nature of which good self-observers were already aware. "Forgetfulness," wrote Nietzsche in 1886, "is no mere *vis inertiæ*, as the superficial believe; rather is it a power of obstruction, active, and, in the strictest sense of the word, positive . . . a very sentinel and nurse of psychic order, repose, and etiquette."[1]

Six years later appeared the first works of Freud in which the theory of repression and transformation was given definite shape. Forel in 1874 had proved the suppression and transformation of instincts in ants, but Freud contended that the suppressed instinct may discharge itself in other forms, and may continue to exhibit itself either in a 'neurosis' or in a 'sublimation'—*i.e.*, a socially approved form of activity.

The Mutual Obstruction of Interests. Colloquially we say of a man suffering from a mental disorder that 'he is all tied up in knots inside,' and this comparison does faithfully represent what in fact has happened. Psycho-analysis, in fact, is essentially a 'jam-probe.'[2] His interests (and we must remember

[1] Cf. Prof. C. Baudouin, "The Evolution of Instinct from the Standpoint of Psycho-analysis," *Psyche*, vol iii, 1922, p. 5.

[2] Anglicé, 'an inquiry into traffic congestion.'

that an interest is an activity springing from a need) instead of allowing smooth and clear passage to one another are in some way mutually obstructive. The working of one is hindering that of others and, it may be, involving activity in others which has nothing to do with the situation and is out of place.

We saw, in describing the growth of the child's mind, that it begins as a system of interests which are very unlike those with which it concludes as a healthy adult. We saw that the infant's view of the world is a reflection of his interests, and the adult's reflection of his. The immense difference in their world pictures corresponds to an equal difference in their interests. Now the most extensive and the most abrupt of the changes in interest occur in early years. Hence the stress which Freud has rightly laid upon infantile experience as a determining cause of later mental life. And further, the most important of the child's interests, and of the adult's, are those which make up the system governing his relations to other human beings. And since he grows up from complete dependence to partial freedom, all the while in peculiarly close contact with his parents, there is nothing surprising in the view that the kind of interest he takes in them and the way this interest changes will have a great influence upon his later life.

The Freudian Theory of Sex. What was surprising and gave the world in general a beneficial shock was Freud's persistence in regarding these interests as sexual. To understand both view and shock we have to remember that the components or germs of a later interest need not be identical with it. Freud saw this, but his alarmed and disgusted critics did not. Instead of assuming that sexual interests appear suddenly from nowhere about the time of adolescence, Freud declared that they were composed of trends which had a continuous history from birth. Naturally enough, early sexual activities differ markedly from later, but, according to Freud, their later trends are determined very largely by this early history and particularly by the precise ways in which the early interests become changed into the later.

We saw (in Chapter X) that according to Watson a very wide range of 'love' phenomena—crowing, chuckling, smiling, affectionateness, etc.—is elicited in the very young infant by patting and stroking it. We saw too, (in Chapter VII) that the sexuality of Köhler's chimpanzees was a much more indefinite affair than adult man's. Any considerable emotional disturbance [1] tended to produce marked signs of sexual excitement and this was so with young apes by no means mature. One possible explanation of this 'overflow' was also touched upon above, in a discussion of chronaxy (Chapter III). Thus a set of unquestionably sexual interests is present from birth and gradually extends, multiplies, and makes more definite its responses and becomes attached to wider and more definite ranges of situations. These trends, originally separate and diffused, later become unified

[1] Cf. also Freud, *Collected Papers*, vol. ii, p. 259.

in the definite sexual character of the adult, who may, therefore, according to the history of this gradual unification, vary very greatly in his sexual make-up. The Freudians have been led largely through the study of certain eccentricities in adults to point to particular infantile situations as the origins of special sub-trends in later life. For example the infant's acts of evacuation, which, as all mothers know, assume great importance in his sight, may, through their special sexual interest, later influence his attitudes to gifts and to money. This is the Freudian explanation of the miser's love of gold.[1] And the same kind of stage-to-stage *transference* (a fundamental conception in psycho-analysis as indeed in all psychology, since it is only substitution or conditioning seen from another angle) would extend the infant's original love of touching and being touched (handling and being handled) into the delight so many find in ordering their lovers about (sublimated sadism) or being ordered about by them (sublimated masochism.) Similarly with the child's passion for displaying himself and for looking at others.

The Complexity of Sex. Of course these germs may be developed in many different ways and the task of tracing the vicissitudes of their growth is highly intricate. On the multiplicity of the infantile sexual components and on the ways in which a dis-

[1] There are, of course, many steps and turnings in such a transference. A lucid account of the child's growth will be found in J. H. van der Hoop, *Character and the Unconscious*, chap. iii.

ordered development can affect later life, Freud himself may be quoted, if only as a contrast to current emotional reactions. "We are faced by a fact; and it is to be hoped that we shall grow accustomed to it when we have put our own tastes on one side. We must learn to speak without indignation of what we call the sexual perversions—instances in which the sexual function has transgressed its limits in respect either to the part of the body concerned or to the sexual object chosen. The uncertainty in regard to the boundaries of what is to be called normal sexual life, when we take different races and different epochs into account, should in itself be enough to cool the zealot's ardor. . . . Each of us in his own sexual life transgresses to a slight extent—now in this direction, now in that—the narrow lines imposed upon him as the standard of normality. The perversions are neither bestial nor degenerate in the emotional sense of the word. They are a development of germs all of which are contained in the undifferentiated sexual predisposition of the child, and which, by being suppressed or by being diverted to higher, asexual aims—by being *sublimated*—are destined to provide the energy for a great number of our cultural achievements. When, therefore, anyone has *become* a gross and manifest pervert, it would be more correct to say that he has *remained* one, for he exhibits a certain stage of *inhibited development*."[1]

[1] Sigmund Freud, *Collected Papers*, vol. iii, p. 62.

The Œdipus Complex. The most important of all cases of transference concern the parents. This brings us to the much-discussed problem of the *Œdipus Complex.* For the little boy and girl alike the two pillars of the world, the all-important centers of the majority of interesting situations, are the father and mother. At first the mother naturally takes first place for both. The very young child's affections are set on the mother as soon as they are systematized enough to be able to be set on anything. This may be originally because she bathes it, kisses it, and rocks it most, thus giving it the major groups of the stimuli which elicit infantile sexual responses. We must not, of course, suppose that the child *thinks* this out, though a rudimentary kind of *working* it out does seem to go on. The child's mental processes are so much simpler and more concrete than our own that any clear intelligible account we give of them will misrepresent them. If we remember this and translate the *verbalized thought* which alone can be used for communication into a far simpler, partly pictorial but chiefly emotional, fabric, we shall escape many misapprehensions. The child's life is a tissue of longings, of wants, satisfactions, and unrests, rather than of thoughts as we know them. It is nearer our dream and daydream existence than our waking.

Projection and Introjection. The mother's (or nurse's) predominance does not, of course, last for long. The father and any brothers and sisters there may be come into the picture and the job of reconciling and adjusting the multitude of different interests which arise becomes very complex. It will help us to understand this process if we remember what was said in Chapter VIII about the lack of fixity in the distinction, as the child makes it, between himself and the outside world. He easily regards both what happens in him as happening outside him (Projection, as the analysts call it) and what happens outside as happening in him (Introjection). The boundaries of his self are not yet established. His thoughts of his father and mother are not and cannot yet be clearly marked off for him from his father and mother themselves, and his interest in them is predominantly selfish. But at the same time their behavior and the differences between them give him all the patterns for his own activities, and in working out these patterns he both projects and introjects continually. He sees himself in them and he finds them in himself. There is nothing in the least surprising, then, if we find him, as we do, constantly behaving to his father as his mother does and to his mother as his father.

The Riddle of the Sphinx. The Œdipus complex is the name for a particular system of these activities. Œdipus in the legend, after guessing the riddle of the Sphinx, became a king and married the reigning queen who in fact was his mother. Freud believes that in the phantasies of every child (or rather in the wish-activities from which phantasies spring) this drama is reenacted. There comes a point when a boy wishes to replace his father in his mother's affections, and a girl wishes to replace her mother. And

Freud holds (which is the point at which opposition chiefly arises) that this wish may be very specific and definite.[1] It varies in many ways, but chiefly with the degree to which the riddle of the Sphinx has been guessed. And this riddle is nothing else than the great problem, for the child, as to how he came to be born. This problem and its clue, the difference between the sexes, inevitably exercise every child enormously. There *may* be something to be said for keeping him ignorant once the desire for knowledge has been expressed on the ground that it gives him his first real training in scientific research, but these advantages are far outweighed by the distortions of his personality produced by an atmosphere of secrecy, and his own inevitable but wildly misleading theories. That he should appear to drop the subject may be convenient for bashful parents, but is really a bad sign. He should—and this is one of the most important practical recommendations that it is possible for psychology to give—have his problem well ventilated for him and be given, not hurriedly as something unpleasant to be got over, but freely and

[1] "Children who have never known their parents have it," says MacCurdy. "Adults whose childhood was cursed by parental neglect and cruelty, in whom filial affection seems unthinkable, will also give evidence for these unconscious tendencies." Of the Œdipus tendency MacCurdy adds: "Of such wide application is this principle that I cannot conceive of anyone who has once found it of use, who has ever understood it, abandoning it" (*The Psychology of Emotion*, p. 94). Another view is that the object of unconscious interest is an *imago*—*i.e.*, an idealized imagined parent, rather than the real one. Interesting light on the equivalent of the Œdipus complex in savage societies where mother-right prevails is thrown by Malinowski in *Psyche*, vol. iv, nos. 2 and 4 and vol. v, no. 3.

without poetic nonsense, all the data which he needs.

The child's crude theories (and no child is without them) of the differences between the sexes are particularly important. The boy, briefly, is proud of his possessions, and the girl rather resentful of what she regards as an unfair deficiency. By very natural analogies the boy may come to dread that he will some day suddenly be turned into a girl. This dread, and the resultant theories and phantasies to which it leads, is known as the castration complex. It may afterwards have startling consequences if he becomes predominantly attached to his father. Certain threats sometimes used to children may favor this dread. In the girl, whose psychology is very much more obscure, perhaps because there has as yet been no feminine Freud, a different complex may develop, though one equally capable of playing a part in after life, an infantile sense of unfair treatment which may greatly strengthen all the other better grounded reasons which women may later have for a quarrel with the natural order of things. The castration complex, for the girl, appears as a notion or fear that she is but an imperfect man.

Conflict and Repression. We come now to the problem of the interaction of all these queer interests as they become more specific. The life of a healthy child from birth until towards five years old may be regarded as a time of more or less independent development of its manifold sexual and other interests. But by growing severally more definite they are obviously heading for a time when they will interfere with one another. One of the chief clashes comes, according to Freud, at about five years over the Œdipus complex. We must not suppose that the boy (*vice versa* if a girl) is then merely in love[1] with his mother and anxious only that his father shall be dead (=vanished). At the same time he may be passionately attached to his father. And out of this contradiction trouble may arise. The child, however, has a vastly greater power of combining contradictory attitudes than the adult.

What happens will largely depend upon how clear (in his sense, *not* in our sense) his ideas are and how adequate to the actual facts they are. He has to find a set of attitudes towards father and mother which will work smoothly together. We can hark back with advantage to the idea of competition for a final common path which was discussed in Chapter III. The child's interests (activities in which his ideas are incidents) have come into conflict. The full solution would be a reorganization in accordance with the facts of the world and society and based upon a recognition of these facts. But ordinarily, of course, nothing of the kind happens, the struggle is far more limited.

The whole situation is vastly complicated by yet

[1] Whether in a sense closely analogous to the adult sense—Freud thinks this is frequently the case—or in some more incomplete and more primitive sense due to the distortions of its false theories or to specialization of some one of the components only of the as yet piecemeal sexual interest. Obviously one such component may be dominant in its love for its father and another in its love for its mother. When this is so conflict may be postponed and difficulties only arise later.

another very powerful interest, the child's desire to be approved of. He has found out on innumerable occasions that direct expression of his more specifically sexual interests is unwelcome. Naturally enough (through introjection) those interests become unwelcome to himself. But they do not for this reason cease. To suppose so has been the immense mistake made by traditional moralists, in the nursery and in the professional chair. They continue, but make a compromise with the wider desire to be well regarded. What looks like a cunning form of deception then arises. The narrower interests have a large selection of ways in which they can be satisfied. Some of them also satisfy the wider interest. If there are enough of these all is well; the others are simply discontinued and narrower and wider interests now merge in socially possible forms of expression. But the former ways may be opened again if for some reason these compromise conditions change. The same kind of compromise may occur between the rival claims in the Œdipus complex situation, but often such a solution is too difficult, or the parents may themselves make it too difficult either by over-indulgence or by ridiculous embarrassment. Then other temporary solutions have to be found.

One common form is the *repression* of the interest either in the mother or in the father. This notion is fundamental; it is also the point at which metaphors usually begin to become misleading. Repression we have insisted is simply inhibition, the universal phenomenon we considered in Chapter III. A repressed wish is a set of impulses cut off temporarily or permanently from the final common paths. If permanently, two possibilities are open. It may find other outlets; or continue, since the need which is its source remains, to bombard the entrance to the common path whenever circumstances occasion the need. Frequently other outlets are found. We shall see later that many ailments which have no adequate organic cause, and are thus classed as 'psychical,' are such outlets. But for the moment let us consider the other case, and let us turn our attention to the need, the source of the wish. This need itself is not a simple thing; it is already, even in a very young child, the result of a co-ordination of simpler needs. It may happen that whereas impulses from the whole up-to-date co-ordinated need cannot get through, impulses from the component needs can; then through a backwash influence the need reverts to an earlier stage of development, and we have what is known as *regression.* The child's comparatively developed sexual interest is transformed to an earlier type. To a type, for instance, for which the difference between the sexes is no longer significant, it returns suddenly from a four-year-old stage to a one-year-old.

Regression. This kind of catastrophe, for such it may be, involves both a lapse backwards of behavior and a reformation of ideas. For here, as always, the child's understanding and its wishes are different aspects of the same thing.[1] But since not its whole mind, but only one out of its interests, has lapsed back, the common result is a widespread disorder, for some of its ideas which have been developed in the interests of its now lapsed interest are also involved in other interests which have not lapsed. Thus further conflicts arise. Partial and permanent regression, in other words, is a bad solution. Brief *temporary* regressions may, on the other hand, be very useful. The parent who can make them in his play with children is a great success.

But there is another way in which repression (inhibition) may influence the need. It may cause it not to regress, but to develop, and this is in fact the main source of the child's curiosity and the development of his understanding. And there is yet a third way out of the difficulty. If the need is not very strong it may satisfy itself in phantasy in the place of action, but, since the plasticity of the play world is so much greater than that of actuality, the influence of the other interests which are barring out actual behavior is likely to transform it beyond any ordinary means of recognition.

[1] And this interdependence of ideas and wishes explains the curious fact that regression leads to forgetting. To remember anything we need partially to reinstate the activity which was originally occurring, and when this activity is banned many of the ideas which formed part of it pass completely beyond the normal power of recall. Hence on the Freudian view the great difficulty for most people of recalling infantile experience. But, as we saw in Chapter VIII, there are other good reasons why infantile memories may be difficult to recall. It is very natural that Freud, having discovered a new principle, should be tempted to apply it too widely. That regression does cause blanks in memory is beyond doubt.

Mechanisms of the Unconscious. A repressed wish is usually described as being forced into the Unconscious, and it is often supposed to be active there in the same way as before, much as a submarine continues as before when it dips below the surface. And between the Unconscious and the Conscious another department of the mind is supposed to intervene, namely the Fore or Pre-conscious, which in complicated ways helps to rule the relations between these domains. It must be realized that these divisions are merely conveniences introduced in order to make exposition more easy. As soon as we forget this they become inconveniences, in fact such a scheme is far too simple, and the real interactions of different interests are far too subtle to be described so simply. It is true that a repressed wish is not thereby abolished, yet we should not suppose it to continue unchanged by repression. What makes it appear to be unchanged is the fact that, later on, behavior may appear which is unmistakably activated by an exactly similar wish. This, of course, is no proof of an underground persistence of the wish itself, any more than the return of Spring each year is a proof that she has been lurking in the soil throughout the winter. What persists in all cases is a certain pattern in the organization of the mind. If the need behind the wish persists and conditions once again allow this pattern to be used, the wish reappears all complete. But that is a very different thing from its having itself been striving for manifestation throughout the interval. For example, given strawberries,

I may at once wish for cream, but this does not mean that a wish for cream has been battering for months at the barred gates of consciousness and has now seized its chance. The point, as we can easily see, is that the specific need for cream only arose with the coming of the strawberries. But with many wishes that, unlike the wish for cream, unfortunately cannot be expressed, the equivalent of the strawberries is always coming. They are always being touched off either by cyclically recurrent organic states, or by patterns in the external stimulation which may be very hard to separate out and distinguish. And since other simultaneous needs and their resultant wishes are in possession of the appropriate final common paths, the wishes these needs give rise to can only find satisfaction either by reorganizing their needs backwards or forwards (regression or development) or by some kind of compromise with their rivals at the gateways to action. It is these compromises which give rise to many of the phenomena of dreams, and in more serious cases to those disorders of the mind which are known as *neuroses*, as well as to innumerable more trifling oddities and mistakes in ordinary life.

Compromises. Such compromises between conscious wishes which interfere with one another are familiar to everyone. A man wishes to take a holiday and also to get on with his work. If he can he takes his work with him and so combines the two. But conscious wishes are only those which are not in too direct conflict with the main systems which the individual is prepared to avow freely and has recognized as belonging to him. Certain sets of wishes he constantly hears acknowledged by others; his mechanisms of projection and introjection lead him readily to recognize these in himself. Others he will find acknowledged only in the best fiction; to these he will give a more private kind of recognition. But a swarm of others long ago came into direct conflict either with the wishes of parents and elders or with other avowed wishes of his own. These wishes are not conscious, and he may easily be quite unable to believe that he has them if to avow them would in any way upset his self-esteem, a matter which very early begins to turn upon the character of his avowed wishes, since to avow some wishes, but not others, is usually the highway to parental esteem.

The compromises between conscious wishes are usually of a different type from those among the unconscious wishes. Conscious wishes often, though not always, adjust themselves to one another in a rational way with due regard to time, place, the situation as a whole and the probable consequences. In comparison, unconscious wishes often show a freakish disregard of all ulterior considerations and express themselves in a totally unreasonable fashion. The explanation of this is usually to be found in their history. For the unconscious wish, like the conscious, has its prototype in infancy, but unlike the conscious it may never have passed beyond the infantile stage of development.

Dream Analysis. The evidence for this is drawn largely from the study of serious mental disorders through the method of dream analysis. In the dream, or rather in one very frequent type of dream, we have a figurative sketch of the solution of a conflict; usually this is an absurd solution, though sometimes, as some notable scientific discoveries show, it may have value. Sleep has cut off the greater part of stimulation, and it has altered the whole scheme of waking inhibitions. Unconscious wishes aroused during the day, then find an opportunity for displaying themselves. But conscious wishes, though greatly weakened, are also still active. The dream is a compromise in which none of the wishes operating may be clearly revealed. It may be interpreted, as a rule, in many fashions, corresponding to the wishes involved. As everyone knows, it tends to be very rapidly forgotten; the conscious wishes reinforced by the waking situation soon make the recall of the compromise impossible. There is nothing particularly mysterious in this. We can cross a stream in a drought which is hopeless in normal weather, and there is no need to suppose any Censor who takes a partial nap with us and is caught off his guard in the dream, or baffled by the disguises of the unconscious. All this is mythological machinery for convenience of exposition. The dream is the product of a transaction between conscious and unconscious wishes and the results during sleep are naturally very different from those during waking hours.

The analysis of the dream consists mainly of

allowing 'free associations,' as they are called, to come into the mind in connection with as many as possible of the recalled episodes and features of the dream. These associations are again compromises between conscious and unconscious wishes. They often show what seems an astounding power of recondite metaphorical allusion on the part of the unconscious wish, as any study of dream analysis will show. But the most interesting feature of such dream analyses is the frequency with which infantile wishes reproducing infantile experiences enter into them. One reason for this is fairly clear and helps to explain why dreams occur at all. Being asleep in bed is one of the few among our activities (if we may call it such) which have continued unchanged since infancy. But there are deeper reasons. Most of the wishes which we consciously discountenance were first outlawed in our childish days. They are new productions of the old needs which had such a stormy history long ago, the needs themselves being reinstated by recent situations—generally bearing a subtle resemblance to our old emotional situations. Hence the great importance of the earlier handling of these situations in childhood.

Transference. This reawakening of an old need by a situation which may have only a remote, or trivial, or purely schematic resemblance to the ancient problem is the work of that transference which we have already considered. It is through transference that all our triumphs come—and also most of our woes. Any and every metaphor, simile, or analogy illustrates it. But whereas analogies and most similes usually bring out clearly the relevant point through which the transference is effected, metaphor—poetic metaphor especially—often leaves this point very obscure. So it is with the points of resemblance through which infantile needs are reawakened in later life. For the child's original classifications were very different from the adult's, and his ways of thinking far less systematic than our own. Hence also the apparent incoherence of such dreams.

The infantile need thus awakened, events tend to take the course originally taken. For example, a child for whom the Œdipus situation led to a clash between his love for his mother and his different love for his father may, when he grows up, have his infantile mother-love reawakened by some chance similarity to her in his wife—as judged, of course, by infantile standards. The effect of this will vary with the outcome of the original clash. In fact, a man's outlook on the world and his attitude to other people, especially women, is largely determined by the manner in which the transference from the parents to the outside world, at school or in the ballroom, has been effected. Suppose that, as may happen, his mother-love was violently repressed, giving place later to a sense of guilt and a horror [1] of any

[1] This horror, it may be remarked, is a defense mechanism and a measure of the original strength of the wish. Psycho-analysts often write as though the energy of the wish were itself transformed into the repressing horror, the libido converted into its opposite, but this seems an unnecessary hypothesis. The horror may be merely a

such idea. Then without his knowing anything about it his attitude to his wife may be seriously affected. In another man a similar awakening of a childish wish may, since the original course of its repression was different, lead not to depression, but to increased affection.

The instance is relevant, for there is reason to suppose that the choice of mates is much influenced by transference from father and mother, and, since a very great proportion of mental troubles arise through maladjustment in mating, the prominence of the Œdipus complex in the psychology of the neuroses is explained. In normal people it is likely that this early crisis was less severe.

Such in outline is the modern theory of the ways in which the mind goes wrong. The whole theory is in many quarters rejected.[1] But its opponents sometimes show either ignorance and misconceptions of it or an emotional attitude towards it which suggest that their theoretical objections are in part *rationalizations*, to use a term which we shall explain in the following chapter.

A number of cleavages have occurred within the ranks of psycho-analysts, and these schisms have led to much unnecessary acrimony. The three main schools—of Freud, of Adler, and of Jung—tend too much to regard their accounts as incompatible.

---

memory of the original disturbance of the triumphant wishes. If the banned wish is still active, the horror will of course be all the greater.

[1] The most elaborate recent attack is that of Wohlegemuth.

But just as there may be for a dream a number of different but equally good interpretations, so it is with all psychical products and phenomena. We are not yet within several centuries of a complete account, and meanwhile any clue which in any way helps to unravel the maze should be followed up.

Organ-inferiority. Adler's distinctive treatment sets out not from the sexual interests, but from what Freud regards as the other main group—the Ego interests. These other interests, built up round the child's desire for power and reflecting themselves in his ambitions, undergo a process of development corresponding in broad outlines to the processes we have sketched. For Adler the key to character lies in the association of what he has named 'organ-inferiority' with a 'superiority' aim (ambition). A defect of which the child is sensible leads him to an effort at compensation, sometimes successful—as in the case of Napoleon, who complained later that he always felt like 'a boiled fowl' at home, where he was bullied by the family. But sometimes the compensation, the desire to obtain power in other ways, may be disastrous. The typical instance is that of the 'malade imaginaire,' who, failing to make himself or herself felt in ordinary life, contrives to turn the rest of the family into a nursing staff. The instance brings out the important point that there is no hard and fast line to be drawn between malingering and mental illness. As Crookshank writes, "Where there is a will not to do, there is always a way of escape from doing what should be done."[1] Most people have plenty of weak spots physically and plenty of awkward problems of mental adjustment, and the tendency to dodge the latter by stressing the former provides a large part of every medical practice.

Moral Re-education. This insistence upon the present problem, as opposed to Freud's insistence upon infantile problems, is in a large measure Jung's contribution to psycho-analytic theory. His famous theory of Types and his doctrine of the Collective Unconscious give rise rather to speculation than to positive results. Jung sees in many, indeed in most, mental disorders what amounts to a moral failure to meet the exigencies of life, which should be set right mainly by a re-education of the individual which aims at making him realize his duties and his work in the world. He is thus much more in line with traditional views of the function of the spiritual adviser than the other psycho-analysts, who, however, are by no means blind to this factor in the situation. They reply that most people are only too well aware of what they ought to do and that the real problem is to discover why they cannot do it. On the other hand, by pointing out that failure to reach a *decision*, with its corollary, a Troubled Conscience, may be the unsuspected cause of ailments regarded as obstacles to such a decision, they can often set the pilgrim on the right track—back, it may be, to his own fireside.

---

[1] *Migraine and Other Common Neuroses* (1925), p. 37.

CHAPTER XVI: THE ABNORMAL

The Borderland. Around the frontiers of the better established part of psychology lies a ring of debatable matters; sometimes these are treated as though they must involve quite new hypotheses and principles of explanation; sometimes an attempt is made to extend the hypotheses already in use so as to include them. There are many who hold that these borderline phenomena—suggestion, hypnotism, telepathy, clairvoyance, and mediumistic happenings in general—will involve in the end a reconquest, as it were, of ordinary psychology by some form of Animism. The hypotheses needed to explain, for example, how a mind can act upon a distant mind (if it does) will, it is held, when they have been worked out, make ordinary orthodox psychology seem unduly timid.

Unfortunately these exceptional phenomena which lie outside normal psychology are notoriously hard to observe. They inevitably remain too often at the stage of the remarkable anecdote. Full verification and corroboration are rarely possible. A quite special criticism is required before they can be accepted as fact; and, in face of the great reserves which their extraordinary nature demands, and the difficulties as regards testimony and even mere accurate description, it is hardly surprising that so much hesitation should be felt by psychologists in admitting them as facts at all. We shall see that different classes of these phenomena stand in different positions in this respect. And such a preliminary sorting out is almost all that psychology can at present do with them.

Suggestion. We may conveniently begin with suggestion, since, although the more striking instances of suggestion are unquestionably abnormal, and in many cases not above suspicion as having been misdescribed and exaggerated, suggestion itself is a quite normal process which can be observed easily enough in ordinary daily life.

In its widest sense 'suggestion' is merely another name for the working of mental processes in general. A stimulus would 'suggest' its response, and this, whether the stimulus be a perception, an idea, or an emotion, and whether the response be a movement, another idea, or a further emotion. In this sense the sight of a theater-bill 'suggests' a visit to the play, or a despondent mood 'suggests' a series of melancholy reflections. But the sense of 'suggestion' prominent in recent discussion, for example in the agitation centering round the work of Liébault, of Bernheim, and of Coué, is narrower than this. Only those suggestions which take place primarily through the operation of unconscious processes are included in the narrower sense. Going to the play or indulgence in gloomy prognostications is ordinarily under our own conscious control. They are *voluntary* activities, matters of the will; but sometimes we may find ourselves stepping through the theater doors when we have strong reasons for being elsewhere, or we may harrow ourselves with thoughts which are the last we consciously wish to entertain. Such impulsions or obsessions are typical examples of the working of suggestion in this narrower sense.

The most interesting field for suggestion is in the control of the bodily functions. As all who suffer from colds are only too well aware, we have very little conscious power of control over what takes place in the nasal passages. It is claimed by the Nancy School—and the phenomena of faith-healing also show it—that unconscious control may be very much wider. Not only functional disorders, but some organic conditions also can be corrected by psychological means. Warts, for example, it is said, can be cured in many cases with great ease by the recitation of an appropriate verbal formula.

But the question arises, why are some suggestions effective and others not? The answer given by the Nancy School is that failure is due to the arousal of a counter-suggestion. They draw a very hard and fast line between the 'Will' and the 'Imagination,' using these terms in their popular sense. It will repay us to examine more closely the distinction. The 'will' on this view, would appear to be the conscious operation of a particular interest or set of interests, whereas the 'imagination'—that is, the picturing or thinking of the end to be reached—allows a variety of unconscious wishes to take effect, and gives less occasion for conflicting wishes to interfere. A consciously formulated wish often seems to act as a challenge to any dissentients there may be in the personality, though in many cases, of course, such a wish is quite effective, a point which M. Coué does not sufficiently stress. It all depends upon the strength of the wish and the extent to which it is in conflict with other wishes, or, as Coué puts it, with the imagination: "When the will and the imagination are at war, the imagination *invariably* gains the day. In the conflict between the will and the imagination the force of the imagination is *in direct ratio to the square of the will.*" This metaphorical statement becomes more plausible when we realize that the "force of the imagination" is the force of the desires and interests to which the imagining is due. We must, of course, be careful in the examples we choose: M. Coué's favorite instance, the undesirability of *trying*, of making an effort, to go to sleep is clearly misleading, sleep being by the nature of the case a state in which effort must be absent. But when, as for example in getting up on a winter's morning, effort is not antagonistic to the desire to seat oneself at the breakfast table, or even perhaps to reach the office before ten o'clock, the exercise of the will is salutary and successful almost daily; and this no matter how powerfully the imagination pictures the rigors of the frore morning air.

Auto-suggestion. The controversy as to whether all suggestion is really auto-suggestion—*i.e.*, whether all suggestion involves the intervention of our own imagination, or whether all auto-suggestion ultimately depends on suggestion from without—

would seem to be due to a common failure in systematizers to allow for the many ways in which the mind works.

There is no doubt that suggestions of external origin gain added force when they ally themselves with auto-suggestions, and conversely an auto-suggestion will be the stronger if some authoritative utterance from a person of prestige—a doctor, a teacher, or a public idol—is co-operating. None the less these two processes may be regarded as distinct, though, of course, an external suggestion which elicits the support of no conscious or unconscious interest will lead to no response; whether this interest be an impulse to conform, or to obey—and Binet reduced all suggestion to obedience—to please the suggestor, or to be a satisfactory platform exhibit. The reason for distinguishing between them is that the motives operating in the two cases are usually diverse; with external suggestion they are largely of social origin.

Hypnosis. This brings us to the problem of the influence of mind upon mind and the vexed question of hypnosis. About 1880 hypnotism emerged suddenly, with the work of Richet and Charcot, from the period of opprobrium which followed the excesses of Mesmer.[1] For a while the most remarkable phenomena were recorded, including the transference of affections from one side of the body to another by

[1] An absorbing account of the history of animal magnetism and hypnotism will be found in the two volumes of Janet's *Psychological Healing* (1925).

means of magnets, anæsthesia, clairvoyance, etc., all leading to the conclusion that the mind could be influenced from without by unknown forms of vibration and radiation. But with the triumph of the Nancy School, which already in the 'eighties attributed everything to 'suggestion,' though without at that date giving any account of it, interest in hypnosis declined. It has generally been supposed that the hypnotizer works upon his subject by restricting the range of his attention, and that this narrowed field of concentrated attention allows the suggestion a free field for operation; while Freud has recently pointed out that fascination and infatuation, the extreme developments of being 'in love,' are but little removed from hypnosis.[1] The effects of Rhythm in poetry, music, and the arts might also be brought under this heading.

The most characteristic phenomenon of hypnosis, as its name implies, is the inducement of artificial sleep. Sir Michael Foster recorded a case where a man had no sense organ left save a single eye. He was half-blind, totally deaf, and insensible to all other stimuli. If anyone closed his remaining eye he promptly fell asleep.[2] The cutting off of the sole remaining field of attention left him no alternative. Another curious corroboration comes from the work of Pavlov. As we have seen (Chapter IV), the interval between a conditioned stimulus and the response (salivation) can be extended to as much as

[1] *Group Psychology and the Analysis of the Ego* (1922), p. 77.
[2] *Text-book of Physiology* (1888), p. 1117.

half an hour. Now if the experiment be repeated without the food being given, there comes a stage when the conditioned reflex becomes quite inactive. "At the same time the animal enters into a kind of cataleptic condition; inert to stimuli, it assumes a particular pose and thus remains rigid, finally falling into a deep sleep from which it can only with difficulty be aroused."[1] The simplest interpretation of this result in psychological terms is that the dog's field of attention is so narrowed down by inhibition that when what is left, namely his expectation of food, is inhibited, he passes into that state of total inhibition which is known as sleep.

There are signs of a reaction against the view that hypnosis is only a phenomenon of suggestion. It was maintained by the late Dr. Alrutz on the basis of a number of ingenious experiments that passes, which used to be so prominent in the procedure of mesmerists and the early hypnotizers, do in fact play an essential part. After covering the subject's head completely with a black cloth, and shielding his arm from currents of air, etc., by sheets of glass, he claimed to have induced by a few downward passes complete insensibility of the skin. Upward passes produced the opposite effect. Precautions against suggestion seem to have been taken.[2]

Whatever may be the truth with regard to these contentions, some of the better established phenomena of the hypnotic state are so extraordinary

---

[1] Pavlov, *British Medical Journal*, October 18, 1913.

[2] *Psyche*, vol. iv, October, 1923; p. 129, ff.

that the slight amount of work which is being done upon them is surprising. For example, very profound anæsthesia can in some cases be produced: so deep, in fact, that a number of surgeons, such as Esdaile and Elliotson in the years preceding the discovery of anæsthetics, employed hypnosis for this purpose. Even major operations—the removal of a leg, for example—were performed without pain by its aid, thought it has been held that there were less phenomena of hypnosis than of hysteria, while one writer went so far as to maintain that the patient was an "impostor" who had been "simulating" insensibility during the amputation. It seems probable indeed that had the discovery of chemical anæsthetics been delayed a considerable development in the practical use of hypnosis would have taken place.

Hyperæsthesia. Another well-authenticated phenomenon is what is known as *hyperæsthesia.* The subject in light hypnosis quite usually displays powers of sensory discrimination much superior to those possible in the waking state. Instances are reported in which he is able to perceive distinctly the details in microscopic slides, and to overhear conversations in remote rooms which would normally be inaudible, facts which would seem to show that we do not usually exploit our powers of perception to the full. Doubtless this hyperæsthesia has a bearing upon many alleged instances of telepathy. In this connection we may recall the controversy, still *sub judice*, between M. Jules Romains and the Sorbonne professors on the subject of 'eyeless sight.' M.

Romains claims to have discovered a power of reading through the skin, for which he gives an anatomical and evolutionary explanation, and which may be revived in a suitable "régime of consciousness"—possibly a form of mild hypnosis. Whether or not the facts are as described—and the late Anatole France was among those who vouched for some of them—the problems raised by the discussion are of unusual theoretical interest and should certainly be further examined.[1]

Post-hypnotic Suggestion. If during hypnosis it is suggested to the subject that at a fixed time after waking he shall perform some unusual act, for example remove his shoes and place them in the bookcase, he will often perform the act at the appropriate moment without fail—showing incidentally a remarkably accurate appreciation of the lapse of time. When asked why he has done this he will usually give some more or less plausible and elaborate answer, bearing no relation to the real reason, known only to the experimenter. Such answers, known as rationalizations, throw a curious light upon the normal working of the mind, particularly in the matter of political opinion.

Telepathy. The evidence for the influence of mind upon mind independently of the recognized channels of sense has long been accepted by a sufficient number of trustworthy investigators to justify the scientific study which is now being devoted to it. The fact that such trained thinkers as Sidgwick,

[1] *Eyeless Sight*, 1923.

James, Forel, Freud, Driesch, Bergson, McDougall, Becher, and Broad, to name only a few of those who have actually written on the subject, are convinced of its occurrence makes the cavalier dismissal of its possibility no longer prudent. At the same time the clear possibility of as yet unguessed-at forms of physical transmission makes the acceptance of telepathy less difficult. We know too little about the nervous system to be sure that an event in one body may not produce a direct effect in another, even at a remote distance. No useful conjectures can yet be made as to how it should do so; but there certainly seems no reason to assert, for example, that special receptive organs would be required. The absence of such organs, then, is no good ground for a hasty return to the primitive hypothesis, the view, namely, that on exceptional occasions the soul, or a part of it, is able to leave the body and travel to distant regions. Nor is an acceptance of telepathy necessarily a step towards Animism. The aim of science is to give an intelligible account of what happens, and to speak in this connection of direct interactions between souls which transcend space or operate in supernumerary dimensions is not, unless something much more definite can be added, particularly profitable. Such accounts, although they may provide a certain emotional satisfaction, actually bring us at present no nearer an understanding of the alleged phenomena. This is in fact a field in which a resort to words which have no definite significance is fatally easy.

Various other phenomena, for which the evidence is less satisfactory, are allied to telepathy and raise similar fundamental issues if they are accepted. Such are clairvoyance and the prediction of the future. In the typical case of clairvoyance the subject, sometimes in a trance-condition, sometimes in what appears to be a quite normal state, reads the contents of an opaque envelope which has been sealed with all possible precautions, or, as in the celebrated 'book tests,' indicates the words or matter of a passage of print in some volume which has been set aside with others for the purposes of the experiment in a distant house, after the most elaborate precautions have been taken to prevent any collusion. In this last instance it would appear that no one whatever knows which books have been set aside, yet the clairvoyant is reported as giving the gist of the passage she has selected sufficiently often to make the hypothesis of chance unplausible. In yet another kind of experiment the medium is handed some object whose history is unknown to all present; it is alleged that sometimes detailed accounts of episodes in which it has been concerned are given. To explain these phenomena by the hypothesis of telepathy would plainly involve something like a central pool wherein the knowledge of all men is stored, a pool whence the medium is able to draw her knowledge. But this is so desperate a conjecture that very much more stringent conditions would be required to establish such occurrences as facts than are required for more ordinary cases of telepathy.

Dissociation. The peculiarities of the trance condition which seems necessary for many mediums are an easier and at present more profitable subject for investigation. These trance states bear a close resemblance to pathological conditions which have been studied by alienists in cases where these borderline phenomena are not in question. There is indeed little doubt that the mediumistic trance is a state of what is known as *dissociation*. The medium claims ordinarily to be 'controlled' by an independent personality. It often appears to be that of a child. Now mild degrees of dissociation are not uncommon. Just as we can digest and at the same time learn to ride a bicycle, so when we have learned to ride we can continue on our way while arguing about birth-control. There is nothing pathological about this, but when the two streams of activity are such that one would normally inhibit the other, and the two cannot be combined into a coherent personality, an abnormal condition may arise. There is a surprisingly large number of people who, if they hold a pencil comfortably in their hand over a piece of paper, while reading a book or talking to others, find that after a little practice the pencil begins to move and write down more or less coherent script. This is known as automatic writing. A set of interests which has been repressed by normal consciousness is taking advantage of this channel of expression. In extreme cases this dissociated set of interests is complete enough to make up a minor personality, and it may be added that provision of the means of expression often favors the development of the disease.

Facial Asymmetry. Many people who have never heard of 'dissociation' are aware that the faces of their friends are not the same on the right side as on the left; and discussion frequently arises as to which side will come out best in a photograph. This facial asymmetry reflects a functional or structural asymmetry in respect of the twin cerebral hemispheres. Conversely, just as Elliot Smith correlates the asymmetry of prehistoric skulls (and so of prehistoric brains) with right- and left-handedness,[1] so we may come to correlate similar brain asymmetries with right- or left-facedness in the matter of emotional expression. In extreme cases the disparity of expression is very marked, and insanity is often indicated by a cocking of one eyebrow. In normal people both halves of the forehead muscle work together, but in states of dissociation one half will work independently. Normally, too, the eyes are directed by the occipital lobes of the cerebral hemispheres after the manner of a pair of horses' heads controlled as in Fig. XIII opposite; but squint may indicate dissociation of this curious faculty of conjugate direction, and the imbalance involved may explain the distrust of many for people who squint as unreliable. Phrases such as 'double-faced,' 'smiling on one side of the face,' or 'laughing on the wrong side,' show a further recognition of this lack of co-ordination. So, popularly, when it is said in

[1] *British Medical Journal*, November 14, 1925.

France that '*le nez tourne*,' an accusation of duplicity is to be inferred. We may compare, too, the very

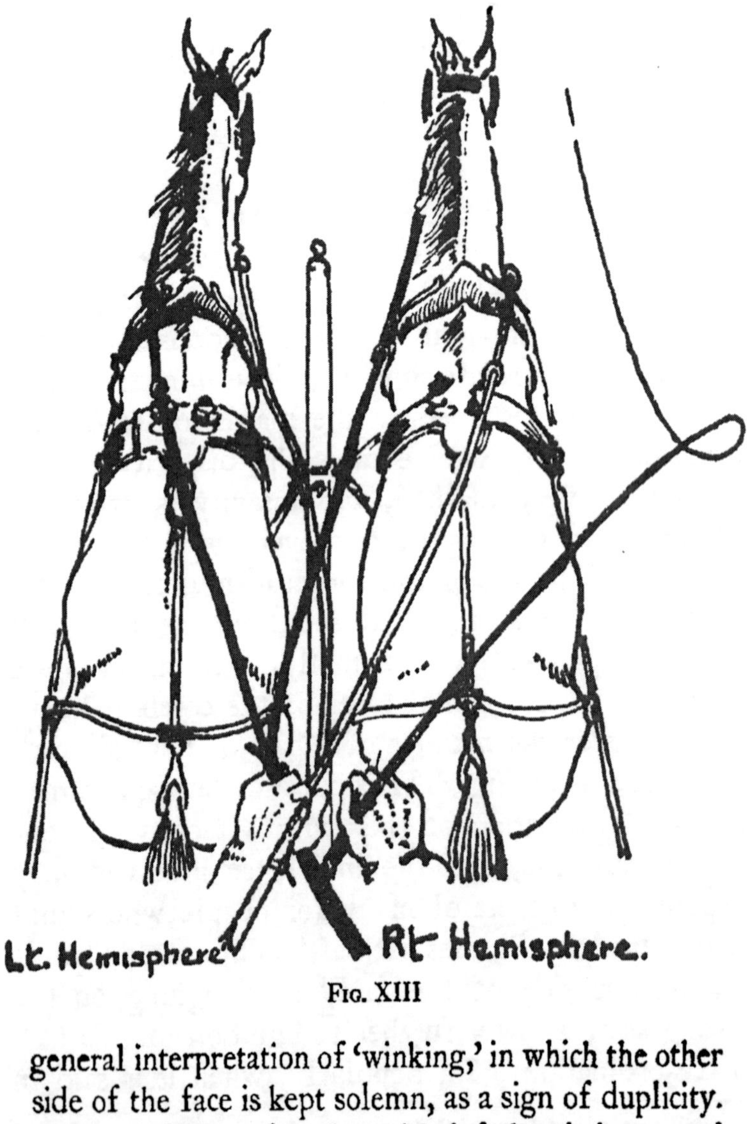

Fig. XIII

general interpretation of 'winking,' in which the other side of the face is kept solemn, as a sign of duplicity. The correlation of squint with left-handedness, and

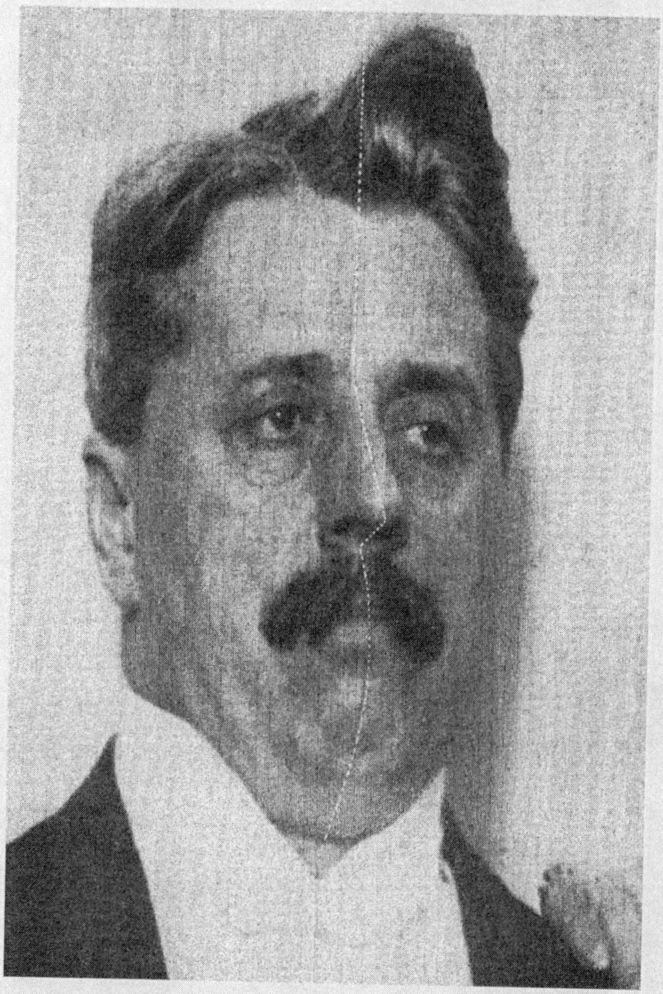

PLATE IV

the possibility of their origin in some infantile reaction to thwarting by a heavy father, are now receiving attention from oculists who are conversant with psychology.[1]

But the psychological bearing of asymmetry extends to the whole personality. In civilized man the *left* side of the brain (connected with the right side of the face and body) is usually the dominant hemisphere. Intellectual development (in right-handed people) depends on the potentialities and predominance of the left brain. The palmists express this by saying that the right hand (governed by the left brain) reveals what the owner has accomplished, while the left hand (governed by the right brain) shows his congenital equipment and inheritance. Hence when a man rises by his own efforts we may expect to see his origins revealed in the left side of his face, his accomplishments in his right.

When two or more such personalities are unified (unilateral control) at a high level of development, we get the various forms of 'genius' which are associated with versatility and synthetic achievement. Thus in the portrait of the distinguished writer on the opposite page—who is also one of the world's greatest psychologists, though he finds it more profitable to call his work fiction—the reader may imagine on the right hand side of the dotted line (the left side of the face) the penetrating humorist who created *The Card*, and on the other side the reflective

[1] See W. S. Inman's contribution to Dr. Culpin's *The Nervous Patient* (1924).

artist whose *Old Wives' Tale* remains a landmark in literature. Facial asymmetry of this type is usually combined with pronounced right- or left-handedness and those in whom it is most marked are often regarded by their less wayward friends as unaccountable and disturbing—"you never know where you are with them." A different type of genius is found, though very rarely, in unified personalities with complete facial symmetry, when both cerebral hemispheres are abnormally developed at a very high level: as for example in the well-known Stratford bust of Shakespeare. Perfect symmetry of face on a low level (the left side of the brain having failed to develop above the right) is seen in certain idiots, criminals, and 'low-level ambidexters.' Moreover, in thalamic diseases hyper-emotivity will be expressed on the side of the lesion, whereas the other side of the face remains relatively quiescent.[1]

Alternating Personalities. A very striking form of dissociation may occur when the lack of co-ordination between two or more mental systems (whether from + Left or − Right or some more complicated disorder) is so great as to result in what is known as alternating or dual personality; those fugues, or flights from reality, which occur in cases of hysteria. Certain drugs, notably alcohol and hashish, or the deep-breathing practices of the Yoga system, are artificial means of inducing them. A great part of

[1] Cf. V. Gordon Holmes and Henry Head on thalamic overtoning (as this phenomenon is called), in "The Thalamic Syndrome," *Brain*, 1910.

the technique of the religions of antiquity was devoted to bringing about similar states, and to-day the trance medium is in many respects the lineal descendant of the Priestess of Apollo. In the trance the medium often utters strange cries, writhes and gesticulates. Raps and voices are heard in all parts of the room, and, strangest of all, physical objects are sometimes reported as moving, even with violence, beyond the medium's reach. Endeavors are, of course, made to control the movements of the medium's limbs, but the darkness or low illumination, and the hubbub that is usually declared to be essential, make any scientific judgment difficult. All that can be stated is that if such phenomena are genuine, physics, physiology, and psychology alike are very far from being able to explain them at present; whether their verification would invalidate any particular view of the nature of the mind cannot, therefore, be decided. In any case such *séances* provide a valuable field for a study of the psychology of belief and testimony.

Calculating Boys. The unconscious is often regarded as a source of all that is most marvelous in the mind. Certainly some of the performances of the very backward nine-year-old child Zerah Colburn, who could instantly declare the factors of six figure numbers and extract cube roots without a moment's hesitation, though entirely ignorant of the commonest rules of arithmetic, require a special explanation. When later on he discovered in part how the feat had been performed, the odd consequence was that he lost the capacity. Apparently at the age of six he had indulged in an enormous number of multiplication sums involving two figures, classifying the products by the last two digits. He then unconsciously remembered what numbers when multiplied together could yield products so ending. The power of finding factors and extracting roots seems to have depended upon this prodigious unconscious classification. G. P. Bidder, a calculator even more remarkable than Colburn, used similar methods, believed in multiplying from the left-hand corner, and never lost his capacity for lightning calculation in all forms. Two days before his death at the age of seventy-two the query was suggested that, taking the velocity of light at 190,000 miles per second, and the wave length of the red rays at 36,918 to an inch, how many of its waves must strike the eye in one second? His friend, producing a pencil, was about to calculate the result, when Mr. Bidder said: "You need not work it: the number of vibrations will be four hundred and forty-four billions, four hundred and thirty-three thousand six hundred and fifty-one millions, two hundred thousand vibrations." This number written in figures is 444,433,651,200,000.[1]

A different kind of calculator was Jedediah Buxton, whose memory for figures was amazing, though he never learned more than the simple multiplication table. Though he was very slow and did little else in his whole life but multiplication, he

[1] Hankin, *Common Sense and How to Acquire It*, 1925, p. 55.

failed to discover that the simplest way to multiply a number by 100 is to add 00. He talked freely whilst solving his problems, and could complete an unfinished problem three months later, taking it up where he left it. He remembered all the free drinks of beer he had had since he was twelve years of age and gave a list of them thus:

D of Kingston	2,130	pints.
D of Norfolk	266	"
Duke of Leeds	232	"
D of Devonshire	10	"
Lady Oxford	280	"
G. Heathcote, Esqr.	160	"
Sir G. Saville, Bt.	20	"
etc.	etc.	

and so on, amounting to 5,116 pints received from 60 persons.

Musical Prodigies. Another precocious capacity which has naturally attracted attention is musical genius. Most of the great composers were remarkable for their early musical development, and in many cases exhibited astonishing gifts of discrimination and analysis. In his elaborate study of the powers of Erwin Nyiregyházi, the Hungarian boy prodigy, Dr. Révész records his analyses of the three chords in Fig. XIV the first time they were played to him at the age of seven.

The Inheritance of Genius. It is natural to inquire how far special capacities are due to inheritance and how far to early environment. But the usual antithesis between heredity and environment is no longer justified. Modern genetics has shown that if we could give the same education for many generations to a number of different human families, we should find that the characteristics resulting from education are inherited characteristics in the same sense as are color of eyes and form of head. "Every creature," adds Professor H. S. Jennings,[1] "has many inheritances; which one shall be realized depending on the conditions under which it develops; but man is the creature that has the greatest number

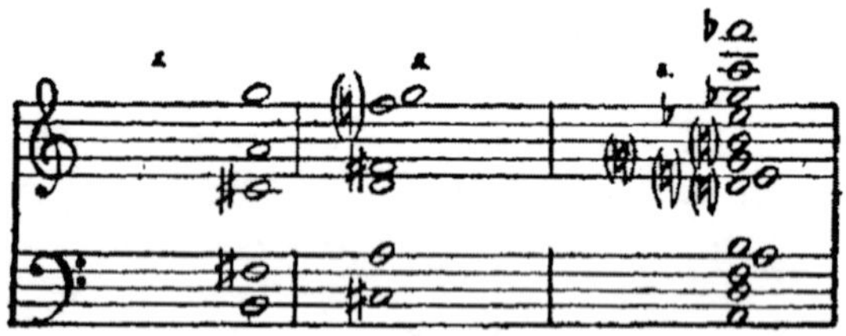

FIG. XIV

of possible heritages. Or, more accurately, men and other organisms do not inherit their characteristics at all. What their parents leave them are certain packets of chemicals which under one set of conditions produce one set of characters, under other conditions produce other sets."

The Great Abnormals. It is useful to realize how many of the greatest figures in history have suffered from grave disabilities and apparently congenital defects which might have been expected to debar them from worldy success. If St. Paul suffered from contagious ophthalmia, as the late Dean Farrar held; if Napoleon was a victim of Fröhlich's dystro-

[1] *Prometheus* (1925), p. 62.

phia adiposo-genitalis, as the late Dr. Leonard Guthrie conclusively proved; if Coleridge was an opium-addict, Dostoevski an epileptic, Nietzsche a martyr to migraine, and Darwin for thirty-six years lived a valetudinarian life (during which he published twenty-three volumes and fifty-one important scientific papers)—we should hesitate to regard good health and perfect normality as the first of human needs.

CHAPTER XVII: LOOKING FORWARD

THERE is no department of human activity in which psychology may not be of assistance or does not promise help. On the other hand, we must not too often expect from psychology light upon topics which common sense cannot at least faintly illumine. Rather shall we find, reinforced and supported on a systematic basis, the fragmentary conclusions which shrewd and observant people have already reached. Before passing to a more detailed account of some of these conclusions we may note that the provision of a general conception of the way in which the mind works is already a great step forward. For example, what is the place of pleasure and pain as moral inducements? How far does sustained activity depend upon partial and increasing success? How far are vivid images useful in clear thinking? Upon these and many similar questions the reader will already be in a position to reflect with a sufficient background of general considerations.

Man's Protracted Infancy. We have seen in Chapter VIII that man, of all animals, has the longest period of infancy. He is the most incompetent in his early months, and has the most complex social environment to which to adapt himself. This is partly due to the immense extent of the social heritage carried by language and institutions, which is now quite beyond the attainment of the individual child without the aid of education. The whole effect of recent psychological discovery has been to confirm the view that the first three years of childhood are of overwhelming importance for the rest of life. The fixity of early trends, and the acquisition of modes of dealing with the environment which are transferred and reapplied to an ever wider circle of situations, make it clear that in many cases education only begins when one of its main tasks has been clumsily finished. Doubtless there is a sense in which the child's first and best educator would be the ideal mother: but the records of child life in the past, in spite of notable exceptions, do not encourage us to envy even those of our predecessors who survived the cradle; and modern economic tendencies are making it more and more necessary to replace the guttering light of nature by a galaxy of well-considered principles and trained assistants. No one readily trusts himself in a car driven by an amateur for the first time. Yet we cheerfully leave a much more difficult undertaking in the hands of an unaided novice. If the modern mother has to be taught how to keep the child's bottle clean, how much more does she need help in learning not to poison its mind with all those unnecessary fears and desires which are occupying the attention of psychiatrists to-day (Cf. Chapters X and XV).

School Education. Further, the study of suggestion shows that everyone with whom a child comes in contact is in these early years, as to a lesser extent throughout his life, an educator. Suggestion leads characteristically to imitation in the simplest sense. "Whenever the dog barks in the child's presence, or the wind whistles through the cracks, or the kitten purrs or rolls upon the floor . . . he will tend to repeat the activity in what appears much like a reflex manner."[1] But later, so early as the second year, this imitation becomes a deliberate activity controlled by a desire to copy what other people are doing and guided by an explicit idea of what this is. The prodigious exercise in imitation, and the prestige which successful imitation thereby gains, are best seen in the acquisition of language. The slightest deviation from the linguistic conventions of the home circle is at once stamped out with a ruthlessness which only a student of phonetics, of dialects and comparative linguistics, can realize. The plasticity of the child's vocal habits and its zeal in imitation make this the golden moment for an initial training in the sounds of foreign languages. A similar linguistic opportunity occurs during adolescence, when those strange aberrations of interest in language for its own sake, the counterpart of the universal primitive belief in Word-magic, hold sway. The power of concentration on what may afterwards be regarded as dreary details is at its height between the ages of seven and seventeen, but at present, as a rule, little advantage is taken of these capacities otherwise than in the interests of formal training.

The Transfer of Training. The great problem thus arises, do formal exercises, whether in Latin Gram-

---

[1] O'Shea, *Mental Development and Education* (1922), p. 51.

mar, in Arithmetic, in Music, or in History, lead to mental development which can be transferred to other subject-matter? The present conclusion, based on methods of mental measurement to which we shall return, is on the whole negative. But of course everything turns upon the precise way in which the formal training is given. If it allows the pupil to discover how, why, and when one step in his exercise follows from another, if it gives him insight into what he is doing, there is reason to expect transference. If it does not teach him how to work, how to think, how to control his inferences and test his conclusions, how to distinguish a general case from a particular, how to weigh evidence, and vary his procedure with variation of the situation, transference is hardly likely to take place, and it is hard to see what there would be to transfer. The primary aim, in other words, of all formal training is to teach the pupil how to handle a varied material so as to reach ends which should be clear to him. But a blind fumbling without any goal in sight, animated by a vague hope of satisfying a largely incomprehensible demand, can teach nothing; and to-day unfortunately most people have cause to resent the loss of a valuable decade largely spent in such pursuits. A suitable epitaph for many a teacher of the old school would be:

> "Here lies One
> Who wasted All his Own time
> And Much of Other people's."

The Case Against Education. It is hardly surprising, in view of the failure of most schools to profit by the findings both of common sense and psychology, that the question, "Is school education doing more harm than good?" is still periodically raised by headmasters of securely endowed institutions, as well as by employers and trade unionists. There is, however, also the consideration that in some way human beings have to be inured to drudgery and unnecessary toil, and that in this respect current education admirably fits a man for the world as he will find it. But this is not an argument of which educationists are proud; and we hear on all sides of the difficulty of finding men and women able to take responsibility, or to do anything they have not already been repeatedly shown how to do.

Vocational Training. The cure for this, from the point of view of the psychologist, is either a formal education both wide enough and conducted with sufficient insight (which involves thinkers as teachers, small classes and a consequent tenfold increase in educational expenditure), or an adequate and enlightened scheme of vocational training. Any discussion of this choice, however, involves social and economic considerations which are outside the scope of the present work. Are we moving towards a general sharing out of unavoidable labor, or towards scientific discoveries and technical applications which will make highly trained intelligence the first essential?

Incentives. In any case the problem of incentives in education remains, and here the arguments presented by advocates of the vocational school are valid.[1] Without some concrete practical problem which is in itself arousing interest, the teacher must rely upon his own personality, upon comparatively feeble indirect inducements, or upon the competitive spirit. All these are motives which in comparison with a genuine interest in the work itself are of low educational value. The most reliable incentive, and the one most worth developing, is the pupil's own sense of his growing command of the subject; for this springs from the self-regarding sentiment which is the nucleus of the personality. Thus a practical recommendation of some importance is that children should be encouraged constantly to measure their capacities not against those of others, but against their own at an earlier stage; and in particular to reflect upon the means by which the improvement has been brought about. The reasonable confidence which this engenders is not to be confused with vanity, and is in fact the surest safeguard against it.

Mental Types. One of the points in psychology which is of most interest to the teacher concerns the recent work on types. The classifications of the past have dealt chiefly with intellectual differences, with contrasting attitudes to special kinds of objects. Thus we get Synthetic and Analytic minds, Intuitive and Logical, Romantic and Classic, Visual and Auditive, and so forth. Recently the speculations of

[1] Kerschensteiner, *The Schools and the Nation*, 1914, chap. vi.

Jung have received much attention. His classification forms a kind of chessboard with four horizontal divisions—sensation, intuition, feeling, and thinking —and two vertical divisions—extravert and introvert. Sensation and intuition are lower level forms of what at a higher stage of development appear as feeling and thinking. In this way eight main types are obtained. But since all these terms are used in special senses, and the whole classification is based on a theory of the collective unconscious and of primordial symbols, which have all the air of being emotive rather than precise forms of speech, the practical value of these types is problematic. Moreover, most people in the course of a day will find themselves fitting into several. Those who employ the terms 'extraverted' and 'introverted' in a broad sense as equivalent to 'practical' and 'reflective' might find the latter, and the many similar pairs which are already in current use, more profitable.

The ancient classification into the sanguine, melancholy, choleric and phlegmatic suggests a more useful line of approach. Recent work on the internal secretions or hormones, though still in its initial stages, makes it probable that not only physique, but character also, is closely dependent on what is known as the endocrine balance. We dealt in Chapter XIV with one of the internal secretions, the adrenalin produced by the adrenal glands, but it should be noted that there are many other glands, of which the thyroid, the pituitary, the thymus and the reproductive glands are the most important. The substances which they produce are carried in the bloodstream and vitally affect the growth and functioning of the tissues. Certain emotions such as fear, rage, and pain are known to be directly related to the discharge of adrenalin, and it seems likely that correlations may in due course be established for other secretions.[1] Another hopeful line is that which relates certain types of physique with particular temperaments and capacities:

> "Let me have men about me that are fat;
> Sleek-headed men, and such as sleep o' nights:
> Yon Cassius has a lean and hungry look;
> He thinks too much: such men are dangerous."

Cassius, in the language of Kretschmer[2] who is chiefly responsible for the alarming vocabulary of this subject, was a 'schizothyme.' Cæsar would have desired him to be more of a 'cyclothyme'!

Moreover, every classification of types must take note of racial and national differences. This is not the place to raise the fascinating topic of man's animal ancestry and the traces of pre-anthropoid evolution in the human organism as a possible basis

[1] The widely read work of Berman, *The Glands Regulating Personality* (1921), is still more open to the charge of uncritical schematizations and *ad hoc* hypotheses than that of Jung, but, like the same author's *The Personal Equation* (1925), it has served to evoke popular interest in endocrine research.

[2] *Physique and Character*, 1925, p. 208. A valuable discussion of these distinctions will be found in E. Miller's *Types of Mind and Body* (1926); an attempt is there made to go beyond the inductive enumeration of Kretschmer by tracing the processes in the neurovegetative system which determine the correlation of the two main types of Mind with the two main types of Body.

for the differentiation of types; but it may be noted that recent work on racial origins has made it probable that the three chief stems of humanity, the White, the Black and the Yellow (Shem, Ham and Japheth), are allied, respectively, to the Chimpanzee, the Gorilla and the Orang;[1] and further, that they are far more intermingled than we suppose.

Mental Tests. It is these multiple possibilities of type differences in one apparently pure stock which make such wholesale methods as are used in mental tests of less practical use than is often supposed. The devoted labors of the vast army of mental testers are slowly laying the foundations for an objective method of comparison, of which the ultimate scientific advantages may be great. It is useful to have a standard even if we do not know what it is a standard of; since it is always possible that this may be discovered. And in due time no doubt correlations between the intelligence quotient and other mental characteristics will be forthcoming. But meanwhile the use of such crude methods in place of the more traditional and leisurely ways of judging ability and desirability is suitable rather for economic and military crises than for a civilization which prides itself upon its complexity and its refinement. There is much to be said for the quick lunch; but there are those who prefer to treat themselves more sympathetically. In particular, such methods are apt to be unjust to the very individuals on whom the future may most depend. Even as things are the genius is

[1] Crookshank, *The Mongol in our Midst*, second edition, 1925.

too often regarded as an imbecile; mental tests in many cases *prove* him to be one. But what can be tested is unfortunately not always what is most valuable. Few experimenters would deny this, but the temptation to make practical social applications in conformity with current standards is strong.

The Future of Communication. The reader will have noticed the stress laid upon language in these pages. The center of interest in psychology has of recent years shifted considerably and the symbolizing activities of the mind are more and more becoming its main concern; but in many respects the significance of this trend has been insufficiently appreciated by workers in experimental fields. The majority of intelligence tests, for instance, are essentially tests in the handling of linguistic material, though they are seldom regarded in this light. Even the best non-linguistic mind naturally makes a poor showing. In some quarters there is actually a tendency to overestimate the importance of the language factor. Many behaviorists in reducing thinking to sub-vocal talking overlook the fact that one of the chief practical problems of psychology is to distinguish verbal from non-verbal thinkers—another, perhaps fundamental, division of the types which are discussed above. And even among verbalizers we must distinguish those who are at the mercy of their expressions from those who are not, a distinction of great practical importance in all discussion. There are some people, and those not the least eminent, who can only be persuaded to change their opinion when they are presented with a formal rearrangement of their own vocabulary, while others can grasp a point, however it is put. In university and adult education generally this is of supreme importance, and the technique by which men can be delivered from the bondage of set phrases in earlier years is slowly being evolved. One of the first tasks of those who appreciate the bearing of this aspect of the psychology of thinking on human progress must be to make conscious the manifold strivings towards such a technique, which are found, for example, in grammatical reform movements, in the study of semantics, in new methods of language teaching, and even in simplified spelling.

Another sign of this endeavor is seen in the steady decline in psychology of the traditional type of argumentation in which the disputants revolve patiently each in his own closed system of linked definitions, and keep in touch with one another only through the fact that each is using the same words, though in different senses. The freedom with which psychoanalysts, behaviorists, and even traditionalists are busy coining new vocabularies is on the whole an encouraging symptom, since it at least prevents the general student who is linguistically plastic from becoming prematurely encaged in too narrow a symbolic system.

But if this happy result is to ensue it is essential that men become word-conscious. A similar multiplication of technicalities is occurring in all the sciences, and is particularly embarrassing in the social sciences. It may lead to great difficulties if not to general unintelligibility and a sterilizing isolation of specialists, unless psychology comes to the rescue by inducing a new attitude towards speech based on an understanding of what is happening when we speak. The important point is to remember that what any thought is 'of' or 'about' (its Referent, to use a convenient technicality) and the formulation of the thought, must never be confused. Every statement is translatable, and translation should form a chief part of intellectual training at all stages; not only translation from foreign languages into our own, though this is at present probably the most valuable part of the general curriculum, but also, and still more urgently, translation from one formulation to another within the bounds of our native tongue. By this means we may best become word-conscious, that is, become able to look beyond our forms of speech to the things we are talking about. A truly sagacious Dictator would make it his first business to create a Word-conscious Proletariat.

The Need for Conscious Control. This need for increased conscious control of the machinery of life is even more evident when we turn to the influence which modern psychology is exerting in medicine. Why have we this sudden universal emphasis on the psychological origin of so much mental and physical disease? Is it not because the problems of existence which a little while ago were so simply solved, have, with the increasing complexity of modern civilization, begun to put a strain upon the old mechanisms? Just as we should take over conscious control of the Words which have set men chasing after so many unrealities, in the same way we must learn to take charge of our Minds. We are beginning to realize, with the aid of the doctor, that our neuralgia, our headache, our migraine, our dyspepsia, and even our phthisis, are, no less than the phobias, the hysterias, the anxieties, and the other neuroses which loom so large in the contemporary social picture, as often as not ways in which we are dodging some awkward situation or decision. We have been evading the issue. We have lost touch with reality. And again, just as we evade the personal problem, so civilization as a whole is evading the cosmic issue. Vaguely apprehensive that the old solutions in their traditional form can no longer be squared with the facts, we either look wistfully backwards, or compromise with some morbific phantom which we conjure up to screen us from the abyss. But we must dare to be wise, and the way to wisdom lies through knowledge of ourselves. The facts which we can least afford to neglect are those which it is the object of psychology to present.

BIBLIOGRAPHY

[The following books have been selected as representative of modern psychological opinion in the various fields covered in outline by the present work, and as likely to be of service to the general reader for the further study of contemporary psychology.]

Adler, *Individual Psychology.*

Baudouin, *Suggestion and Autosuggestion.*

Bayliss, *Principles of General Physiology.*

Bergson, *Matter and Memory.*

Bernard, *Instinct.*

Brett, *History of Psychology* (3 Vols.).

Broad, *Mind and its Place in Nature.*

Burt, *The Delinquent Child.*

Cannon, *Bodily Changes in Pain, Hunger, Rage, and Fear.*

Child, *Physiological Foundations of Behavior.*

Collins, *Colour Blindness.*

Collins and Drever, *Experimental Psychology.*

Crookshank, *Migraine and other Common Neuroses.*
The Mongol in our Midst.

De Sanctis, *Religious Conversion.*

Dewey, *Human Nature and Conduct.*

Dorsey, *Why We Behave like Human Beings.*

Ellis, *The World of Dreams.*
Psychology of Sex (6 vols).

Fox, *Educational Psychology.*

Freud, *Collected Papers* (4 vols).
A General Introduction to Psychoanalysis.
The Interpretation of Dreams.

Gordon, *Personality.*

Gregory, *The Nature of Laughter.*

Hart, *The Psychology of Insanity.*

Helmholtz, *Sensations of Tone.*

Herrick, *Introduction to Neurology.*
Neurological Foundations of Animal Behavior.

Hobhouse, *Mind in Evolution.*
James, *Principles of Psychology.*
Jung, *Psychological Types.*
Koffka, *The Growth of the Mind.*
Köhler, *The Mentality of Apes.*
Kretschmer, *Physique and Character.*
Lange, *The History of Materialism.*
Leuba, *The Psychology of Religious Mysticism.*
McCurdy, *The Psychology of Emotion.*
McDougall, *Outline of Psychology.*
Physiological Psychology.
Mitchell, *Structure and Growth of the Mind.*
Morgan, *Instinct and Experience.*
Ogden (C. K.) and Richards, *The Meaning of Meaning.*
Ogden (R. M.), *Hearing.*
O'Shea, *Mental Development and Education.*
Parsons, *Colour Vision.*
Perrier, *The Earth before History.*
Piéron, *Thought and the Brain.*
Pole, *The Philosophy of Music.*
Pratt, *The Religious Consciousness.*
Prince, *The Dissociation of a Personality.*
Révész, *The Psychology of a Musical Prodigy.*
Rivers, *Conflict and Dream.*
Richards, *Principles of Literary Criticism.*
Rignano, *The Psychology of Reasoning.*
Russell, *The Analysis of Mind.*
Schrenck-Notzing, *Phenomena of Materialization.*
Semon, *Mneme.*
Shand, *The Foundations of Character.*
Sherrington, *The Integrative Action of the Nervous System.*
Stern, *The Psychology of Early Childhood.*
Stout, *Analytic Psychology* (2 vols).
Thomson, *Instinct, Intelligence and Character.*
Thorndike, *The Psychology of Learning.*
Tischner, *Telepathy and Clairvoyance.*
Titchener, *A Text Book of Psychology.*

Trotter, *The Instincts of the Herd.*
Van der Hoop, *Character and the Unconscious.*
Warren, *Human Psychology.*
History of Association Psychology.
Watson, *Behaviorism.*
Wilson, *Aphasia.*
Woodworth, *Psychology.*

INDEX